THEY'RE TALKING ABOUT
REX REED AND HIS BOOK

"@*'!'!"!'#@?&¢%! ! "—*AVA GARDNER*

"*The young man who wrote all those scandalous things . . . the Now Kid, the jet set's latest instant celebrity . . . the most entertaining new journalist in America since Tom Wolfe and the most unprincipled knave to turn name-dropping and voyeurism into a joyous journalistic living*"

—Time Magazine

"*I love him veddy much. He makes me suffer*"
—Melina Mercouri

"*Ferociously intimate, detailed dissections . . . There is nothing impartial about Rex Reed. Whether turning his feature pieces into a theater of cruelty, or his articles into Swiftian examinations of the warts and cicatrices of the famous, Reed has rewritten the rules of interviewing . . . Lots of people hate him*"
—Newsweek Magazine

(TURN THE PAGE FOR MORE)

AND TALKING . . .

"*If I had an affair with Jack the Ripper, the offspring would be Rex Reed*"
—Jacqueline Susann

"*A saucy, snoopy, bitchy man who sees with sharp eyes and writes with a mean pen . . . His prose is lush, and full of metaphors that are literally delicious . . . It is impossible to read this book without wondering how on earth Reed gets his subjects to say the things they do*"
—The New York Times Book Review

"*He's tough, man, but he tells it like it is. The most honest thing ever written about me*"
—Peter Fonda

"*Reed admits that some of those he has interviewed no longer speak to him, and it is not difficult to guess why*"
—Chicago Tribune

"*I'd like to write about him*"
—Sandy Dennis

AND TALKING . . .

"Cast aside your movie magazines, gang, and plunge into this juicy little volume. Rex Reed has caught your favorite people off-guard, and he tells it like it is"

—Indianapolis Star

"Made me sound like a gun moll"

—Natalie Wood

"Reading Rex Reed is like going to a party where he's the host and half the celebrities are loathsome, half are lovely, and the lot is pretty damn lively"

—Boston Globe

"He has antennae most people haven't even heard of"

—Angela Lansbury

"Frank, irreverent, mod, cynical, funny"
—Milwaukee Journal

"Beautiful, man, beautiful!"

—Bill Cosby

And you'll have your own comments
to add when you finish reading—
DO YOU SLEEP
IN THE NUDE?

Other SIGNET Books of Related Interest

Do You Sleep in the Nude?

By Rex Reed

A SIGNET BOOK
Published by The New American Library

The pieces on Peter Fonda, Ava Gardner, Warren Beatty, and
Governor Lester Maddox first appeared in *Esquire*;
Marianne Moore and Lotte Lenya in *Queen*;
Mike Nichols and Bill Cosby in *Cosmopolitan*;
and Jean Paul Belmondo and The Living Theatre
in the *New York Magazine* of the *Herald Tribune*.
Everything else appeared in *The New York Times*.
For permission to reprint these articles, the author
wishes to express his thanks.

Library of Congress Catalog Card Number: 68-20116.

This is a reprint of a hardcover edition published by
The New American Library, Inc. The hardcover edition
was published simultaneously in Canada by General
Publishing Company, Ltd.

SIGNET TRADEMARK REG. U.S. PAT. OFF. AND FOREIGN COUNTRIES
REGISTERED TRADEMARK—MARCA REGISTRADA
HECHO EN CHICAGO, U.S.A.

SIGNET BOOKS are published by
The New American Library, Inc.,
1301 Avenue of the Americas, New York, New York 10019

FIRST PRINTING, MARCH, 1969

PRINTED IN THE UNITED STATES OF AMERICA

For my mother and father,
who inspired and guided me
when nobody else could

and for Liz Smith, Rick Winter,
and Seymour Peck,
who encouraged me
when nobody else would

CONTENTS

INTRODUCTION

REX REED ON REX REED. Easy. Let's see, I guess I'd better begin . . . no, not *there*. How about the time . . . forget *that*.

The name is real. Of that much I'm certain. I was born in Ft. Worth, Texas, at a time when the big stars were Brenda Frazier and Hitler, and for the first ten years of my life I moved around from one Texas oil town to the next (with time out at the age of two to appear on a radio show in Pampa saying my ABC's, which made me something of a smarty-pants before I ever heard of a typewriter). My memories of that period are all mixed up with Betty Grable musicals and greasy pit barbecues and people dancing around bonfires doing the Bunny Hop. Then my family moved to Louisiana and Mississippi and we lived in everything from a motel near a Tobasco sauce factory to a crumbling Southern mansion near Natchez—anywhere there was an oil boom. I remember that old house in particular because it was covered with bougainvillea vines, red as pomegranates, and came equipped with a Negro cook with a glass eye who used to make Creole gumbo in the kitchen while I sat around the table reading Nancy Drew mysteries. I have tried to write about my childhood, but Harper Lee and Carson McCullers had lived it first (don't laugh, but *The Member of the Wedding* is the story of my life). That's one of my hang-ups.

By the time I hit college I had attended thirteen schools and had a pretty good idea of what the South was all about.

The first thing I did was write a steaming editorial called "The Price of Prejudice" which almost got me expelled from Louisiana State University. It was reprinted in *The New York Times* and I was accused by the Ku Klux Klan of being paid to attend journalism school by the NAACP. "Not true," said my father, "but if they're interested, have them give me a call. He's costing me a helluva lot of money." It was the beginning of a long and relentless relationship with controversy.

I have been a jazz singer, a performer on a weekly Louisiana TV show (it also featured my old buddy Elizabeth Ashley, who also later headed for New York and made good), a pancake cook on an oil rig in the Gulf of Mexico, a record salesman at Bloomingdale's, an actor in a summer stock company in the Anaconda Copper Mine in Butte, Montana, and the editor of a college literary magazine started by Robert Penn Warren.

I've been writing as long as I can remember. When I was twelve, I read my first Salinger and wrote a series of short stories, always set in New York, in which somebody invariably ended up committing suicide in Schrafft's. I won a national short-story contest when I was a senior in college, and Eudora Welty, who was one of the judges, has been after me ever since to write fiction.

The interview game happened to me quite by accident. I went to the Venice Film Festival two years ago and sent an interview with Buster Keaton to *The New York Times* unsolicited. At the same time, I sent an interview with Jean Paul Belmondo to the *New York Magazine* of the now-defunct Sunday *Herald Tribune*. I had two checks waiting for me before I left Venice, and I've been the fly in the celebrity ointment ever since.

I don't have any particular philosophy about interviewing celebrities. I don't really do interviews at all. I am not a reporter (I've never worked for a newspaper in my life) and I hate that word. I just kind of follow people around and they tell me about their lives and I tell them about my life and suddenly a story forms in my head. I write what I see, sense, touch, smell, and taste. I don't give a damn about the established traditions of the Hollywood interview, because I am not part of the era when Marilyn Monroe used to sit down to breakfast at the Polo Lounge and tell Louella Parsons about Joe DiMaggio's batting average. I'm more interested in what people look like when they take off the goo at night. If I have any philosophy at all, it's cancel the moon, turn off the klieg lights, and tell it like it is.

Actors? They are sensitive, frightened, complicated people

who have dark, goblin sides to their personalities. Show me one who hasn't clawed his way to the top and I'll show you one who isn't really an actor. The only difference between actors and writers is that while there are many good actors with very few roles to play, there are very few good writers with lots of space to fill. So if you are any good at all as a writer you have a better chance of survival. Otherwise, both jobs are a crap shoot.

My biggest problem in writing about celebrities is that because I was once an actor I have an empathy for their pain which often leads them to tell me more than they realize. Print a few of their candid remarks and suddenly you've got a reputation for being a bastard. Natalie Wood treated me like her long-lost college boyfriend (I don't think she went to college), but she hasn't spoken to me since I wrote a funny description of how she sat on the floor of a New Orleans hotel room eating eggs Benedict off the coffee table, opening a bottle of Dom Perignon with her teeth, and doing Russian imitations in her nightgown. Now she tells everyone I made her sound like a gun moll. Sandy Dennis is one of the kookiest girls I ever met, but when I printed that she had dirty feet and ate cold sauerkraut out of a Mason jar and served ginger ale in a champagne glass full of cat hairs she nearly went into a coma. You can't win, and frankly I don't care try.

I used to stay up nights with stomachaches, swallowing Tums like Life Savers, worrying about whether people would like me. Now I know the silliest thing a writer can do is let other people make up his mind for him. I have never *ever* set out deliberately to be bitchy to anyone in print, but the conditions often dictate the results. There is no other way to write. The pieces in this collection on Warren Beatty, Michelangelo Antonioni, Governor Lester Maddox, and Barbra Streisand speak for themselves. I have never been afraid to call a spade a spade.

The best interview I ever had was with Shirley Knight, a daring young actress who says all the things other people say at cocktail parties but are afraid to say in the Sunday papers. I also liked Angela Lansbury, Robert Anderson, Lotte Lenya, Melina Mercouri, Lucille Ball, and Marlene Dietrich. And some of them even like *me*.

Otherwise, what can I tell you? I love Mexican food, Southern Gothic writers, horror movies, fireplaces, people who tell the truth, corn on the cob, Dr. Pepper (which I cannot find in New York), old movies, Céline, and ketchup on my steak.

I hate phonies, liver, unions, organized labor, organized behavior, politics, milk (which I'm allergic to), subways, the

New York Transit Authority and most of its personnel, New York stores that won't give charge accounts to free-lance writers, and writers who write about themselves.

REX REED
New York City, November, 1967

P.S. Although the title of this book—the age-old interview question—never appears once in this collection, I'd like to thank Sidney Skolsky, who thought of it first, and Arthur Laurents, who reminded me of it later.

Michelangelo Antonioni

IF THERE is anything more excruciating than sitting through a Michelangelo Antonioni film, it's sitting through a Michelangelo Antonioni interview. Like a scene from one of his movies, the experience is a symphony of tedium. The setting is a room at the Regency, the color design is drab: beige ceiling, beige walls, beige floor, beige suit, beige trousers, beige face. The one splash of color is Antonioni's bright purple tie, which he occasionally fingers with no particular fondness. An interpreter from the Italian Cultural Institute who never takes off her beige raincoat sits in profile in an uncomfortable-looking beige chair facing him, like Whistler's Mother. People speak, but do not communicate. They talk, but never touch.

There is no beginning to the interview, just as there is no real beginning to an Antonioni film. It is 10:30 A.M., but he has been up since six and seems irritated that the press could not start arriving then. He speaks when he feels like it, without animation, not always in response to a question. He is tall and dignified, like the gray-templed counts in Italian vampire movies, with a kind of screening-room pallor only the very rich or very famous can get away with without being called unhealthy. He insists he is neither rich nor famous, but "very unhealthy." Everything about him twitches. His lips twitch, his eyes blink, his head ticks. He looks at his watch occasionally and yawns a great deal. Sometimes he makes a sudden undefinable noise, like a yelp. As one observer points out, it is like being in the same room with an old dog that is having a bad dream.

"I hate my films, and I do not wish to talk about them," he begins, then proceeds to talk about them anyway. "Since I just finished *Blow-Up* it is still too early to tell about that one. All of the other films I did with my stomach, this one I did with my brain."

15

Why is Blow-Up *different from previous Antonioni films?*

"Because before I am questioning the relationships between men and men and this one is about the relation between men and reality."

Does this indicate a new trend?

He fingers his cigarette. There are no treetops in the room to focus on, so he angles in for a close-up on the ashtray. Then he gazes out of the window behind the interpreter. Everyone waits breathlessly for the answer. A few minutes pass. "Wait until the next film and see."

Why were you attracted to the idea of making a film in English?

"I wasn't." He yawns. The interpreter smiles. It beats a hard day behind the desk at the Italian Cultural Institute.

Why did you pick London?

"Simple. Vitti was there making *Modesty Blaise* and I go there to see her often. She suffered very much making that film. You cannot make a film about a myth and then destroy the myth. I hated that film. Joseph Losey makes better films with men than with women. I think he hates women. Me, I love them. They are the most important invention in the world for me."

American women included?

He thinks. Close-up of Antonioni thinking. "I don't know any."

If you like women so much why is there so little happiness in your films. So little love?

His lips twitch nervously and he cracks his knuckles. A look of physical pain brushes across his face like a sudden wind. "Because . . ." Another long pause between the "because" and the rest of it, but it finally comes. "Because I don't think there is any love in the world. Nobody is in love. This is good, because there is less jealousy that way. Also, there is no feeling for family. No religion. Most people of the new generation are dreamers. LSD and mescaline are better for them than love. This is especially true in London. Another reason why I make *Blow-Up* there."

Is this why your films never have conventionally happy endings?

A startled look. "All of them have happy endings. The people never come together, but they like it that way." Oh.

It is rumored that the Italians do not appreciate your films as foreigners do. Will you continue to base your work in Rome?

"I hate Rome."

16

Do you plan to make more films in London, then?

"No. I nearly went crazy there."

Will you continue to work in color?

"Yes, I like the color in *Blow-Up*, although I nearly had a nervous breakdown without my own art directors and my own cameramen. Only about seventy percent of it worked out. The English thought me mad, but I thought them mad, with all their unions and rules. I wanted the photographer to see things in a colorful way. Now everyone talks of the wonderful grass and the wonderful trees but I painted the grass with green paint and. I painted the streets and the buildings with white paint. I even painted the tree trunks. Everything. Since this is not a novel but a short story, I wanted a subdued unity of tone. I got effects you cannot get in laboratories. Also, the light in London makes everything look metallic and white so the colors are filtered through the air the way the human eye sees them."

Would you like to direct for the theater?

"I hate the theater."

You are reported to treat your actors roughly, at times even refusing to let them read the script. How important are the actors to your films?

The question produces a neurotic effect better left undescribed. "Actors are only a small element. Not very important. I could use amateurs and get the same results. I only use professionals to get certain shadings. My films are visual. This is the language of film. I speak through cameras, not actors."

Besides Vitti, do you like any of the actors you've worked with?

"Some."

Jeanne Moreau?

"Interesting woman."

Richard Harris?

A castor-oil grimace.

Mastroianni?

A shrug.

Vanessa Redgrave?

"Wonderful!"

Many people wonder why such well-known actors as Vanessa Redgrave and Sarah Miles chose to appear in such tiny roles in Blow-Up. *Is it because they desired the experience of working with you?*

"Who knows?"

Do you think most actors are really unaware of whether a scene is working or not?

17

"I don't want actors to direct themselves. I am their judge. Their opinions are too limited for me. Mine is the only complete vision. American actors think too much. Actors should not think. The worst actor I ever worked with and the worst trouble I had with an actor was with Steve Cochran in *Il Grido*. The only other American I ever worked with was Betsy Blair. She was no trouble. Actors are like cows, you have to lead them through the fence."

Do you think American actors are overpaid? Elizabeth Taylor now gets one million dollars per film.

"Ridiculous. No actor is worth so much. Zefferelli now directs her. I guess he needs the money. This, too, is ridiculous. He is not as well known as I, and he should not make as much money as I. Still, I would *never* dare direct a film as a showcase for an actress who was making more money than me. That is insulting."

Were there any films in your youth which enhanced your desire to become a filmmaker?

"Eisenstein."

Any American films?

"No."

What films have you admired recently?

"Only *Pierrot le Fou* and *8½*. No American films. I go today to see Andy Warhol's film. I am told we make movies alike. I also think *Scorpio Rising* is lovely."

Would you consider working in Hollywood?

"If I control completely everything from the script to the lipstick on the actresses. If not, no. Two years ago I almost made a western here but I learned the script had already been prepared, and the actors already hired, so I lost interest. I don't care about money. I have no money. I own an Alfa Romeo and a few paintings. Those are the only things I own."

Do you read the critics?

"Never. They are idiots. What upsets me most is that when they praise and flatter me it is always for the wrong reasons. In Italy, they are bribed by the producers, who can easily corrupt them. Give them some money, they will like anything. Also, they write too much about me, I forget what they say. I pay no attention. I don't try for anything. There is no such thing as an Antonioni camera angle. If there is any one thing I do often it is to focus on inanimate objects instead of people to reduce things to an abstraction and demonstrate the lack of feeling in people. Other than that, you don't need critics to tell you how to understand my films."

What do you think of film festivals?

"I hate them. If you win, it's o.k. If you lose, disaster. I also hate premieres. I despised the New York premiere of *Blow-Up*. The audience was insulting. Also, they did not pay to get in."

What will your next film be about?

"It will be very violent. I cannot make a horror film, because nothing scares me. I cannot make a comedy, because nothing amuses me except sex. I mostly make films about unhappiness."

Are you unhappy?

The question is followed by about two minutes of silent inertia. Then he gets up and leaves the room. When he returns, his eyes blink and his hands shake. "Happiness is complex and only an occasional thing. I am better since I get my marriage annulled."

Isn't that difficult to get in Italy?

"Yes, but it is also difficult to do films in Italy. I do both. I am Antonioni."

The question of the annulment left only one more subject to be—hopefully—explored. *In America, we have seen many photos of the Rome apartment you share with Monica Vitti. Does your new marital freedom indicate a future plan to make her the next Mrs. Antonioni?*

He pauses, makes a stuttering sound, closes his eyes, and for a moment it's an even guess as to whether he'll ever speak again. "Come to Rome and find out," he grins wryly.

There is no ending. He blows a smoke ring. The interviewer blows a smoke ring. And somewhere, up near the beige ceiling, the smoke rings almost meet. Long, lingering, interminable fade-out of the two smoke rings almost touching, then dissolving into nothingness. That is how you know an Antonioni interview—like an Antonioni film—is over.

Barbra Streisand

ONE THING about Barbra Streisand: to know her is not necessarily to love her.

19

Barbra is always late. She hates being interviewed, distrusts all photographers, and is as nervous about publicity as she is about her own performances. Reporters covering her second CBS-TV special, *Color Me Barbra*, even had running bets on just how late she would be for each appointment. The answer, from this corner: very.

The damp, gray hotel room in Philadelphia is charged with tension. The date was for one o'clock; it is nearly three. Somewhere, in a suite high above, Barbra is pasting sequins on her eyes. She wanted Pablo of Elizabeth Arden, but he takes five hours. Barbra hates to sit still that long. In the corner, a kindly CBS press agent pours Scotch from a bottle sent up by room service. People come and go, telephones ring mysteriously. Everyone smiles nervously. The taping is scheduled to begin at the Philadelphia Museum of Art in two hours. "Barbra is very unpredictable; to tape songs for the show, we rented a studio from seven to ten last night; I got home at four A.M.," says the press agent wearily.

People drop by to give opinions. "She's changed," says her personal publicity girl, a pretty blonde with pierced ears dressed in a green-chenille (like the bedspreads) blouse, pants, and paratrooper boots. "She used to sing her guts out; at the end of 'Happy Days' she sounded like she was screaming. She'd never do that now. When she was in *I Can Get It for You Wholesale* she used to beg the press agent to get her interviews so she could get a free meal. Reporters used to stare in horror at the table piling up with hors d'oeuvres, three appetizers, two soups, celery tonic, tomato juice, a main course, and four selections from the dessert tray. Now everything's going so smoothly she only worries about details, refinements. She knew her work so well in *Funny Girl* she never worried about the singing, but about the dust on the plastic flowers or why the blue light failed on Cue eighty-two. Closing night she was still giving notes to the orchestra on what they were doing wrong."

Word comes, from on high, that the superstar is ready for her audience. Three and a half hours late, she plods into the room, plotzes into a chair with her legs spread out, tears open a basket of fruit, bites into a green banana, and says, "Okay, ya got twenty minutes, whaddya wanna know?"

What's the new show like? "Like the old one. They're like book ends. The first one was great, ya know? So this one's gonna be close as it can be. Whadda I know from TV? I hire the best people in the business, then I let them do everything for me. I don't take chances. I'm payin' the bill, it's my problem, right? I coulda got Frank Sinatra and Dean

Martin to clown around just like everybody else does on their specials, but who needs it? I got complete creative control here, so I do it my way, right?"

How will the show differ from last year? "Instead of Bergdorf's, the first part's in a museum," she says, munching on a bunch of grapes. "I move around in front of the paintings and sometimes I turn into the paintings, get it? The costumes are mostly designed by me, borrowed, rented, or remade from my old hock-shop wardrobes. The second part's in a circus, and I sing to all the animals. The last part's the concert. Just like last year. Different songs, same feeling."

Eight people have moved into the room. All of them check their watches and make her very nervous. Some of them answer her questions for her. "Barbra does not like the image that comes with being a glamorous star," volunteers one. "She doesn't like parties; she's afraid people ask her because she's a celebrity, not because they like her."

"Yeah. Like whatchamacallit—"

"Joshua Logan."

"Yeah him. He threw this party for Princess Margaret, ya know? Elliott even wore a tuxedo. We were so miserable we cut out for a Ninth Avenue delicatessen, my favorite restaurant, where they still got great greasy french fries and the best rice puddin' in town. No raisins, ya know what I mean?

"Listen, all my life I wanted to be famous. I knew from nothing about music. I never had a Victrola till I was eighteen. I used to buy clothes in thrift shops. Now I don't go there no more 'cause people bother me. Besides, they've gone up. I always dreamed of a penthouse, right? So now I'm a big star I got one and it's not much fun. I used to dream about terraces, now I gotta spend five hundred dollars just to convert mine from summer to winter. Let me tell you, it's just as dirty with soot up there on the twenty-second floor as it is down there on the bottom."

At 5 P.M. the museum closes and the cameras are ready. An armada of armed guards line the doors with name tags for everyone official. Disgruntled reporters and unhappy photographers line up in a Renaissance hallway for clearance. "Barbra gets very upset if anyone who isn't official watches her," says a cameraman. Outside, the Philly branch of her fan club peers through the beaded glass windows carrying a sign that reads, "Welcome Barb." "Barbra has a fan club in prison," offers the pretty press agent.

At 7:30, Barbra emerges looking like a banana-split nightmare in a floor-length, op-art gown of hand-sewn sequins in twenty colors and six-inch triangle earrings with bolts of lightning through them like Superman emblems. Mondrian eyes sharpened with mascara and boyish hairdo slicked back behind her ears, she looks more like a male hairdresser than a girl, but she is ready for the first number. A twenty-five-man production crew, a registered nurse, her personal staff, and a few favored members of the press watch as bongo drums blare from portable speakers and Barbra shimmies past walls filled with Cézanne watercolors and Matisse still-lifes shaking on their brackets. The number is repeated a dozen times before choreographer Joe Layton bounces through in white tennis shoes and white turtleneck sweater crying, "It's awful. It needs work."

Rest time. Barbra sits in a deck chair in front of the color receiver and eats salted nuts and Life Savers from a rumpled paper bag. There is no camaraderie, no teddy-bear playfulness with her crew, no exchanges of bon mots or even dirty jokes common to most sound stages. She speaks only when spoken to, trusts only those close to her, and ignores everyone else. Mostly she just eats and stares at the gorillas peering out from a Rousseau jungle on the wall. When the nuts are gone, she brings out a half-eaten bag of potato chips. A maid occasionally fortifies her with Kleenex to wipe her hands. A guard stops her from leaning against Renoir's "The Bather." "Cheez," she retorts, "just like New York. Pardon me for breathin'."

By 9:30 the test pattern is adjusted and the color cameras are ready for the fourth tape of the first song. A cameraman crushes out a forbidden cigarette on a valuable piece of a hundred-year-old Romanian oak while a guard isn't looking. "Let's go, Barb!" "I gotta get up?" cries the star. Hard looks from Joe Layton. Barbra gets up, pulling up her panties through her skirt.

"She's no dumb broad," says a CBS official. "She heads two corporations—one packages her specials, pays for everything, then the profit she makes is the difference between her expenses and what CBS pays her. This includes her salary. It's a one-woman show, so it would be very weird if she was not the boss."

By 1:15 she comes out in a floor-length black-satin maid's outfit with white over-apron, which she designed herself. Elliott Gould, her husband, arrives to hold her hand, wearing an official label so the guards will let him in. Barbra runs past twelve pillars and up thirty-five stone stairs singing "Yesterdays." Then she collapses in a corner eating hot pastrami, sour green tomatoes, kosher pickles, and stuffed derma from paper containers. "My gums hurt," she cries, sticking her fingers into her mouth. The crew throws color cables over the balcony of the museum's Great Hall, missing by inches a valuable Alexander Calder mobile and a priceless seventeenth-century Flemish tapestry. A museum official screams. Two guards rush forward. Barbra bites into a fish stick and adjusts her false eyelashes.

Barbra's manager, Marty Erlichman, comes over. Marty is a friendly, bearlike fellow who discovered her in the kitchen of the Bon Soir fresh out of Erasmus High School, a skinny, big-nosed girl with pimples who had a ninety-three average and a medal in Spanish. When he met Barbra he was a small-time talent agent working out of phone booths on Broadway. Now he heads his own company. "For nine months I tried to get her a job. Every record company in the business turned her down. 'Change the clothes, change the nose, stop singing the cockamamy songs.' Now it'll start all over when she hits Hollywood to make *Funny Girl*. They'll want to make her into Doris Day. But she sells the public Barbra, nothing else. She's never been bastardized or exploited. The main thing she's gotta learn is not to trust too much. The public is very fickle. Ten million people love you when you're an underdog on the way up, but nine and a half million of them hate you when you hit the top."

At 2 A.M. a group of teen-agers appeared at the museum with a kettle of hot chicken soup. "Just give it to her," they yell through locked doors. "Could she just wave?" Barbra is busily chewing sour green-apple gum (her current favorite) in a lavender-and-silver Marie Antoinette costume with lavender wig and purple ostrich plumes. 'Get rid of the creeps. These jerks follow me everywhere. Sometimes they get my autograph three or four times in one night. Whatta ya think they do with all them autographs?"

The action continues through the next day, with no sleep. Barbra playing a guillotine scene in the French Revolution. Barbra doing "something based on Nefertiti" in the Egyptian Room. Electricians and reporters curl up on tabletops and behind potted palms, catnapping. "If the star gives up, everybody gives up, I gotta keep smilin'," says Barbra, swallowing an aspirin.

Back in New York, part two was achieved through sheer terror. Barbra danced out onto a pomegranate-and-pistachio-colored three-ring-circus set. A baby elephant named Champagne roared so loud at the sight that a baby llama nearby did a somersault. Barbra sang "Funny Face" in an orange ringmaster's costume. The horse reared. The penguins got

23

sick under the hot lights and had to be carted off to a refrigerated area behind the set. The leopard refused to pose. Barbra fed grapes to the baboon, which lunged at her. Barbra tripped and forgot her words. "Print it," yelled Joe Layton, "if nothing else we got the tiger's face in."

To make matters worse, the show was half-live, half-prerecorded. Barbra had to worry not only about being trampled to death, but when to come in on cue. Contempt hung in the air like moss. The show was behind schedule and the overtime was costing the star money. Four electricians chased a pig across the set and damaged part of the back-drop. The lion broke out of its cage and had to be replaced. As uncontrollable as their temperaments were the animals' nature habits, for which several takes were loused up by the broom-and-shovel detail. Barbra hated the animals and the animals were frightened to death of her. The only friendly moment came when she sang to an anteater named Izzy. "He must be Jewish," she said, as they touched noses.

More than thirty hours were spent on the circus segment, which runs only a few minutes on screen. Barbra's temper exploded. "Too many people not connected with the show. Too many people staring at me." The press was removed to the control room.

By week's end, there was nothing left but the concert. She came out in a pale creamy gown with pearl-drop earrings and pale-mauve lipstick, standing on a white spiral staircase under blue-turning-lavender lights, switching on the charm to the teased-hair girls, the screaming teen-age fans—clowning, joking, kvetching with her little dog Sadie ("a hooked rug that barks"). For the first time in the week of temper tantrums, torment, uncertainty, and bleary-eyed exhaustion, she turned on her juices, and the talent showed. The Brook-lyn accent was gone, the magic shone through. Barbra the terrible—rude, arrogant, anything but a lady—was Barbra the public figure—charming, almost appealing.

By midnight, 400 hours of hard work were over. The grips packed up, the set was struck. "Great show! She'll make millions on the reruns," said a control-room engineer. "Give me Julie Andrews any day," said an electrician, wiping his forehead. In her dressing room the star of the show was told she could finally go home to bed and, for the first time that week, Barbra Streisand was on time.

Warren Beatty

I WAS STANDING on the U.C.L.A. campus, under a sailboat sky, not far from a psychedelicatessen which sells everything from avocado hand cream to Ravi Shankar records, asking college students what they thought of Warren Beatty. Nearby a stunning girl in a leopard-skin balaclava helmet was intensely involved in watching the ritual of a campus maintenance man scrubbing the side of a building on which someone had written JESUS WASN'T DRAFTED with green paint. "What do you think of Warren Beatty?" I asked. "Who's *that?* I never heard of him," she said crisply and walked away so fast her spray net crackled in the sunlight.

Next, came a young man with a large button on his car coat proclaiming ORGASMS FOR SALE OR TRADE. "Oh, yeah. Isn't he the one who used to run around with Natalie Wood? Naw, *naw,* I never saw any of his movies, but I sure wouldn't mind getting together with Natalie Wood. . . ."

And so on. "That slug," said an Indian girl carrying a small telescope. "Warren Beatty! G'wan, you're putting me on," said a geology student with a slide rule hanging from his belt. "What are you—some nut from *Candid Camera?*" On the fifth try, a Tuesday Weld-type in a Rudi Gernreich minicoat scratched the knee of her Bonnie Doon panty stocking, applied a fresh coat of pomegranate lipstick, and replied: "Sure, isn't he the one—let's see—who got arrested not long ago for beating his dog?" "That was Tab Hunter." "Well, I mean, same difference."

And that's what happens when you ask the public. Back in New York, I had skipped the public and asked Those Who Know, and from them I heard that Warren was a draft-dodger, a Communist, that he had two illegitimate children living in London, that he had been arrested three times by the Los Angeles vice squad, that he was a sadist who loved to invite ten girls to his hotel room at one time and not show up, that he wore black leather pants and carried a whip when

25

he was not working, and that "at least fifty women were seduced by him," as one man swore. Above all I learned that Those Who Know knew everything but the truth.

The Truth—as I came to find out—is that nobody knows very much at all about Warren Beatty, including Warren himself. Other than the fact that he had never appeared able to make complete sentences, his old interviews—during the period when he was the hottest thing since Dr. Pepper—turned up nothing.

How would you describe yourself, Warren?
"Sloppy. That's how I'd describe myself. Sloppy."
What do you look for in a role?
"For instance, if I started working. . . . And some of the questions I don't have answers to. . . . Something hits me, it hits me. . . . I read something and I say, Oh I *know* that moment. You never know what it is you really look for . . . it's like . . . but . . . you a . . . dum . . . generally speaking (he spits something out of his mouth) . . . I would think. . . ."

LIKE THAT. Another look at his films—eight of them in seven years—proved that he was not untalented. Three, in fact—*Splendor in the Grass, All Fall Down* and *Mickey One*—showed that he just might be one of the few young actors in films who have more on the ball than a forty-six-inch chest. Still, Warren's relatively brief fling at trampling out the vintage where all those Hollywood grapes of wrath are stored has earned him a reputation for being the most *enfant* of the *enfants terribles* since Baby LeRoy hit W. C. Fields over the head with a bottle. The women in his life—perhaps the only people to know him well—refuse to talk. Once, in a New Orleans hotel room, I asked Natalie Wood about him and she walked out of the room. His directors? Except for Arthur Penn, no director has worked with him twice.

And yet . . . and *yet.* Warren's every waking hour is spent trying to convince people he is a responsible guy. His major interest in life today is to change that old image. He has just produced a film in Texas called *Bonnie and Clyde,* about Bonnie Parker and Clyde Barrow, who conducted a crime spree through the Southwest in the Thirties. Warren financed the project, with aid from Warner Brothers, and press releases out of Hollywood these days proclaim "Warren's grown up."

"Denise Minnelli threw a party at the Bistro last month and Warren didn't even *go!* He's really changed!" That from a friend. And from Warren: "Now that I am in my late twenties,

I find there are other things in life than just having a ball."

Estelle Parsons, an actress in *Bonnie and Clyde*, says, "He had a great respect for the other actors, he ran everything himself, made all the decisions, contributed very important comments, and we all got paid on time. It's a game out there in Hollywood. The people who make the crazy demands and do the bizarre things are the ones who don't get kicked around. Maybe that's what Warren had to do in the beginning to get ahead." Diana Michaelis, who works for V.I.S.T.A.— a volunteer arm of the War Against Poverty—phoned from Washington to tell me she thinks so much of Warren she has asked him to make a recruiting pitch to the young people of America to stir up interest in national welfare. "He went out and talked to our volunteers on the edge of the Watts area and we found him to be a very genuine person sensitive to the problems of the times. Besides, in America people are much more likely to listen to a celebrity."

At the King Cole Bar I talked to Robert Benton and David Newman, two men good and true, who wrote the script for *Bonnie and Clyde*. "You won't get Warren's story in an interview. It's all movement, motion, girls. He drives up and down the Sunset Strip with one hand on the wheel, waving at everybody. He's very *now*, with his own vocabulary, his own way of doing things. He was a terrific producer. We went into a meeting at Warner's and Warren said, "This is what they're gonna ask, this is what we're gonna say," and he was right. He's a great wheeler-dealer. Get him in a car. One time we were looking over locations in some little town in Texas— they all look alike—and some girl spotted him. "Hey, mister, you Warren Beatty?" she said, backing up four times in an old Buick. Warren did ten minutes of *shtick*."

Then they described a scene, typical of the kind of thing that happens every day to Warren the Hipster:

They are stopped for a red light. Warren is hanging out of the window. "Hey, man," says a man in the next car.

"Hey, man," says Warren.

"What's happenin'?"

"Nothin' much happenin'."

"Hey, my place, man. Eight o'clock. A freaky scene."

"What kinda freaky scene?"

"A few girls, man. Real *freaky*."

"Well, it wouldn't be much fun without at least eight girls, man."

"Oh. Okay. Later, man."

"Later."

"Who was that character?" asks Newman.

"I never saw him before in my life," says Warren, giggling and stepping on the gas.

The best evaluation came from a famous actress who appeared with Warren in a film. Over cheeseburgers at The Ginger Man she whispered confidentially: "Warren is really two people. You see him on the screen and that's one thing. He's no actor and never has been. His working habits are unorthodox and difficult to understand, but that's mainly because he doesn't know what he's doing. He has always gotten by on the screen by faking it. It's almost as though the moon has to be in just the right quarter and the winds have to blow just the right number of miles per hour from the east before he can even function. The *other* side of Warren is more interesting. He can be youthful, charming, debonair. Every eye at the table is on him. He is musical—plays wonderful piano—and he's very interesting when he isn't hung up acting. But of course this is the side he has never shown to any writer to my knowledge. He is always too busy playing roles. That seems to be necessary to his own kind of survival. So I think it would be impossible to write about him, because you will never see what he's really like. You will only see all the roles he wants you to see him play."

THE HOLLYWOOD SUN rose like a big pink seedless grapefruit over the date palm trees out by the Beverly Wilshire pool. I was up early, waiting for a call from Guy McElwaine, Warren's Hollywood press agent, who had promised to phone at ten A.M. I sat around the hotel, sharpened my pencil, and got my questions ready for Warren.

At eleven, McElwaine phoned. "Meet me for lunch at the Brown Derby in one hour," he said briskly. The beginning. Will the real Warren Beatty stand up and sign in, please. "Will Warren be there?" I asked. "Your parrrty is disssconnected," purred the operator.

Two hours and several Bloody Marys later, McElwaine sauntered elegantly into the Beverly Hills Brown Derby, called "the Veda Ann Borg of restaurants" by people who know it well. McElwaine settles into the booth and orders a chopped sirloin steak. "No French fries," he says, fondling a waistline that is threatening to get out of hand. "You don't *look* so tough," he says, peering over his wraparound sunglasses.

Guy McElwaine sounds like the inscription on a tombstone in the King of Cornwall's graveyard at Tintagel. Actually he is a boyish, thirty-one-year-old ex-ballplayer who has been blasted by almost every writer in Hollywood for protecting his clients from exposure to the indignity of the printed page. (Mention almost any writer of any reputation and he'll sneer, "Yeah, *he* took a swipe at me in print.") A swinger. Checked tweeds, striped pink shirts, paisley ties, a regular face at The Daisy. It is clear almost instantly (and from the way he later nudges up to Warren) that he is quite confused about his own relation to the stars he handles. As one of his acquaintances says, "He wants so badly to be a celebrity himself that he goes around drenched in cologne, wearing loud clothes and living in the spotlights of his clients. He has a pretty tough ego to feed." There are two kinds of press agents—the no-nonsense guys who expose their clients to the proper media because that is what they get paid for, and the professional hand-holders. McElwaine fits into the second category. Warren needs him. Like most of the young successes in show business, Warren is smart enough and rich enough to get anything he wants, but he's not stable enough yet to provide his own built-in reassurance.

McElwaine talks a lot about his current wife, Pamela Austin, and loves to tell how she made $100,000 last year for a few days' work. She's the petunia-eyed blonde who nearly drove the World Series off the air by announcing repeatedly, at disturbingly regular intervals, "The Dodge Rebellion wants yeeewww!"

There is still no sign of Warren. Will he show up for lunch? McElwaine's conversation avoids any pinning down of exact times and dates, but there is a casual mention of, "Well, I guess we'd better try to get some kind of schedule going between you and Warren." Mostly it's just peppered and salted with exclamations like, "Who needs writers? All they want to do is make movie stars look like asses!" And "Richard Warren Lewis can't get a job in Hollywood because of all those vicious pieces he writes for *TV Guide*." And "Joe Hyams is another writer who has nothing but contempt for Hollywood press agents." And "Bill Davidson used to be very good, but he can't get people to see him anymore." Etc. Putting on the scare. But never quite making it, because with each new horror story about each new big-name writer he doesn't like, it becomes increasingly more obvious that what he's really afraid of is a hatchet job on Warren Beatty.

"I have the names of a group of people here who told me not to let you do this story at all," he said suddenly in his best Edward G. Robinson imitation, pulling out of his vest pocket a crumpled piece of memo paper. "Whaddya think of that?" I told him I didn't think much about his list and when could I see Warren?

"I wouldn't blame you if you went back to New York and sued us for a million dollars and you'd probably win the case," he said. I told him I didn't come three thousand miles to sue *anybody* and when could I see Warren?

He started to grin, realizing the corniness of the situation. "There's nothing you could write about him anyway that could harm him professionally. He could walk down the street naked and it wouldn't hurt him. Did you know he's the Number-one film star in Cambodia? In Iran they released three of his films in one *week*—a regular Warren Beatty film festival." I asked if it would be possible to maybe follow Warren around for a few days, see him in action. McElwaine blanched. "Probably not. That's up to Warren. You have to win his confidence first." I asked him what he could tell me about Warren. What time does he wake up? "Whenever I call him. Sometime in the afternoon, usually. Listen, I know there are a lot of people in this business who don't like Warren, but that's because a lot of people want to *be* like him. They're jealous. Hell, he's good-looking, he's successful, he could have just about any woman he wants in the whole world. He *knows* everybody. All the foreign directors like him. Truffaut. Karel Reisz wants to do a film with him. He's very intelligent. He has total recall. He can remember every phone number of mine for years. And *women!* He can look at a girl and say, 'Her number is OLeander - - - - and she used to have a London exchange that was GROsvenor - - - -' *Fantastic!* Let's go see Nancy Sinatra."

We're heading out Santa Monica Boulevard in McElwaine's '67 chocolate-colored Mercedes-Benz convertible toward PJ's where Nancy Sinatra (another client) is rehearsing a rock-and-roll act to take to Vietnam and I'm wondering what Nancy Sinatra has to do with Warren Beatty, and McElwaine is answering: "Why don't you do a story on Nancy?" He plunges through the traffic, pushing his sunglasses up on his nose, telling wild inside stories about Hollywood, all prefaced with, "This is not for publication, *but. . . .*"

PJ's swarmed with rock-and-rollers. McElwaine hugged Nancy Sinatra. Nancy hugged McElwaine. They both wore dark glasses. He produced the cover of her new album, which showed her in a pale bikini photographed, in a Roger Vadim effect, by a camera that looked like it had Vaseline smeared across the lens. "I hear we sold twenty thousand copies already on the cover alone." Nancy blushed and went on with her song. . . . ("Shh-Shh-Shhugar Town . . .") And that's how we frittered away the afternoon, consumed in a roar of over-amplified dissonance. The beat. Gets ya where ya live. The in-crowd. "Is Warren coming here?" I asked over the noise. "Warren's meeting us for drinks later," was the reply. "Why don't you do a story on Nancy?"

Back in the safety of pink sunlight, bouncing off the windshields of all the Hollywood sports cars like sequins, we headed for McElwaine's office. "That's Nancy's fiancé," said McElwaine, driving past a photographer pulling into the parking lot at PJ's. "Does her father ever say anything about her life?" I asked. "Only when he's asked, otherwise Frank stays out of it. Listen, this is no kid. She's been married and divorced once. She's a grown woman!" It still didn't seem like a very good reason to do a story.

Back at McElwaine's office (pink everything, with teeny-boppers to answer the phone and plastic plants and a super-intercom system which allows everyone in the office to listen in on calls whenever he flips a switch), he handed me a book by Roddy McDowall. "Why don't you do a story on Roddy?" Finally, after leafing through six magazines, all featuring stories on his clients, I was told Warren was on the phone. "Yes, Warren, he's here now." Cupping his hand over the receiver: "Warren wants to know if everything's okay. He has lots of contacts at the hotel and he can get you anything you need."

"Ask him when I can see him," I said.

"Yes, sure, everything's fine. I'll talk to you later," he said, hanging up. "Well, I gotta get some work done."

He promised to phone me at five o'clock for cocktails with the star. One of the teeny-boppers drove me back to the hotel, with a running narrative on her life and a complete rundown on her qualifications for pictures. At eight P.M. I dialed McElwaine. "Oh," he said, "I was just going to call *you*. Warren can't make it; he's tied up at the studio. I'll phone you first thing in the morning."

At three P.M. on my third day in California, the call came through, like a voice singing hosannas from on high: "Warren will see you now."

AN ORANGE SUN was collapsing under the weight of a sky full of smog as the car pulled through the gates at Warner Brothers. The studio in late afternoon looked like an old deserted airbase I lived near as a small child; the hangars had long since been closed down, the aircraft dismantled and hauled away for scrap, and all that was left were memories for the calendar to smirk at. Production was crawling. The sound stages—where Bette Davis went blind in the flower beds, where Bogart fired at endless hoodlums in Chicago alleys, where Doris Day pinched S. Z. Sakall's cheeks into colorless hamburger and Joan Crawford had once slapped the faces of countless admirers on her way to the governor's mansion—were inactive and closed to the public. Warehouses filled with Busby Berkeley tap shoes and Cary Grant drawing rooms—padlocked. In one of the labs *Bonnie and Clyde* was in the editing stage, and somewhere, behind those massive bolted doors down one of those concrete alleys, *Camelot* was shooting. Otherwise, a fine pink dust settled crazily over the lot and the ear was assaulted by the sound of silence.

Warren was in his office—a tiny pink room at the end of an empty corridor in a tiny pink stucco building that looked like a temporary wartime army hut for training-center personnel. He was sitting on top of his desk, talking animatedly on the phone to a music publisher about the score for *Bonnie and Clyde*. "Let's go with a hillbilly sound. No, I do *not* want bossa nova." He was playing the role of busy executive, with McElwaine beaming nearby, but there was something wrong with the scene: he was wearing a wrinkled white shirt with two buttons missing, so that his navel showed, and across his face was a cut, where he had slashed himself shaving.

Up close, without the makeup and the lights, he looks like the well-bred right guard on some winning high-school football team; one of the guys from the right side of town hanging around with the moths on a lightning bug-sticky small-town evening in summer: sea-spray eyes, slanted like pecans, constantly squinting because he is nearsighted and too vain to wear glasses when he first meets strangers, footsteps shuffling and slightly unsure, hair healthy and unruly, hands trim, fingers long—not masculine-accepted stubby, but rather delicate and sensitive, like a pianist's (which he once was). When he looks he stares and when he talks he does so in a voice which is not immaculately precise, like most movie stars who dabble a bit in phonetics, but rather slow and cumbersome, wrapping his vowels around his tongue like bacon around a fork. Warren, in fact, does not look or sound like a star. It is not until later, when you have known him, that you begin to notice the desperation to be liked, approved of, the fear (the greatest terror of his life, to be exact) of being considered unintelligent. At least four or five times during our talks, he would turn to me defiantly and say, as if in self-assurance, "I *am* intelligent; I *know* I am intelligent."

He led the way, past crumbling, vine-colored tennis courts once used by Al Jolson and Ruby Keeler, now sorry reminders of the past, with cracks in their floors, down palm-lined walks where Judy Garland had cavorted as Mrs. Norman Maine in *A Star Is Born*, across parking spaces marked "Reserved—for Richard Harris" or "Reserved—for Jack Warner," to his dressing room. He slammed the door. "Now-uh, let's see," he stammered, trying to be polite, still not trusting me. "There is, far as I can see, no reason to do a story on me. Most of what I have to say you couldn't print anyway. Most movie stars are not interesting, so to sell papers and magazines in the fading publications field a writer has to end up writing his ass off to make somebody look more interesting than he really is, right? What it all boils down to is publicity because somebody's got some movie to sell, right? What do I need with publicity? You want to see me driving up and down the Sunset Strip in my car picking up girls, right? Well, you don't think I'd be stupid enough to let you see *that* side of me, do you?"

"Gay Talese came out here and got hot under the collar because it took him three weeks to see Frank Sinatra," McElwaine echoed. "Hell, Mia Farrow doesn't even see Sinatra until the lights go out."

"You've got a reputation for being an *enfant terrible*," snarled Warren. "Let me give you some advice. If you're gonna knock the Establishment, don't make any mistakes. I know, because I used to be an *enfant terrible* myself. You write a story mentioning Natalie Wood's hairdresser and it turns out he was really her makeup man. People don't like that sort of thing."

These boys play a pretty mean game of war, I told myself. Three days under the coconut trees and I was already getting my third lecture—in fractured French—and I hadn't even done the interview. I listened to about an hour of diatribes against various "goddam writers," including a juicy description of one who should have his "ass filled with buckshot" for writing a story which made Joshua Logan sound effete, and another particularly boring attack on the old standbys—the McGuire Sisters of journalism—Richard Warren Lewis, Joe Hyams and Bill Davidson. "Joe Hyams used to write a bitchy article putting down every blonde starlet who set foot in Hollywood and he ended up marrying one," said Warren, who had once been treated to one of Hyams' ace profiles. Warren leaped to his feet, remembering a doctor's appointment.

We drove back to Beverly Hills in his pantherlike black Continental with black leather upholstery. Why not a Jag or even a Firebird with a regular gas overhead cam six? "I like big cars, it's as simple as that." He rents them in whatever city he happens to be in, turns them in when the ashtrays get full. We avoided the freeways, stuck to the boulevards. Warren was careful not to answer any questions, since McElwaine had gone to great lengths to insure the use of a tape recorder, which he insisted he would supply. Warren ripped through the traffic, like a professional cabdriver, his face clouded with surly pain. A beautiful girl with skin the color of buttered cocoa pulled alongside the car in a confetti-colored sports car. Nobody said anything. The two drivers just looked at each other and grinned. That was the first glimpse of something I had heard about, and would see again: the Beatty charm, quickly blossoming and just as quickly dismantled. ("Warren wants the entire world to want to go to bed with him," a friend of his told me earlier. "And what he really is unable to take more than anything else in life is rejection.") The girl in the other car knew him. She flashed her teeth in a Gardol glow. "Warren, can I pass you?"

She did. "That would be one of the most beautiful girls in Hollywood, but she's carrying the weight of the entire civil-rights movement on her shoulders," said Warren. Then he went back into his Charlotte Brontë mood. I was losing him.

"You must know half the girls in Hollywood." I couldn't believe I had said it, but I was clutching at straws. *"That* is such a stupid question I don't even know how to answer it," he sneered. He was right, but it produced a laugh from both of us, and that, at the moment, seemed better than nothing.

He never did tell me why he was going to a doctor, but he was inside the clinic half an hour. I waited in the car. When he came out, he seemed cheerier and invited me up to his pad. We parked in the basement of the Beverly Wilshire and waited for the elevator. He was still harping on the hazards of the interview, concentrating with deadly precision on Barbara Walters of the *Today* show, who had recently called him one of the most impossible interviews of her career in front of millions of viewers on Johnny Carson's *Tonight* show. Warren seemed particularly insulted by her, blaming the failure of the interview on her questions, and was deep in some kind of analysis of female interviewers in general when an elderly lady in a uniform stepped off the service elevator.

"Hello," he said, beaming his wall-to-wall grin.

"Oh, *hello*," beamed the woman, who only a moment before had been doubled over in pain.

"How are you feeling?" asks Warren.

"Oh, so-so," she answers, remembering, rubbing her back.

"I'll have several shirts and some suits for you tomorrow," he says, flashing such a smile that the lady forgot all her aches and grinned girlishly back at him.

"That's the cleaning lady," he says, after she hobbled away. Charm. The boy's got it. ("You should see him at a party," says a female friend of his. "He can walk into a room full of people like Merle Oberon and Myrna Loy—you know, the older beauties—and be so debonair, so wolfish, he has them purring and eating out of his hand in minutes. He's like honey in a beehive.")

Warren lives on top of the Beverly Wilshire Hotel. Most of the suites there have Spanish names; Warren's is called La Escondida. It is only the size of a two-room New York apartment, with Pablum-colored decor and few closets, but it is considered the "hotel penthouse," probably because it has one outstanding feature: a magnificent terrace with a CinemaScope view of Los Angeles that looks like the opening credits of *A Star Is Born*. There is, before you see the terrace, an immediate sense of transitory impermanence about the pad: what looks like four days of room-service trays piled against the door, a week's phone messages crumpled on the floor and on the tops of bureaus, stacks of books (he was halfway through Kazan's *The Arrangement*). We step over a pile of LP's, movie scripts, unanswered mail with month-old postmarks, a typewriter, typing paper. "I'm writing a movie, but I can't tell you about it yet. It's hard work—keeps me up till six A.M. Come on, I'll show you where I live."

We go out to the terrace, where Maya Plisetskaya reportedly sunbathes when she's in town from Russia, with its deck chairs, umbrellas and a view of Mount Baldy in the distance. There is a building which looms above and hovers over this terrace, guarding it like a sentinel. It used to have a name but when the owners of the building moved their business, they took down the name and left just the word BUILDING. It makes Warren furious when anyone notices. Yevgeny Yevtushenko, the Russian poet, once visited his pad and, noticing the sign instantly, made a comment to the effect that only a capitalist society would find it necessary to remind the world that a building was a building. Warren has never quite forgiven him for that, and when I remarked that I thought it quite funny he seemed doubly annoyed. "These New York guys come to Hollywood and see all the lights and say, 'It's phony.' I hate to tell you but the cultural swing is to the West. I love Los Angeles—the temperance, the weather, the girls. I have no family, though, so I'm really a commuter, though. I have no family, no kids that necessitate my being in any one particular place for a very long period of time. Three years ago I had a big Hollywood house with two pools and a tennis court, but I gave it up. I only had it so when Leslie's kids were in town they'd have room to play."

We talk about the growth of Los Angeles, "Nothing's old out here. You want old, go back to New York." Then he springs his memory game. "I'm learning a lot about myself— like I have a photographic memory. Name me a dinner party I was at years ago and I can recite the menu, tell you what everything tasted like. I can remember the way rooms smell, and anything of a sexual nature—all the sexual encounters in detail—and the phone numbers of people I knew five years ago. Ask me a phone number in New York."

This was the part of the story called Gaining the Star's Confidence. "What's Sardi's?" I asked, playing along.

"LAckawanna 4-0707," he answered correctly. "Now give me a number."

"CIrcle 6-1000." He thinks, cups his hands over his eyes. He doesn't know. "Warner Brothers—your own studio," I tell him.

"Well, it always works better with *people's* numbers and it always fails when you're trying to show off. People are the things I care most about in life. One of the things that has begun to mean a great deal to me is to keep relationships with people fertilized and up-to-date. That's probably why I remember every phone number—because when it answers I know there'll be a person on the other end." He looked sad and a little lonely, like a rag doll thrown in a corner by a bored child. I went home, with a date to see him at eleven the next morning, convinced that Warren Beatty was one helluva misunderstood nice guy.

The next morning I phoned him to let him know I was on my way. He was asleep. "What're you doing today?" he asked, yawning, then dropped the phone. "I'm supposed to be seeing *you* . . . the *interview,* remember?"

"Oh, yeah? Well, let's see . . . Christ, what a night . . . there's not much . . . you could if you wanted to . . . come on up . . . we'll have lunch at two. Is that all right? You're sure. . . ."

INTERVIEWING WARREN is like asking a hemophiliac

for a pint of blood. We sat out on the terrace with the palm trees blowing down below and the phonograph playing Kurt Weill music as loud as the volume would go. "It's Morton Gould. Do you think that's square? Maybe I'm a square." The idea seemed to worry him. He was wearing the same wrinkled clothes from the night before and looked exhausted. Mostly he is exhausted by boredom and he is almost always bored if he stays in one city, one room, one situation, too long. Once, when he was telling me about an unknown actor he hired for *Bonnie and Clyde,* I asked if that was dangerous for box office. "The only thing that is dangerous," he said, looking me straight in the eye, "is boredom. I want to get out and do things that are different—not sit around and dwell on my own excrement."

There were two tape recorders, a special requirement for the interview, a tiny Norelco that operated on cartridges and a larger Wollensak which had been borrowed from a girl friend. Warren puttered around a few minutes, shaking them, holding them up to his ear. They were both broken. "Forget the tape recorder. I'll trust you." The day before he had seemed angry because I had once written about Natalie Wood eating eggs Benedict. "I'll never let you catch *me* off guard like that," he said. Now he picked up the phone and called room service. "Hello, room service? This is Warren Beatty. BEATTY! In the penthouse. I'd like some food. Two orders of eggs Benedict, please. Uh—let's see—listen—don't let this be a disaster, but I'm changing my mind. Make that *one* order of eggs Benedict and one Western omelet—and, dear, make the Western *soft.* You got that? Yeah, *soft.* Every time I order them they come hard and I am going to have to start sending them back."

I asked him why he lived in hotels. "I guess because it prevents stagnation, settling down. I get a certain amount of amusement out of knowing I can pack up and move tomorrow. I used to be fairly squirrel-like about keeping things but I've stopped that too. I don't want *things.* I usually have a piano but I stopped that too, because when I have an anxiety I go to the piano and then I don't work out the anxieties on the other work I should be doing. I don't want houses or cars. I rent everything. I have four suits and a dinner jacket. The rest of my things are stored in warehouses. There have been other times when I've been deeply involved with a woman— if it was not what it should be, all creative impulses came to a standstill. That doesn't mean I won't get involved anymore, because you never know what you're gonna do, do you? I wouldn't want to think of myself as cautious, but I guess I am becoming more cautious, I think a very short relationship where you tell the truth to somebody is in many ways more satisfying than a longer relationship where truth becomes more painful."

I asked him if, now that he had become a producer of films as well as an actor, he had fewer anxieties about life? "Yes, but more anxieties about death. I'm afraid to die, aren't you?" He was pacing, arms folded like Napoleon, occasionally reaching inside his shirt to scratch himself. "Hey!" he said suddenly, turning around and pointing at me. "I didn't do any interviews during the movie and now I'm doing a few and it's sounding corny. Does that sound like I'm putting you down? One thing is sure—every time I talk to someone I say to myself after, 'Why did I pontificate like that?' I feel very foolish. It's a struggle to determine just why or *if* you should be interested in me, but you're here so I guess you are or *somebody* is or somebody wants to sell a movie. I don't know . . . it's all so trivial."

I asked him if money was important. "It's becoming *less* important. It's very important when you have a very small amount of it, but when you're comfortable, money ceases to be a remedy for much. For me, anyway. I don't know how sensible I am about currency. I don't even know how much I have. I trust the man who handles my money. On the other hand, when I was producing *Bonnie and Clyde,* it was important to know where the money went, what it went for. Money is chips. It's all tokens. I don't know what it's all about. One day a dollar is worth X, the next day it's worth Y."

Warren was trying. He was really trying to give an intelligent interview, and he was saying all the things he considered important to escape the old cornball labels. "Audiences don't give a damn about statistics. I don't give a damn. We're endowing our imaginary audience with the same tastes, same likes and dislikes we have ourselves. I get the feeling that even with the inflationary costs it's become an almost economic necessity in theatrical motion pictures as opposed to TV to move into unsafe areas statistically." I didn't have the slightest idea what he was talking about, but I was writing like heck. "I want to do more comedies. I've only made two. I guess it's two. Was *Kaleidoscope* a comedy? I never knew what that picture was, not that you had to know what it was, because it was what it was."

The food arrived. Warren nearly burst into tears explaining to the Spanish waiter, who spoke no English, why he would have to send him back to the kitchen. "The toast is not buttered and I ... like ... well ... what can I do? What would *you* do? So you see ... If I don't send you back you'll never learn anything ... and that's why ..." The waiter left, muttering something in Spanish. Warren devoured his omelet in seconds, then continued pacing, occasionally swooping down like an enormous sea gull to nibble on the uneaten portion of my cold eggs Benedict. "Don't you eat these?" he asked, pointing at the truffles on top. "That's the best part," he said, swallowing them.

It seemed like a good time to ease him into a discussion of the past. He was born in Richmond, Virginia, in March, 1937. He grew up in a red brick Colonial house in Arlington, the son of Ira O. Beaty (Warren later added an extra "t"), an educational-psychology professor turned real-estate man, and Kathlyn MacLean Beaty, who taught acting. His sister Shirley (who later turned her mother's maiden name into MacLaine for professional use) was three years older, and as children they used to dress up in top hats and parade around the house. ("By the time he was five he was a wow imitating Boyer, then he went through a Milton Berle stage," says his mom.) But Warren was no sissy. He was president of his class and a star center on the Washington and Lee High football team. At seventeen, he went from Arlington to Washington and got a job with the National Theatre as a rat-watcher. "The manager was a nice man who could see he had a kid here who loved the theater. I asked for a job in the alley—doing anything. They were doing a revival of *The Skin of Our Teeth* with Helen Hayes. There were several entrances through the alley, and since there had been an incident where a rat bit an actor, Equity required they hire someone to stand in the alley and make sure no more rats ran into the theater. It probably relates to my behavior around the doors of studio executives *now*."

He graduated from high school to ten offers of football scholarships, but he turned them all down to study drama at Northwestern. I asked him if he ever wondered what his life would have been like if he had played college football. "No. I haven't seriously given that more than [cupping his head in his hands, rubbing his eyes] twelve minutes thought. At first, the football field seemed a good place to do something. A guy actually became an all-American. He was big and he was tough." The story becomes very important to him. His eyes narrow. He sees it, like a scene from a movie. "He was from Ohio. I rather liked him. One night I came home late to the freshman dorm and they said, 'So-and-so is really sick, got drunk tonight, and he's been asking for you. He vomited in the men's room.' 'How sick was he?' I asked. 'Go in and see.' I saw, for one second, a whole cabbage, a carrot, an unchewed lamb chop—I said, 'Man, I'm too sensitive for *this!*' and I quit." Instead, he sang a song about an Indian in a varsity show and became a hot campus item with a pretty co-ed named Ellie Wood, who is now married to Robert Walker, Jr.

Warren quit after a year and never went back to college. He counted his savings and went to New York, where he lived in a twenty-four-dollar-a-month room, on West Sixty-eighth Street, occasionally played the piano at night in a little place called Clavin's Bar—gone now—on East Fifty-eighth Street, and supplemented his income by working as a bricklayer's assistant, construction worker and sandhog on the third tube of the Lincoln Tunnel. He also studied acting with Stella Adler, who "equipped me with a certain amount of arrogance—arrogant self-confidence, I should say—which enabled me to bluff my way through a few sidescrapers." Most of the time, though, he lived on peanut butter, stalked girls on the streets of Manhattan and lay in bed with a case of hepatitis. I mentioned the hepatitis and he turned crimson. "How did you know about *that?* What else do you know?"

Somewhere during this period—between Northwestern and his first break on Broadway—Warren had a serious rift with his family. Today he still refuses to discuss his parents *or* his sister Shirley, who by that time had already been discovered in *Pajama Game* and featured in an Alfred Hitchcock film. "Did you communicate with them during this period?" I asked. "There's communication and there's communication," he replied, freezing up. Then, "It's been traumatic for my mother and father to have raised two kids who have become successful in a way-out profession." And Shirley? "I think I learned to talk to my sister later than anyone else. Little things build up—you build up a little head of steam—and pretty soon you have to go into a conference on disarmaments. Just in the last two years we've become able to communicate."

When he recovered from the hepatitis, Warren landed a job in a religious early-morning TV show, which led to a part in a winter stock production of *Compulsion* in New Jersey. William Inge and Joshua Logan were in the audience. Zip! A star is born. Etc. Logan wanted him instantly for *Parrish* (the part later went to Troy Donahue). Inge wanted him to play a stud in his play, *A Loss of Roses*. That was the beginning of Warren's reputation, less than enviable, for being difficult, arrogant, moody, hostile, uncooperative. From

40

he beginning the show was plagued with troubles, not the east of which was Warren himself. Shirley Booth was the tar and Warren was nobody, but as the rehearsals wore on, t became obvious to everyone in the cast that Inge had made a mistake. Warren refused to cooperate with Director Daniel Mann. By this time he had met Joan Collins, the first n a long line of *amours,* and she was traveling with him, to he rest of the company's annoyance. He'd arrive twenty to thirty minutes late for rehearsals, hold up the cast in private directorial conferences, change the lines. Dennis Cooney, Warren's understudy, was kept on call to replace him on a moment's notice. Mann said, "Warren won't listen to me, he's going to do nothing until opening night and then he'll play on he sex appeal and charm and all the crap and do something onstage we don't even *know* about."

According to people who worked on the show, Mann wanted to fire Warren, but Inge defended him as merely an insecure actor who would be great in the part if given a chance. Gradually Warren began to take over the show while the leading lady's role shifted in perspective. At the end of the first tryout week in Washington, Shirley Booth walked out of the show, and the emphasis changed to the role played by Carol Haney, making her debut in a drama. The play was a disaster, but Warren got good reviews. Twenty-five performances later, he was off to Hollywood. He now says he doesn't want to return to the stage because "I don't want to go through the mess of doing a play just to win the approval of four critics who decide whether you're going to be allowed to keep doing the play. That's a bore."

In 1960, through William Inge's help, Warren was cast in his screen play of *Splendor in the Grass,* directed by Elia Kazan. By now he was engaged to Joan Collins. When she left for Europe to film *Esther and the King,* Warren went to New York to film *Splendor* and met Natalie Wood, whose husband Robert Wagner spent the summer of 1960 watching the co-stars fall in love. Joan Collins smelled more than splendor in the grass, flew back three times, but by August, 1960, Beatty and Natalie were going everywhere together saying, "We're just friends," and collapsing in fits of laughter. While Wagner was selling Natalie's Hollywood mansion with its his-and-hers salt-water swimming pools, Warren (who nobody had ever heard of a year before) and Natalie (who nobody cared about a year before) became an item. The columns exploded with the news: suddenly Natalie, who was separated from Bob, was dating Warren, who used to be engaged to Joan, and Joan was dating Bob, who used to be

Warren's best friend. And if you think *that* was confusing, it *was*, because Bob used to date Joan before he married Natalie. A *Time* correspondent on the scene at the time filed this dispatch from Hollywood: "Last time I saw them they were all sitting in a screening room watching *Splendor in the Grass*. Joan laughed a lot in the picture. Natalie wept."

Splendor established Warren as a *cause célèbre:* he got on a few covers and the ladies of the Hollywood press awarded him the much-despised "Sour Apple" award for "Most Uncooperative Actor in Movies." His price went up overnight to $200,000 a film. Through the help of William Inge again, Warren landed the role of an Italian gigolo who seduces Vivien Leigh in Tennessee Williams' *The Roman Spring of Mrs. Stone*. Lotte Lenya, who won an Oscar nomination for that fiasco, says: "I owe him a lot. Like most women, Vivien had a tremendous crush on Warren. He kept her so occupied that she allowed me to steal our most important scenes together. One night we were watching the day's rushes together and Vivien gasped, 'Oh, how could I let you *do* that to me?' and I said, 'But dalink, you were very busy this afternoon and had no time to rehearse.'"

In 1962, William Inge maneuvered him into his third film, *All Fall Down*. That was the end of their professional relationship. Inge wouldn't discuss Warren, but Warren still calls him "a nice man."

All Fall Down was a surprisingly sensitive film, but some of the critics flew up the wall over Warren. "Beatty's acting consists largely of picking his nose and mumbling one sentence speeches," said *The National Observer*, and Bosley Crowther summed it all up in *The New York Times:* 'There is one fatal flaw in the arrangement of elements in this film that makes it implausible, unnatural and extremely hard to take. It is the essential arrangement that everyone in the story is madly in love with a disgusting young man who is virtually a cretin. At least, Warren Beatty plays him so he seems like one. . . . Surly, sloppy, slow-witted, given to scratching himself, picking his nose, being rude beyond reason.' "Bosley Crowther has never liked me," says Warren, "but I don't like him either, and I told him so once in Sardi's."

When he refused to play John F. Kennedy (the President had suggested him) in *PT-109*, the papers had a field day roasting him in effigy. "Unbelievable!" yelled Producer Bryan Foy. "Actors today will drive you crazy if you pay any attention to them. The kid has got a mop of hair like the

President but if all I needed was a mop of hair for this part, I could get Jack Benny to play it."

PT-109 was a lousy picture and so were the others Warren turned down. He knew what he was doing. "Success was very difficult to adjust to in the beginning," he says. "I became stimulated by the gravy of being a movie star, but I didn't want to work just for the sake of working. So I dabbled in this and that. I became unnerved by the anarchy that seemed to exist in the movie establishment—all of which blended into a series of very good times, good food, a lot of good-looking girls, and a lot of aimless fun. I worked with Clifford Odets on a script. I drank wine. I sat in a lot of easy chairs and I listened. I met people like Jean Renoir, people I had only heard about before, in Paris and London. I was becoming an adult. I didn't want to pass up really tasting my early twenties in order to churn up momentum. I just didn't do *anything* until finally I was flat broke and I had to go back to work."

The film he chose was *Lilith,* the last film directed by the late Robert (*The Hustler*) Rossen. Everyone had high hopes for it, but *Lilith* was in trouble from the first day's shooting. A Gothic story of life in a mental institution, it was shot mainly in an abandoned airplane hangar at Roosevelt Field on Long Island, where Lindbergh took off for Paris in 1927, and in an old mansion in Oyster Bay owned by an executive of the Dime Savings Bank. To this day the cast and crew of *Lilith* mention Warren's name as though they have just bitten down on a strange green bug. According to them, he was impossible. He exasperated Rossen fighting over lines—once delayed a scene for three days demanding the line, "I've read *Crime and Punishment* and *The Brothers Karamazov,*" be changed to "I've read *Crime and Punishment* and *half* of *The Brothers Karamazov.*" He sulked, refused interviews, annoyed the crew by holding up scenes to have his hair cut, angered the other actors by wearing four undershirts under his shirt to make himself look big-chested.

At the end of the picture, at the wrap party, the word got out that Peter Fonda and several of his friends were going to beat up Warren and throw him in the lake. Hortense Schorr, a kindly woman who was the picture's publicity consultant, says: "We were terrified. We had to keep Peter and Warren on opposite sides of the room. The Columbia executives got very nervous and the word was out—'Get Warren out of here!' " One of the guests was elected to drive Warren back to New York. He remembers: "They didn't get Warren, but the next day I discovered that the house had almost been demolished. The door to Warren's dressing room was ripped off the hinges, glasses and candles were smashed, wigs were missing, the lawn wrecked."

Warren diplomatically refuses to discuss *Lilith*, but it is clear that he blames everything on Rossen. "He had diabetes, a bad heart, a drinking problem, and boils inside his skin which later ruptured and killed him. He was dying during the picture and didn't know it. His family didn't even know it. He was a sick man and the picture suffered as a result. I don't want to talk about it because it would sound like I was kicking a dead man." When it was finally released, Jean Seberg got rave reviews and Warren once again was roundly panned. Bosley Crowther wrote in *The New York Times:* "A muddy performance by Warren Beatty doesn't help.... [He] has a sodden way of moving and a monotonous expression that suggests *his* character should be getting treatment."

Word of Warren's behavior on *Lilith* spread through the industry, but Arthur Penn went to see it anyway, and hired Warren for *Mickey One*, a low-budget film with a sixty-day shooting schedule made in Chicago in such bizarre locations as the New Republic Cafeteria and Hugh Hefner's swimming pool. Something magical happened to Warren under Penn's baton. He shaped up. He took direction. He worked twelve to fifteen hours a day and never complained. And he turned in the best performance of his career, proving that he was not untalented when he cared enough about a project to work for his living instead of merely posing in front of a camera with a pocket comb.

Offscreen, Warren was still in there pitching with the glamour girls. Natalie Wood, who had followed him to the set in Miami for *All Fall Down*, had long left the scene; Joan Collins, who had followed him around in Washington years before, had married Anthony Newley; and Warren, at the age of twenty-seven, had begun his most serious romantic entanglement to date with thirty-three-year-old Leslie Caron who was very much on the scene in Chicago. In February, 1965, Peter Hall, the director of the Royal Shakespeare Company in London, divorced Miss Caron, charging adultery with Warren in Chicago, Jamaica and Beverly Hills. Warren paid all the court costs.

He moved to London for a while, where he made two films—*Promise Her Anything* with Caron, and *Kaleidoscope*. Both were colossal bombs, like all the others, but the former was particularly notable for its mediocrity. (PROMISE HER ANYTHING—BUT DON'T TAKE HER TO THIS, screamed Judith Crist's headline in the *Herald Tribune* and, in tiny letters

44

sually reserved for B pictures in Forty-second Street grind ouses, the portly *New York Times* announced: *Promise Her Anything* Has Dual Opening with Baby as Star.)

Meanwhile the parties went on, at the rate of one every week, in Miss Caron's five-story Georgian town house on Montpelier Square in Kensington. Warren had five chauffeurs in London. All of them quit. "Sometimes he goes into a house and says he'll be out in five minutes—it's sometimes five hours," moaned one of them. Warren's birthday party in March, 1966, made all the society columns. James Fox and Charlie Feldman and John Huston and Vanessa Redgrave and Anjanette Comer and Christina Ford and simply *every-body* had a super time talking about skiing and the British elections, wore pants suits and flowered ties and danced till dawn when they all ended up at breakfast and you could hear the shrieks of "Dahling" all the way to Chelsea. It ended, like all the Beatty idylls before it, in flames.

SOMETHING STRANGE had happened to Warren's California sunshine and a crazy-bleak winter breeze was blowing across the terrace. We moved inside, where he turned over the Kurt Weill record and played the flip side. Warren doesn't smoke and doesn't drink (I've known him to sit in Arthur and sip six ginger ales in a row), but he was cold and felt like a little nip. He picked up a brightly wrapped package left over from Christmas, and began to tear it open. "This was a thirty-year-old bottle of bourbon made in 1936, which I bought as a gift for practically nothing. I wondered why it was so cheap. Then I found out it's only good if it's kept in a keg, so now I'm giving it to myself."

He opened the bottle and we drank it straight from room-service glasses. He noticed me glancing around the room, and immediately shifted to a new role—the tour guide. "Here is my poetry of Yevtushenko, here on this table is my jar of 5,000 super protein concentrate vitamin pills. I get *The New York Times* every day—an eccentric thing to do in a Beverly Hills hotel, don't you think? Here is another book I'm reading—*Khrushchev: A Career*, by Edward Crankshaw. Have you read it? You really should. I've learned to speak Russian without a teacher—from pocket books. When I don't understand a rule in one book I just go to another." There was no mention of Maya Plisetskaya, the Russian ballerina he had been linked with in the columns, and, one suspected, the real reason for his interest in linguistics.

"These," he continued, "are colored sheets of paper. On the white sheets I write the crap and then when it gets better

45

it goes to the pink sheets. By the time it gets to yellow, it's an idea." He scooped up the papers scattered across the rug and hid them under a stack of folders on the coffee table. "Here is an article on the economic situation in England, which I clipped from a weekly newsmagazine purchased in the hotel drugstore..." he was really letting me have it now..."and *this* is an article I wrote on Mabel Mercer. *That* is an empty bottle of Jack Daniel's. I have *here* fifty pages of a screenplay I'm writing in longhand. *This* is Sea & Ski suntan lotion. And *here*"—he strokes it with affection—"is my leather-bound producer's case on *Bonnie and Clyde* ... shooting schedules the script, legal files, contracts, budgets, actors' salaries...."

I asked him if he'd like to talk about how he became a producer, what kind of money he expected to make on the film. "Talk to my agent."

"Well, then, would you say—"

"*No!* I wouldn't say that. Whatever you say I wouldn't say I only say what *I* say."

I asked him if he'd care to talk about the women in his life. He seemed stunned, as though I had hit him suddenly in the locker room with a wet towel. "*What* women?" "Well, all the women you've been seen with since you became an actor. The list reads like *Who's Who*." "You said it, man, I didn't. I never discuss money or personalities. Its nobody's business but mine."

"You mean you deny the affair with Leslie Caron?"

He looked very tired. "I look back on that with enormous, overwhelming sadness." Why had he never taken any of his relationships as far as marriage? "We move in a time when tranquilizers, polygamy, so many alternatives are offered to working out the difficulties of a marriage. This business of you go with a person, you live with a person, you marry a person, you divorce a person, you marry *another* person— there is no substitute for the particular depth that is provided by time. Why don't you ask about the value of monogamy and the genius it requires?" He was showing those wide, Pepsodent molars again.

"Do you feel you don't really know yourself well enough yet to take on the responsibility of marriage?"

"I don't want to say that. I just want to be able to tell the truth."

"What do you mean by the truth?"

"A man tells the truth to a woman. A woman tells the truth to a man." Oh!

He was bored. He was lying down now, his head tilted to a

45-degree angle on the sofa, looking up sideways. I asked him why, if he wanted so desperately to project a new image as a responsible filmmaker instead of just another actor, interviews were so detestable to him? "They embarrass me. I have a pretty good antenna for when somebody is bored, and then I get the feeling some gigantic economic machine is forcing us to sit down and talk to each other. I've been badly burned by interviews. They usually take the *enfant terrible* approach, anyway. If someone wants to attack me, my sensitivity has long since evacuated that scene."

Warren was also beginning to evacuate the scene. And that's how I left him. A kid from Virginia, restless from having everything too soon, bored with himself, desperate to become a pillar of the movie world, not really sure if he was or was not a superstar, with no easily obtainable public to insure him of the right answer, listening to his Kurt Weill records, howling at the moon rising over his terrace like a slice of lemon peel in the California night, and falling, warmly and bearishly, asleep.

A few weeks later, I saw Warren once more. He had just been to a party thrown by Lynda Bird Johnson at the White House. He met me in a bar. He was sipping orange juice and I was drinking a Whiskey Sour on the rocks. He was being very surly with the waiter. ("Whaddya want, you want money?") The waiter fled. He was very nervous about the story. "I want to make a valuable contribution to this business, to produce worthwhile motion pictures!" he kept saying. I told him about the students at U.C.L.A., and he became furious. "Anybody can get five jerks to say *any*thing!"

Maybe so, but I already knew what Warren thought about Warren. What about the public? We left the bar and walked for five blocks along Eighth Avenue, elbowing our way through the theater crowds. Not one person showed any sign of recognizing Warren. We paused in the onslaught of normal, everyday subway-riding Joes on their way to a hockey match at Madison Square Garden. Nobody yelled, "There's Warren Beatty!" Nobody came near him.

I went home frankly worried. Maybe I wasn't being fair. So what if Warren Beatty acts like a jerk? When he's far from the maddening Hollywood hysteria, shut off from the bleach-blonde starlets busily buying baby sharks for their swimming pools, out of touch with the phonies filling his head with how they're spending $2,900 on totem poles for their front yards featuring handcarved faces of all the members of their families—away from all the silliness, Warren seems like a nice guy. He doesn't own a Maserati or a sixty-eight-foot yacht or a twin-engine Cessna or an Andrew Wyeth original or a projection room with his own 35mm print of *Potemkin* or a Cardin blue pinstripe suit or a beach cabana on the isle of Sylt. I like him for that. And so what if he comes on strong? If you had, at some point in your life, been swooned over by Vanessa Redgrave, Natalie Wood, Joan Collins, Faye Dunaway, Leslie Caron, Inger Stevens, Princess Margaret, Maya Plisetskaya, Lee Radziwill, Candy Bergen, Julie Christie, and God knows who else, wouldn't you be full of it?

I reached for my notes, ready to tear them into eight hundred little pieces and eat them for Sunday brunch, when I heard a knock at the door. It was my upstairs neighbor—a stereo addict, film buff, sports-car driver, *Playboy* reader—who had dropped by to borrow a bottle of Scotch. One last chance.

"What do you think of Warren Beatty?" I asked suddenly.

"Is *he* still alive? I used to see him in the circus."

"That's *Clyde* Beatty!" And that's when I covered the typewriter and went to bed.

Carson McCullers

> (*Carson McCullers was a friend and an advisor whose personal courage was as inspirational to me as her literary output. This is the last interview Mrs. McCullers ever granted. Shortly after it appeared, she died in a Nyack hospital, at the still-young age of fifty, on September 29, 1967. The world has been a sadder place to be ever since.*)

INCREDIBLE, YES. But it actually happened, right there in Brentano's, where they're supposed to know better: The clerk turned to me and said, "Carson McCullers? I never heard of him."

Even in an age super-gimmicked as it is with flying saucer

and LSD, it seems unbelievable that anyone could forget. The flash in the pans make a million and vanish into the woodwork, but she remains one of the dozen or so American writers to reach the top echelon of greatness. She was a legend almost from the beginning—a wiry slip of a girl with bangs and a crooked-tooth grin in sneakers and a baseball cap, who, at the tender age of twenty-three blossomed like a sunflower on the literary scene and, like Dilsey in Faulkner's *The Sound and the Fury*, stayed on to endure. Gore Vidal says, "The publicity was the work of those fashion magazines where a dish of blackeyed peas can be made to seem the roe of some rare fish, photographed by Avedon."

Yet there was more to it than that. Her novels—*The Heart Is a Lonely Hunter, The Member of the Wedding, Reflections in a Golden Eye, Ballad of the Sad Cafe, Clock Without Hands*—her plays and her short stories explored the depths of the human heart like no writer before her and cemented her place forever in the history of letters. She had come to New York from Georgia at the age of seventeen, lost her tuition money to Juilliard (she wanted to be a concert pianist) on the subway, and lived in a boarding-house for sailors on the Brooklyn waterfront. When her first novel was published in 1940, she became a celebrity, the troubled darling of the fashionable people like Edith Sitwell and Cecil Beaton. With the late *Harper's Bazaar* editor George Davis she established the only important literary salon in America in an old Brooklyn brownstone called February House, where the boarders included Christoper Isherwood, Richard Wright, Thomas Mann's son Golo, Oliver Smith, Jane and Paul Bowles and Gypsy Rose Lee. Gypsy provided the cook, W. H. Auden kept house and they all chipped in on the groceries. Their friends who came and went at all hours of the night were people like Anaïs Nin, Leonard Bernstein, Salvador Dali and his wife Gala, Marc Blitzstein, and Aaron Copland. Already one of New York's most controversial figures, she became one of its most famous playwrights with *The Member of the Wedding*. She drank champagne and ate raw oysters with Isak Dinesen and danced on a marble tabletop with Marilyn Monroe. Even after ill health and personal problems forced her into a life of seclusion in her country house in Nyack, she was flooded with letters from critics and fans throughout the world— schoolboys writing term papers on her work, new generations discovering the poetry in her books, scholars begging her to lecture.

What happened? The years brought her fame and money

but the one thing she never enjoyed was good health. The victim of a conspiracy of troubles, she suffered, at twenty-three, the first in a series of strokes that crippled her and threatened to destroy her career. In 1947 she lost the lateral vision in her right eye and entered a brief period of total blindness. One night in a Paris chateau she was reading a revision of *Wedding*, written by a script doctor who later sued her unsuccessfully for $50,000. Exhausted and unhappy because he had almost destroyed her play (and because at that point no one had yet been willing to produce it), she rose to get a glass of water and fell prostrate on the floor, where she remained for eight hours until discovered by a neighbor. She was constantly attended by her friends Kay Boyle and Truman Capote, but her left side has been paralyzed ever since. In December, 1953, her husband, Reeves McCullers, committed suicide. In 1955, her mother, whom she had depended on since childhood, died in Nyack in the house where Carson now lives. She suffered acute cardiac failure and has since suffered from chronic rheumatic heart disease resulting in numerous operations at the Columbia Presbyterian Hospital to relieve the spasms of her left arm and hand. In 1962, after she developed cancer of the right breast (now arrested) double surgery was performed in a final eight-hour operation on the nerves in her left hand. Fears of being permanently bedridden and her overwhelming desire to write goaded Carson into walking with a cane, but bouts of double pneumonia set in and she fell on the bathroom floor and shattered her left hip. Now she moves about only in a wheelchair and is able to write only by pressing one finger on her right hand to the typewriter keys. "Everyone," says one of her friends, "has someone—a husband, a wife, or a lover. But Carson lives strictly on the will to survive."

And to prove it, she picked up the phone recently and called a public-service ambulance to drive her to New York, where, in a hospital bed in the middle of a lavish Plaza Hotel suite the size of a small baseball diamond, she held court. She had a few things on her mind—her new story about a civil-rights march in *Redbook* magazine, the musical version of *Member of the Wedding* Mary Rodgers is preparing for Broadway, and the film John Huston has just made of *Reflections in a Golden Eye*. Ray Stark, the film's producer, told her he would pay all of her expenses if she and Ida (her Negro cook, housekeeper and faithful companion) would make the trip. Carson said she needed a holiday and Ida said, "It sure is good to eat somebody else's cookin'." So here they were, ordering up scorpions from Trader Vic's and giggling like two debutantes in an old Diana Lynn movie.

Carson sat up in bed, thin and frail, like a quivering bird, with dark, brilliant eyes and an aura of other-worldness about her: Frankie Addams grown up, sipping a bourbon toddy from a silver goblet, smoking endless cigarettes, talking cheerfully, and admiring the chrysanthemums and anemones sent by her friends. "On February 19 I was half a century old. Ida made a pineapple tree out of toothpicks, cocktail onions, cheeses, and cherries, and there were so many flowers it looked like somebody had been laid out. Mercy me, far from it. I feel better than I have in years. This spring Ida and I are going to Ireland to visit John Huston's castle. He sent us two first-class round-trip tickets and he will meet our plane with an ambulance which will take us to the country. He has promised to take me trout fishing and the change of scene should do wonders for us both. Do you know John Huston? A lovely man. I was first approached about a film of my book by Sir Carol Reed. I said, 'Sir Carol, I don't think it can be done,' so of course we forgot it. Years later, Huston came to my house in Nyack. We sat on the back porch and looked out at the flower garden my mother planted there, and I thought it over. If two top directors were interested, maybe it had a chance. Now I'm thrilled over it and can't wait for the opening night. John said it could be done in two different ways—as an art film, which I was not interested in, or in the grand manner with a great cast. What a cast! I've known Marlon Brando ever since he was in *Streetcar* and of course my beloved Julie Harris was Frankie Addams and I love her very much—she's been to my home many times. Elizabeth Taylor wrote a lovely letter to me from Rome. The Filipino houseboy is played by a wonderful young man named Zorro David, who is a hairdresser at Saks Fifth Avenue. Imagine that. I think they will all be superb in it. I have always been drawn to the beauty of words and I am fascinated by the vocabulary of films—marvelous words like *stills* and *rushes*. So far I've only seen the stills, not the rushes, but they look beautiful. Ray Stark, who loves to play practical jokes, phoned me and said, 'I've seen the film and I have to tell you that as a professional you must understand it's not good.' 'Not good?' I repeated, my heart breaking. 'No, it's *great!*' I hope he's right."

A knock at the door admitted Flora Lasky, Carson's long-time friend and lawyer, with a gift. "I suppose it's too late to persuade you to give up smoking," she said sternly.

"I suppose so," replied Carson impishly.

"Then you might as well smoke in an elegant ashtray," she said, presenting her with a sea-green dish encrusted with jewels from the Virgin Islands.

After she left, Carson said, "I don't know what I'd do without my friends. They are the 'we' of me. I can't get out of bed at all now. I broke my leg and can no longer walk." She grinned her Raggedy Ann grin. "The sad, happy life of Carson McCullers. Sometimes I think God got me mixed up with Job. But Job never cursed God and neither have I. I carry on. Every morning around nine Ida comes to my house and prepares breakfast for us, then I try to write, whether I feel well or not. I've been a writer so long I have to—and *want* to—do it. There are awful days when the pain is so intense I can't write. Those are the dreadful times, and I drop out for a while, but I always snap back again. The doctors make me drink prune juice, so I'll go to the bathroom, and I hate that. So you see there are things I have to put up with, like it or not."

What about that musical version of *Member of the Wedding*? Might it break the bones of her fragile play? "Well, I just won't allow that to happen. It all takes place in a kitchen, so I don't see how they can do much dancing. It would be simply awful if Berenice Sadie Brown went into some elaborate tap-dance production number with pots and pans. But John Henry and Frankie were always singing and dancing around the kitchen, so that wouldn't be too out of place." Still her favorite among her works, it took her a solid year to write the first sentence. When she saw the film version of *Wedding* in a little movie house in Macon, Georgia, the scene in which Ethel Waters holds the children on her lap singing "His Eye Is on the Sparrow" was cut. She has never recovered from the shock and has higher hopes for both *Reflections* and the forthcoming film of *The Heart Is a Lonely Hunter*, which will star Alan Arkin. "That script was written by another Southerner named Tom Ryan, so it has much of my original feeling in it. I wouldn't trust a Northern writer with it."

Another knock at the door and in came a young college boy from Long Island who presented a speechless Mrs. McCullers with both an oil portrait he had painted of her and a copy of the record album "Judy Garland at Carnegie Hall." The scene was embarrassing, but not untypical of the adoration students have for her today, when her novels are being taught in college English courses. "I was so nervous about meeting her I didn't sleep all night," he said on his way out.

"Astonishing!" she cried, when he was gone. "One critic mortally wounded me when he wrote that I had corrupted young people. I don't think that is true. I get along with them. Edward Albee was very young when he came to me to ask permission to adapt my *Ballad of the Sad Cafe*. He rented a small cabin with no electricity on Water Island and I sat up all night on the beach while he read it to me. However, when I saw it on Broadway I was disappointed. Edward had his own genius and I thought he was just cooling his heels working on something of mine. He should've been working on his own plays. There was no dialogue and no action in my novella and I told him it could not be done. I don't know how he feels but I still think I was right."

She talked into the afternoon about New York ("not for home folks"), books (after much prodding, she admitted her favorites are *Sons and Lovers*, Dostoievski, Tolstoi, "and Mr. Faulkner, who makes me blush like a bride"). With long, elegant hands turned out like ivory carvings, she described her house in Nyack, a Southern Gothic Victorian building the color of vanilla ice cream right across the street from the Methodist Church, where she greets her guests in long white nightgowns and tennis shoes. She works slowly, even slower since she has been incapacitated, admits belonging to no school of writers ("Most schools copy *me*"), and pays no attention to vogues that come and go in fiction ("Who," she asks, "is Jacqueline Susann?"). Her next books, she says, will be a collection of stories about Negroes she has known in the South ("The speech and feeling of one's childhood is always inherent to me as an author and Negro speech is so beautiful") and, eventually, a journal about her life, her books, and why she wrote them. "I think it is important for future generations of students to know why I did certain things, but it is also important for myself. I became an established literary figure overnight, and I was much too young to understand what happened to me or the responsibility it entailed. I was a bit of a holy terror. That, combined with all my illnesses, nearly destroyed me. Perhaps if I trace and preserve for other generations the effect this success had on me it will prepare future artists to accept it better."

"It's time for Sister to take her nap now," Ida interrupted.

"That," added Carson, "is orders from headquarters."

And that is where I left her, surrounded by clouds of pillows and lost in her own memories, fortified by No-Cal orange soda and a bedside apothecary shop of assorted rainbow-colored pills, like Easter eggs on a white table. "Good-bye," she whispered no louder than the sound of a ripe rose falling off its stem.

Mike Nichols

(*Although he might deny it, Mike Nichols, at thirty-six, is one of the few real geniuses of the Sixties. Everything he touches turns to gold, a fact of life which has earned for him a Midas mantle. Any active file on Mike would have to be updated every two weeks. Therefore this story, which first appeared in* Cosmopolitan *in 1965, seems almost obsolete. In the intervening three years since I wrote it, he has successfully directed stage productions of* The Odd Couple, The Apple Tree, *a Broadway revival of Lillian Hellman's* The Little Foxes, *and* Plaza Suite. *For films he has directed* Who's Afraid of Virginia Woolf? *and* The Graduate, *and for his next movie it is reported he will receive the highest salary ever paid a motion picture director—$1,000,000. All of which makes him more of a wizard now than he was three years ago. But I thought it might be fun to see what he was like then, and it is with this in mind that it is reproduced here.*)

AT TWO O'CLOCK in the afternoon on New Year's Eve, I sat in Sardi's sipping a Black Russian, listening to Guy Lombardo playing "Auld Lang Syne" on the Muzak, and waiting for Mike Nichols. He was half an hour late. He is always late. And as a friend had told me just a few days earlier, "The older he gets the later he gets."

At the age of thirty-three, it is not surprising. Looking back on the many facets of his amazing career, I was only surprised he has not yet been hospitalized from nervous exhaustion and overwork. Since he and Elaine May exploded on the entertainment scene in 1958, I had come to equate them with those very special pleasures in life, doing for comedy what avocados had done for food or what Kurt Weill had done for musical comedy.

Their brilliance as social satirists, tickling the ribs of the world with razor-sharp pins of self-analysis, had made them the undisputed leaders in the field of sophisticated laughter. Then, in 1961, after 30 improvised performances on Broadway, they came to a halt. They were fed up with business managers, publicity photos, newspaper interviews, conferences, luncheons, and autograph hounds. They stopped throwing crumbs at a begging audience of millions of discriminate fans who had previously asked politely for cake. Their lives, they said, had become "a million deals" and they wanted out.

Elaine wanted to write plays and Mike set out alone to prove himself adept at practically everything—a Pantaloon conjured up by Pirandello, a character indeed in search of an author, ready and determined to burst into every role in life and play them all brilliantly. He tried writing (with Ken Welch, he provided the sketches for the classic evening at Carnegie Hall with his pals Carol Burnett and Julie Andrews, wrote a guest column for John Crosby, and a parody of Italian movies for *The New Yorker*). Then he had a go at acting (played the Dauphin in Shaw's *St. Joan* at the Vancouver International Festival; starred in Elaine May's Broadway-bound *A Matter of Position,* which closed out of town because the audiences loved Mike, not the play; and made television history as a psychotic undergoing group therapy on *Playhouse 90*).

All of it made him very unhappy. Then he discovered directing and hit a home run. He had already been the guiding hand for a hilarious summer-stock potpourri called *The World of Jules Feiffer,* which never got to New York, when producer Saint Subber took a big chance and asked him to direct a bit of soufflé called *Barefoot in the Park.* The rest is theater history.

In case there is anyone left who still thinks of Mike as "Elaine May's partner," examine this: In the professional theater of 1965, where the life-span of practically everything is determined by the size of the next theater party, he is the director of three of the biggest smash hits—*Barefoot* (which recently marked up its 500th performance), *The Knack,* and *Luv*—for which the lines of both theater-party agents and private citizens waiting to buy tickets, if placed end to end, would reach halfway to New Jersey.

In New Orleans, his television commercials for Jax beer

55

are as popular as Creole gumbo. His radio spots for the Peace Corps have probably been responsible for more enlistments than a stack of Joan Baez records. With Elaine May, he still does weekend broadcasts on *Monitor,* and the two of them are signed for six comedy appearances on *The Jack Paar Show* throughout 1965. As if that were not enough, he is now directing a new Broadway show called *The Odd Couple,* written by *Barefoot*'s Neil Simon, and Hollywood, not to be outdone by Broadway, has finally beckoned with a solid gold forefinger: come June, Nichols will direct Richard Burton and Elizabeth Taylor in the movie version of *Who's Afraid of Virginia Woolf?,* followed by two more films—a movie version of Joseph Heller's novel *Catch-22,* and *The Graduate* for Joseph E. Levine.

Before we agreed to meet for lunch, I had tried to seek a few clues to the Nichols personality. One of his close friends is free-lance writer Gloria Steinem, a lovely, dahlia-like girl who, it may be remembered, was the much-publicized undercover Playboy bunny who later wrote up her experiences in a national magazine. "It's hard to be with people who are joke funny; you have to struggle for a topper," she said over coffee at the Coffee Mill. "But Mike is basically an actor. He finds situations themselves funny, not gags, and he blends his own ideas about humor into the things he directs. With people, you have to be straight. He knows when you're pretending or just dropping names. He accepts people on their own levels, and his friends always turn to him in emergencies. There's always a part of him that remains private, though. He's not a bleeder."

Has success changed him? "No, but it seems to change everybody else. For instance, it is now very difficult for him to go to parties or be himself in public. Because of his commercial success, a lot of people think he's fair game. We went to a party in Greenwich Village recently where he was insulted by the same crowd that used to love to sit in greasy cellars and applaud him when he was living on twelve dollars a week—you know, the ones who read the *Village Voice,* or have two things published in the *New Republic.* A man came up to him and said, 'I just finished a play—but I'm not giving you the script. You wouldn't understand it.' That sort of thing really hurts him, you know. He has become sort of a 'fastest gun in the West' and people who used to like him are now out to get him."

Then I went to see *Luv,* where tickets are so hard to get that the stage manager told me, "The FBI couldn't get in there with a pass key." I had to stand, but it was worth it.

Luv is so stamped with the mark of Nichols that on opening night Henry Fonda remarked, "If nobody had ever told me Mike had directed a show, I'd have seen him in it. The things I loved so much in his performing I loved in his directions."

Although it is funnier seen than described, there is something inescapably Nichols and May about a suicide addict who puts on a bathing cap before he jumps off a bridge, or a wife who bursts sentimentally into choruses of "Love Cast a Shadow Over My Heart" as her husband reaches his hand inside her blouse à la *Tea and Sympathy*.

Backstage I found two of *Luv*'s three cast members, Eli Wallach and his wife, Anne Jackson, wrapped in terry-cloth bathrobes. "I refuse to contribute another word to the already growing rumor that Mike Nichols is a genius," said Wallach. "Besides," he winked, "everybody knows it's true." He put down the copy of *Chaplin* he was reading and went on. "With our Actor's Studio method training, we were taking it all too seriously, with a tendency to work for each line, breaking up all the clichés in the show. Mike would say, 'Play them as clichés.' I remember Annie couldn't do one particular phony-wife line. She would say, 'But Mike, it's not me.' And Mike would say, 'Just act it the way you act on David Susskind's *Open End!*' It worked!"

Later, over vodka and orange juice, I told Anne Jackson what Neil Simon had said about Mike: "He gets into the actors not only a sense of improvisation, but also a feeling that they had just thought of the lines that minute. If he would direct Shakespeare, it would come out the same way—as if Hamlet had just thought of to be or not to be."

"Absolutely right!" she cried. "He's patient, but he's also strict. I'm terribly insecure in the rehearsal stage. Well, Mike wouldn't allow me to waste my time worrying about whether it was working or not. He freed me by making me do end results right off the bat and it was good for me. He's also very stubborn, but he believes in what he's after and he's committed to that belief. If I had an idea, he'd say, 'Try it, but I don't think it'll work.' He was always so sure, but he's so well-grounded in his commitments to what he instinctively knows is *right* that I think there lies the essence of his brilliance as a director."

I was thinking about all of this, and also about how it must have felt after the opening of *Luv* when *Time* magazine called him the "most gifted new director in the American theater since Elia Kazan left Constantinople," when the glass doors of Sardi's flew open and in from the snowy December day sailed Mike himself, blowing frosty smoke from a cris cigar and looking a bit like a merry red-nosed Pinocchio in black sweater.

In person, he suggests a Steinberg drawing of a cro between Peanuts and Gertrude Stein. There is a patch of blu sky in his almost hidden eyes, a wall of regal forehead ju above, and a tired, smiling mouth—all coming together t form a face like an unbaked johnny-cake, rising to a summ just under a patch of wheat-colored hair which parts "a cording to whichever direction the wind is blowing th day."

"Happy New Year. I'm exhausted," he said for an opene settling down between two framed caricatures of Brook Atkinson and Tammy Grimes. Then he ordered a bullsh and a large dish of scrambled eggs, and started talking. H spoke quietly and thoughtfully, and there were times durin our conversation, due to his ponderous noncapacity fo speed, when it was even money as to whether he would eve speak again.

He told me what he had been doing since *Luv* ha knocked Broadway on its jaded ears: "Well, I flew to Londo for three weeks, working on the screenplay for *Public Ey* with Peter Shaffer—we hope to persuade Julie Andrews, Re Harrison, and Marcello Mastroianni to be in it." [It neve came off.] "Then I spent ten days in Hollywood in confer ences with Jack Warner on *Virginia Woolf* and directed th national touring company of *Barefoot in the Park* wit Myrna Loy, and arrived back in New York on Christma Eve, left that night to spend Christmas with my mother i Philly, and winged back to town in time for Sybil Burton' twist party for Dirk Bogarde."

He had just come from his fourth day of rehearsals fo *The Odd Couple,* which will open in March, making fou Nichols-directed plays running simultaneously. "This one' about divorce from the man's point of view, which has neve been done, you know. Art Carney and Walter Matthau ar roommates who end up fighting so much they're almost read to go back to their wives. It's very funny. You never see th wives, just all the great-looking broads—just like in rea life!"

Nichols, who has been married twice, is not using his ow experiences as a basis for his direction. "I have no formulas I don't do anything consciously; I just find it as I live m life." Living his life, he says, includes a pad in New York (where, according to a friend, "shirts, ties, and socks droo from unclosed drawers and framed pictures of horses an

ps hang lopsided on the walls"), a baby daughter named
isy, sporadic reading tastes ("mostly Russian writers"),
d "seeing millions and millions of movies." He reads maga-
es irregularly, subscribes to *Dog World* ("I don't have a
g anymore, but they keep sending it"), never reads *Vari-
'. He likes classical music ("especially *Rosenkavalier*")
d occasionally cooks spaghetti.

In spite of the money he has made, he claims only three
xuries in life: (1) a Lincoln Continental convertible; (2)
 Arabian riding horse, Max; and (3) a brand-new tower
artment in the Beresford, which he has not furnished or
oved into, but which has tower windows through which he
n look out and survey the city he has conquered.

We talked about the jobs he had held before he broke into
e big time eight years ago. He told me he had once
rked in an office for two days, then when he had to file
phabetically he told them he was going to the men's room
d never came back. Then he drove a truck for the post
ice in Chicago and quit because he "couldn't find a single
ddress"; he was a soda jerk at Howard Johnson's and got
ed when he ran out of patience naming all fifty flavors of
e cream, turned to a new customer asking the same ques-
n, looked him straight in the eye, and said "Chicken." He
oveled manure, played folk music on an FM radio station,
en acted as a jingle judge in a mail-in contest.

"Those were crazy days," says Mike. "I studied with Lee
rasberg in the same class with Carroll Baker and Inger
evens and was scared to death. And I was always broke. I
d a little broom closet in the West Eighties, right off
entral Park, and there were two girls across the street who
ed to feed me and lend me carfare. They were always
aking fancy fondue things and I'd raid their icebox until
ey got smart. One day I was so hungry sitting in class that I
alked out, went to a supermarket, and stole a cheese! Now
often think of going back to that market and returning the
eese, but I haven't figured out a way to do it without
tting caught."

When he couldn't sponge or steal a meal, he'd head for the
earest Automat, where he'd buy a cup of tea, go back for
ore hot water (free) and some oyster crackers (also free),
ix the crackers with ketchup in the hot water, and—
resto!—a good actor's excuse for tomato soup.

"The closest I came to complete misery was when I ate a
hole jar of mustard."

"How does one eat a whole jar of mustard?" I flinched.

"Slowly and painfully."

59

Then he went to the University of Chicago ("where eve body talked a lot and nobody ever went to class") and r Elaine May in a production of Strindberg's *Miss Julie*; t hated each other on sight. Then one day they met again the waiting room of the Illinois Central railroad station a improvised a scene together about two spies that had them stitches. They started doing the same sort of thing in vari cellar cafés on Chicago's South Side, and later formed Compass Players with Shelley Berman, all practitioners o sort of modern-day *commedia dell'arte*, the spontane comedy of Renaissance Italy in which strolling players i provised their skits and lampooned their age.

During those years they were both determined to ke their personal lives private. They used to tell reporters thi like "We live very quietly and date occasionally; right n we're seeing Comden and Green." Today Mike talks ope and frankly of their work. "The success of the thing depe ed on people understanding each other's ideas very fast with a minimum of words and as much rapport as possib Our ideas got through to each other very easily; we h instant rapport, like instant coffee." He still laughs at gossip columnist who referred to the "wonderful comic ents of May Nichols and Eli."

Then there was the year on Broadway with the reco breaking *Evening with Mike Nichols and Elaine May*, which they brought down the house with scenes like the m trying to save his soul and his last dime from the telepho company ("But what if you jiggle something with your elb or something and I lose my dime, Operator?" "We do n work with our elbows, sir") or their travesty of Southe writers, with Mike playing "Mr. Alabama Glass," telli Elaine's P.T.A. group that the heroine of his latest play, *Po Makes Me Sick in the Summer*, has just watched her h band, Raoul, commit suicide and has "taken to drink, pros tution, and puttin' on airs." If they hadn't decided to call quits, they would probably still be running today.

"We had to end it while we could still face each other. V just got bored. We're both very restless types." (During t run, while they were capturing the hearts of their audienc they were both trundling off to their psychiatrists twice week.)

In directing, Mike says he has found himself. "I used turn purple with fright before going onstage; now I lo opening nights, when everyone is scared but me. I just had call from Leslie Caron and Warren Beatty, begging me to in a movie with them. 'You'll get used to a set and all t

60

ghts before you start your own picture,' they said. But I said
). I never intend to act again as long as I live. Besides, I'm
)ing what I've wanted to do for ten years right now. I've
ever been happier."

Of his direction, drama critic Walter Kerr once called it
2½ hours of winging it, without ever sloshing into an
nfriendly cloud." Neil Simon, the author, says, "Mike start-
d directing because he wanted to grow. Now he's the Num-
er One director on Broadway." Lillian Hellman says: "I
ways knew Mike had it in him. I'm just so proud of him now
go around dimpling as if I had given birth to him."
lizabeth Ashley says, simply, "Mike's a goddam Super-
an."

She's probably right. He has an IQ of 180. His maternal
randmother wrote the libretto of the opera *Salome* for
ichard Strauss. His grandfather, Gustave Landauer, along
ith Martin Buber, formed the Independent Socialist party
1 Germany and was murdered by the prewar Nazis in
919.

Because of all this, and because his father was a Jewish
octor, his family had to flee Berlin, where Mike was born in
931. Mike and his brother (now a doctor in Minnesota)
ame over on the *Bremen*—the last ship to leave Germany
efore the real trouble started. "We had little ID tags around
ur necks and we knew only two sentences of English: 'I
on't speak English' and 'Please don't kiss me.'"

By the time the rest of the family had reunited in New
York, Mike had gone "crazy wild for Corn Flakes and
.oca-Cola." There was never any money, although Mike
vent to some chic schools on scholarships, like the Walden
chool in Manhattan, "a wild progressive school where they
alk about psychiatry and everything when you're fourteen
nd you learn French from playing cards." Mike's father died
1 1944 of leukemia, and his mother remarried and moved to
'hiladelphia. Then he became eligible for college, registered
t N.Y.U. but hated it violently: "On the first day of classes
hey made us stand up and sing something like 'Oh grim, gray
'alisades,' so I quit. It seemed like a school I really didn't
vant to go to, anyway."

He finished his eggs and ordered a pot of coffee. I asked
im about money. "When you don't have money, you spend
ll your time pretending you don't need it. Then when you
ave it, you need it more. I consider money very important,
n that it gives you freedom never to do anything you don't
ave to do just for money, if that makes any sense. I guess

61

what money really does is free you from thinking about it altogether."

Had his attitudes changed toward life since he had attained a new and respected position as a top-flight director? "Listen I can still go to a really terrible movie like *Send Me No Flowers* and love it. I mean I love really lousy things. The only difference is that now I look at Doris Day and I see a series of stationary two-shots, where I used to see freckles. You know what I mean?"

He loves movies, especially the late show on television which he watches religiously. "I grew up on a diet of movies and I'd still rather see a movie than a play. But then I'd rather direct a play than write one, and I'd rather write one than act in one. But I get a kick out of everything I see. I think there are too many hateful people around who are bored with themselves and their work, so they end up hating everything. I hope I never get that way."

He loves New York and never wants to live anywhere else but admits it is bad for him. "I am hopelessly lazy when it comes to lifting barbells and all that nonsense. Living in the city I don't get much exercise. Also, this is the only city in the world that still has movies coming on at five o'clock in the morning. I practically never get any sleep." It is not at all unusual for him to set his alarm clock for four A.M. to see an old Eric Blore movie, or catch Gale Sondergaard vamping it up in *The Spider Woman Strikes Back,* a passion he finds difficult now that he has to be up at seven-thirty to go to rehearsals. "Sometimes if I miss the endings, my friends call me up and tell me."

His friends are people like Betty Comden, Adolph Green and his wife, Phyllis, lyricist Stephen (*Gypsy, West Side Story*) Sondheim, Barbara Harris, novelist James Baldwin, the Leonard Bernsteins—"and Elaine, don't forget Elaine!"

They usually play "in" parlor games like guessing the characters people played in old movies or doing charades on street corners while waiting for crosstown buses. One of his favorite evenings recently went like this: dinner with Gloria Steinem, Julie Andrews, and Julie's husband, set designer Tony Walton, at Luchow's, followed by the four of them dancing down Fourteenth Street toward Klein's and acting out movie endings. "Julie was marvelous; there she was all pinched together, pretending to be drinking tea and then rolling her eyes skyward toward some terrible make-believe noise. Can you guess what she was doing?" To his disappointment, I confessed I didn't have a clue. *"Breaking the Sound Barrier,* of course. We all got it right off."

Mention *Virginia Woolf* and he turns eggshell white. "I ay love movies, but I loathe Hollywood. And what a movie begin with out there! So much is resting on this. I'm afraid it's no good they'll kick me out. But I refuse to worry," he aid, clutching the edge of the table for support.

Change the subject to Elizabeth Taylor and his mouth elaxes into an almost angelic smile, with eyes that take on e glow of a small boy who has just bitten into his first piece f divinity fudge. "She's divine. People are always coming up me and saying rude things like, 'Elizabeth Taylor? It's the tupidest casting I ever heard of.' Well, I say wait and see. Everyone is going to be surprised. Personally, I consider her ne of the greatest cinema actresses the screen has ever roduced. I've seen *A Place in the Sun* eighteen times, and I on't know anyone in the business who could've done what he did in *Suddenly, Last Summer*. I still see her in *Cynthia*, oughing and frightened and crying her eyes out because she an't go to the prom with Jimmy Lydon, or trying to steal ane Powell's boyfriend in *A Date with Judy*. Every time you ick up a magazine you read all the wrong things—about her ragic loves, her tragic life, her tragic future. It's all bunk. he's one of the happiest people in the world, and a great ampy girl. I like her because she knows how to handle sucess and still have fun. Most of the new kids who are becomng big stars don't have any fun with their lives or their uccesses."

Guy Lombardo had started up another chorus of "Auld Lang Syne" on the Muzak. Mike looked at his watch and panicked. He had to get ready for his idea of a swinging way o spend New Year's Eve: going over to Lillian Hellman's nd watching Lena Horne on television.

"It's been painless," he said, rising to go.

"But we still haven't talked about half the things I wanted o talk about—Hitler, the Beatles, discotheques, Veda Ann Borg—"

"We'll finish it the first evening there's a good Maria Montez movie on the late show!"

Then he gave a cheery wave and rushed out of Sardi's almost as abruptly as he had come in. I caught one last glimpse of him, pulling up his collar around his nose like a puppet whose strings have just been pulled satisfactorily, pirouetting through the Forty-fourth Street traffic toward Shubert Alley: reminding me not at all of a famous New York director, but more of a harlequin dancing in the wind.

Lucille Ball

SCENE: A movie set where Lucille Ball is making *Yours,*
Mine and Ours—her first picture in five years. California sun
blazes down, melting people, cars, ice in the extras' Dixie
cups. On the exact spot where Bette Davis drove Joan Crawford bananas in *Baby Jane* it's Christmas; a fifteen-foot tree
with three tons of tinsel beckons cheerfully, holly and pine
cones hang from Tiffany-glass chandeliers, Christmas cards
dangle on satin ribbons, Christ in the manger entertains
lavishly on top of the family piano, a turkey dinner waits
invitingly to be eaten on a table set for sixteen people in an
1893 Victorian house surrounded by fifty pots of fake trees.
People wait for the star. They talk. "She's tough," says a
Hollywood columnist, "the pressures of being a star and the
responsibility of being the president of a $30-million-a-year
corporation have turned her into something frightening."
"You'll think you're talking to a man," warns one of her
aides. Still they wait, sweating in the glow of the Christmas
tree lights.

ACTION: Lucy is here. Wearing something pink, orange-
popsicle hair flaming in the breeze, sucking a butterscotch
ball. "It's hot in here; I paid for air-conditioning, where the
hell is it? This used to be the old Hopalong Cassidy set—I
think they left some of their fleas." She sounds tough. But—
"Don't believe that guff. I have enough trouble worrying
about the studio during the day. When I get home at night, I
take care of my family. I go home in this terrible heat and
jump in the pool. After years of being in this routine, I've
learned to budget my hours and my energies. I reserve. I
don't let things tear me apart at the wrong times. The most
important thing is what I have to do at the moment. If I'm
driving down the street, I think of nothing but the wheel. If
I'm making up, I think of only my lipstick. I only go to other
people's sets in cases of extreme emergency; usually they
come to me."

You could see, beyond the sound stage, the vast complex of studios called Desilu, which Lucy bought from her ex-husband, Desi Arnaz, in 1962 with three million dollars borrowed from the City National Bank of Los Angeles. In five years she had moved into Howard Hughes' old offices and, flitting back and forth from the sets of her TV shows to the green-chintz chairs in her executive suite, had turned thirty-six soundstages and sixty-two acres of real estate losing nearly a million dollars a year into the biggest gold-mine TV-producing facility in the world. No wonder they call her tough. What other Hattie Carnegie hat model and redheaded, lame-brained Goldwyn Girl from Jamestown, New York, had come that far? "Listen, honey," said Lucy, poking me in the knee, "if I was going to turn into a man I would've done it a long time ago. I've been in awe of most men all my life. It never occurred to me how an executive should be. I've been *told*. But when I took over this job I decided to do it my way. My ability comes from fairness and a knowledge of people. The rules were here before I took over. My job is just to keep everybody happy. I never wanted to be an executive, but when my marriage to Desi broke up after 19 years, I couldn't just walk away from my obligations and say forget it. We were an institution. Life takes guts. If you don't take chances you'll never bathe because you might get dirty again; you'll never eat because you might get sick. So I took on all of our responsibilities, but I ran my studio like I run my home, with understanding for people. I hate to hire and fire. Now I've just sold the whole damn thing to a bigger corporation and pretty soon they'll take my name off the door and I'll be free, open for everything. It's really exciting. But I have to work or I'm nothing. I had a few weeks off from the *Lucy* show, so I decided to make this film. It's about the Beardsleys—that man with ten kids who married the woman with eight of her own. It's a family film—the only kind I'll do. I hate all this violence and 007 stuff they're making now. Turns me off. Wait a minute, they want me in this scene. If I forget you're here just yell 'Lucy!' and I'll come running, honey."

Between takes she attends staff meetings, board meetings, story conferences, production, administration, and financing meetings—and signs checks. She does an interview by seating you in a pink-canvas, white-fringed deck chair with LUCY written across the back while she stands facing you, placing one hand on each arm rest, crossing her legs, looking you straight in the eye, and puffing away on cigarettes people are constantly offering her from crumpled little packs lying

65

around the set. When she thinks of something, in the middle of a sentence, she jots it down and sticks each message to herself on the steering wheel of her car with Scotch tape. It's not unusual to find ten of them taped on at the end of the day.

She went back to work. "Do I look perspiry?" she asks a grip. "I don't want too much white on my face. Charlie, can you get a new angle on that dolly?" She knows every term, every lighting fixture, every prop man. James Agee once wrote that she "tackles a role like it was sirloin and she didn't care who was looking." It's true. She does a shot with Henry Fonda, who plays her husband. A perfect take. The blue eyes flash and the Lucy grin cracks out like the morning sun. "Cut! Let's do it again. There's a shadow on Hank's chin, Mel, move that light three inches to the left. Now stay where you are, Hank." They did it again. "I liked the first one, Mel, but I'll look at them both later in the projection room." Fonda kissed her. Van Johnson, the third star, beamed. "She's the same girl she was at MGM," he says from the sidelines.

"Now, let's see, where was I? Oh, yes. I know people who are big stars in this town, who make hundreds of thousands of dollars a year, who are miserable because they don't know their own requirements for happiness. I deal in people rather than deals. That may not be much of a definition of success, but it's a helluva start. Being able to recognize what makes you happy. When I had my first little money saved—I mean *little*—a few hundred dollars or so, I brought my whole family out here from New York because I realized it was no fun without someone to share it with. Money has never been important to me. You just have to take my word for that; I can't prove it. But when I didn't have it I never felt the squeeze. It was fun to have no dough. I had knocked around New York as a showgirl, but I never held on to those jobs more than a few days. Then I was a model on Seventh Avenue. I worked hard and I was ill for two years from the work and missed out on everything. I was only eighteen, but I even learned from that. It taught me that without your health, you ain't got nothin'. Remember that, kiddo. I had no survival technique, so I didn't survive. But where I was different from the other dumb showgirls is that I learned from every experience and some of them don't. I also had a grab on respectability. My grandparents had raised me to have a conscience. I was very observant. I watched the other girls make their mistakes. I turned down a lot of so-called 'opportunities' because they were only 'maneuvers.' My ambition wasn't high, I just wanted to work. I came out to Hollywood to do an Eddie Cantor picture with twelve or fourteen showgirls, right? They had more experience, more money, knew their way around. Yet I made it and they didn't. Why? Maybe because they turned down more working jobs or social opportunities and I did just the opposite. As a result, I've never been out of work in this town except for two hours once between contracts. Then I got type-cast in *I Love Lucy*, but even when my marriage to Desi was falling apart I never got tired of Lucy. If you love your work it helps make up for the mistakes you make. That was a terrible time in my life. All those B pictures and all those years as Lucy and I felt like I would get out of my rut if I did a Broadway musical, so I did *Wildcat*. Ugh! You know, I learned something there, too. It was the first time in my life Lucy didn't venture an opinion. I hired the best people in the business (I *thought*) to do what they do and they didn't *do*. I should have shouted some and maybe it would have been a better show, but I was tired. It was the first time in years I had been free. I had my divorce and I wanted to move bag and baggage away from trouble. I backed the show with my own money, sank thirty grand in an apartment, and settled down for a long run. It was never anything more than a female *Rainmaker*, but nobody told me how bad it was. Except the gypsies in the chorus. They knew everything. Finally I began to listen to them and they were right. But you know we were SRO from the time we opened, and when you're a hit, the powers that be are inclined not to change anything. When I left, they almost carried me out in a coffin. I had to give them back $165,000 outta my own pocket—the most money ever refunded, they said—you can check it. I had fallen on a Bob Hope picture and healed on the outside but not inside. The antibiotics they gave me killed the red corpuscles in my body, so when I got pneumonia there was no way to fight it. I also had broken fingers and a cast on my left hip. But I was fixing and changing up to the night I closed. Now I don't think I'll ever do another play. The loss of the days and contact with the outer world is terrible. You don't sign up to do a flop, you sign for a long run, and I don't have that kind of time anymore. But I learned something good, even from a horrible experience like *Wildcat*. I learned the people came to the theater to see the Lucy they knew and I didn't give it to them."

She now lives with her husband, Gary Morton, her two kids by Desi Arnaz, three poodles, a Belgian barge dog ("Great watchdog—I've seen her sit for seven hours guarding an avocado seed") in a million-dollar house in Beverly Hills complete with a Victorian billiard parlor, screening room, and bars on the windows because ever since the kids were babies she's had kidnap threats. "I don't set up rules for my kids. I never said a word to them against their father. They've come to know that he's not easy to understand, but he's much better now. The girl he's married to is a doll. I've rented him some space in one of my studios and he's working again. I'm observing now, watching to see how much of my philosophy of life has rubbed off on my kids. I'm a twelve-hour-a-day watcher. I've been as good a mother as I know how to be and so far they have not disappointed me. The only thing I ever missed was Little Desi's graduation from grade school. Or maybe a Little League baseball game now and then, but my mother or Gary is always there. I keep up with the times through them. One night they asked if we could show some movies, so up went the paintings and on came *Thunderball*. Five adults and a few kids sitting around. Well, the blood is spurting, the bullets are flying, the sharks are biting, and then this 007 guy climbs into bed with this dame and I yelled, 'Stop the film! What the hell kind of picture is this?' My daughter, who is sixteen now and in the middle of a big romance, said, 'Oh, Mother, my God—we've seen it three times!' So I showed *Blow-Up*, that awful Italian thing. Well, that was worse. I said, 'I have had it, get me a Western.' And so help me they're in the fort, see, with the Indians coming through the gate, and I'll be damned if the girl doesn't make the sign of the cross, rip her clothes off, and climb on top of this cowboy—Rod Taylor or somebody— and they're crawling all over each other in bed like there's no tomorrow! Ugh! Everybody's taking their clothes off but me. You'll never catch me in the buff, kiddo."

She went into a close-up. "We blew another light, Mel. Hell, what's the matter with everybody?" She was Lucy the exec again, anger flashing beneath the pink rouge. Then she winked at Van Johnson and stroked the head of a child playing one of her eighteen kids. "Straighten up, Jennifer. Smile, Van." Tough? Yeah, sure. About as tough as an Easter egg.

When she gave the order, they closed up the set for the day. "C'mon over and see how I live, kiddo. We touch in our house. I come home dead tired and if I feel my kids stiffen I say 'Honey, don't stiffen up, Mama needs you tonight.' I never say, '*You* need.' I tell them, 'There's so little time. Your friends have you so many years, your teachers have you so many years. We'll have to wait till you come back home with your own kids to have you again. Let's take advantage of the kisses and hugs while we have them.'" She walked into the pounding heat of the Hollywood afternoon, yelling over her shoulder in her best boss-lady voice, "Lock that door, Sam. Don't take those flats down—I want to see them tomorrow first thing. And get that goddam Number Two hookup fixed." Then she climbed into her metallic-gray four-door Silver Cloud Rolls Royce sedan with the notes stuck to the steering wheel with Scotch tape and headed home to put on the coffeepot.

Gower Champion

FEBRUARY, 19, 1967.

GOWER CHAMPION LOPED across the living room of his thirteen-room penthouse that looks like a Sonja Henie set from *Sun Valley Serenade*, gazed down through the beaded glass windows overlooking Central Park, and said, "I've been lucky." It was the understatement of the year.

At forty-five, he may just be *the* most important director of musicals on Broadway. That makes him a ravishing success in a dying business and he knows it. He has piloted the ship on four musicals, all of them hits: *Bye Bye Birdie* brought back teenagers, *Carnival* brought back balloons, *Hello Dolly* brought back legends of what Broadway used to be like before the unions took over, and in his new miracle, *I do, I Do!* he even manages to make a tidal wave of clichés look charming.

It's the old story of the hoofer who made good, only this hoofer is no Pal Joey. Everybody likes him. Carol Channing calls him a "scrumptious little ol' doll." Robert Preston says, "I may never work for anyone else as long as I live." And Mary Martin ... well, get *her* started on the subject and you have to send out for sandwiches: "No matter what ever happens in our careers—our lives—together or separately, nothing, but nothing, could ever replace or equal the months with Gower ... of sheer joy, magic, enlightenment, professional pride...." That sort of thing. The press agent for *I*

Do, I Do!, in fact, says the Preston-Martin-Champion team is the most professionally in love trio he has ever encountered.

It's all enough to send you straight to the medicine cabinet for a glass of mouthwash. Then you meet the ex-hoofer who made good and you begin to see what they mean. "I *am* nice," he admits, giving up his post at the beaded glass windows, running his fingers gingerly across the polished grand piano, tilting his boyishly well-bred face toward the carpeted staircase leading to upstairs walls lined with framed Al Hirschfeld cartoons of himself and his wife Marge. Then he walks across the room like a prize Dalmatian who is so sure of his position in that elegant kennel called show biz he can afford to bark at his own tail, throws another log on the elegant fire, digs his fists down deep into the hand-sewn pockets of his seventy-dollar, fire-engine-red, gold-buttoned Battaglia sweater, and sinks into an overstuffed easy chair. "As I said, I *am* nice, which makes dull reading. What can I do to be more colorful? I could say shit a couple of times if you like."

Offer rejected, he put on an Andre Previn tape that bleated softly from hidden speakers in the wall, tapped the toes of his bedroom slippers on the butterscotch rug, and continued. "When you are just a dancer nobody cares much, but when you become a big hot name everybody suddenly expects you to be a bit of a bastard. When you're not, they're stunned. Maybe that's why I get along so well with David Merrick. I know all about his reputation for meddling in everything he produces, but he really leaves *me* alone. We had a few problems out of town. Mary Martin had bursitis in Boston and missed five performances and it nearly drove me wild. Also, Mary and Bob are not dancers and every time I tried to get them to dance, it just looked pretentious. Some of it still looked phony right up to the last five days in Cincinnati. But I have a very strong visual idea of how it's going to turn out. Then I adjust my blueprint to the special requirements of my performers. Fifty percent of my success depends on them. I can stage, I can give ideas, but I can't guarantee *any*thing. I can't make people good. Sometimes I'm lucky. Channing was a dream. Anna Maria Alberghetti got very bad toward the end of *Carnival,* but Mary Martin is receptive to everything. I'm happy about *I Do* first because Mary had such a disaster in *Jennie* and she needed a hit. Also, I wanted to show the big shots that something different and off-beat could go on Broadway. Very few people have pointed out how really different this show is.

"I am fascinated by gimmicks. *Carnival* I didn't really like until I got the idea of the bare stage with the roustabouts changing each set before the audience's eyes. I didn't even want to do *Dolly* until I got hooked on the idea of that ramp. The musical theater is a blind alley. It's a disgrace that nobody is writing anything original. Somebody's gotta have the guts to throw out all the formulas. We broke down a lot of taboos in *I Do, I Do!* Still, even when you succeed, you have to worry about whether the right people will see it. It seems like all the people who love the theater are out there in the street and all the wrong people—the ones with the expense accounts and the bubble hairdos—are inside sitting in the orchestra seats. We should have a straight two-dollar ticket in the balcony so the kids can come, but the terrible thing is that when you have a hit, greed sets in. I'd make a rotten producer, because I'd let everyone in free and never make any money.

"When directors and actors can't get together and put on a show out of love, or when I can't even have a simple reading of the script in my own house without everybody worrying about how many hours they are rehearsing or what salaries they will draw, things are sick. The whole Broadway situation makes me sick at my stomach."

It's been coming a long time, that outburst. Ever since he did his first shuffle ball chain at the age of eleven in a Friday afternoon Hollywood dance class, up through the ranks in the sweaty backstage dressing rooms of sleazy night clubs from here to Zanzibar, until the movies discovered him and he landed smack in the middle of the glitter up there on top of the cake, Gower Champion has been earning the right to land at least one good stiff clout on the jaw of the industry that spawned him. When he was fifteen, he and a childhood friend, Jean Tyler, went to the Cocoanut Grove in Hollywood where Veloz and Yolanda were holding a dance contest between appearances in MGM musicals. Just like the old Judy Garland-Mickey Rooney movies, "Gower and Jean" beat out all the Harvest Moon Ball types, lied about their ages, and went on the road as a team. Two kids, eating cake instead of cornbread. But even though he never finished school, Gower was intelligent, and it wasn't long before the cake tasted stale.

"It was the era of the dance teams. Every hotel had a room with a team doing the tango in it. When the army called in 1942, I was delighted. I was sick of show business and sick of living out of trunks, and I didn't want any part of it." Three years later, he was standing on the curb in front of

71

MGM with discharge papers in his pocket, looking for a job. "I hated it, but it was the only thing I knew how to do. I could make good money dancing and it was better than working in chop-suey joints or grousing around looking for a job—Christ, when I think of how *lucky* I was!" He landed an MGM contract, spent a lot of time at the beach, and made "one rotten picture—*Till the Clouds Roll By*—in which I danced across the screen in strawberry-pink hair with Cyd Charisse."

Disgusted again. His girl friend from junior high school, Marge Belcher, was in New York playing a witch in *Dark of the Moon*. Reunion. Then, real wedding bells instead of sound effects in a Jane Powell number. And, to pay the rent, they pulled the old act out of the closet, jazzed it up, and hit the road, living out of trunks again. "You danced whenever you got a job and you went wherever the job happened to be. We finally worked our way west into the Mocambo, a tiny place about the size of a four-room apartment, full of posts and pillars—it was awful, but we needed the money. Like a B movie, we were an immediate smash and it was New Year's Eve every night. The act had a lot of hokey-pokey stuff in it, but it had class too, and we got an offer from MGM to make musicals and we took it. Some of those musicals were big bombs, but we made enough money to stay off the road, take up gardening, and enjoy living like normal people for a change."

A red-nosed, golden-haired cherub in a red snowsuit came thundering into the room, followed by Marge Champion and hot coffee. The cherub, age four, was named Blake, after the Champions' friend, film director Blake Edwards. Another son, Gregg, age eleven, was at school. "Are you talking about the MGM musicals?" asked Marge, as Gower rescued the cherub from knocking an arrangement of eucalyptus leaves off the top of the grand piano. "We had a lot of fun and made some good friends. Some of the MGM stars saved their money. Others ... very depressing. But don't worry about some of those game girls like Ann Miller. She was always getting married, but each time it was to somebody richer, so she's o.k. We used to call her Annie Crow because she chattered all the time. Annie the Bird Girl. Jane Powell looks wonderful. Now that her kids are old enough she'd like to do a Broadway show. Monica Lewis I saw the other day on Fifth Avenue. I was in a cab, or I would have said hello."

"Monica Lewis? She married some agent who got shot by Walter Wanger." Gower beamed as Marge congratulated him

72

on his memory, then chased the cherub out of the room. "He sounds like Nanette Fabray when he laughs, that kid."

"Suddenly," said Gower, "we were famous but musicals were over. We finished off Esther Williams in her last film, then we finished off Betty Grable in *her* last film, and it was back to the closet for the old act again. We didn't care, because we never thought of ourselves as movie stars anyway." They went on a tour with Harry Belafonte in *Three for Tonight*, for which Gower did the choreography, sneaking Belafonte in and out of white hotel lobbies in the South. Gower tried to perform and choreograph too, but his heart wasn't in it. "One day Charles Laughton told me I was trying to be a whore and a madam at the same time. I decided I'd rather be a madam. I turned down the choreographer job on *My Fair Lady* to become a director. When *Birdie* opened I said I'd take off the tap shoes if it was a hit and never go back to dancing. I've kept my word."

Later, he would turn another David Merrick musical, *The Happy Time*, into more box-office gold, but for now he was unemployed once more. "I'm a big success but I'm out of a job again. People tell me how good I am and I still wonder, 'Christ, am I *really* any good?'"

Marge's big eyes blossomed like petunias in the doorway. "He's been fan-*tast*-ically lucky," she said. Even coming from her, bursting with wifely pride, it still sounded like the understatement of the year.

Ava Gardner

SHE STANDS THERE, without benefit of a filter lens against a room melting under the heat of lemony sofas and lavender walls and cream-and-peppermint-striped movie-star chairs, lost in the middle of that gilt-edge birthday-cake hotel of cupids and cupolas called the Regency. There is no script. No Minnelli to adjust the CinemaScope lens. Ice-blue rain beats against the windows and peppers Park Avenue below as Ava Gardner stalks her pink malted-milk cage like an elegant

73

cheetah. She wears a baby-blue cashmere turtleneck sweater pushed up to her Ava elbows and a little plaid mini-skirt and enormous black horn-rimmed glasses and she is gloriously, divinely barefoot.

Elbowing his way through the mob of autograph hunters and thrill seekers clustered in the lobby, all the way up in the gilt-encrusted elevator, the press agent Twentieth Century-Fox has sent along murmurs, "She doesn't see *anybody*, you know," and "You're very lucky, you're the only one she asked for." Remembering, perhaps, the last time she had come to New York from her hideout in Spain to ballyhoo *The Night of the Iguana* and got so mad at the press she chucked the party and ended up at Birdland. And nervously, shifting feet under my Brooks Brothers polo coat, I remember too all the photographers at whom she allegedly threw champagne glasses (there is even a rumor that she shoved one Fourth Estater off a balcony!), and—who could forget, Charlie?—the holocaust she caused the time Joe Hyams showed up with a tape recorder hidden in his sleeve.

Now, inside the cheetah cage without a whip and trembling like a nervous bird, the press agent says something in Spanish to the Spanish maid. "Hell, I've been there ten years and I still can't speak the goddam language," says Ava, dismissing him with a wave of the long porcelain Ava arms. *"Out!* I don't need press agents." The eyebrows angle under the glasses into two dazzling, sequined question marks. "Can I trust him?" she asks, grinning that smashing Ava grin, and pointing at me. The press agent nods, on his way to the door: "Is there anything else we can do for you while you're in town?"

"Just get me *out* of town, baby. Just get me *outta* here."

The press agent leaves softly, walking across the carpet as if treading on rose glass with tap shoes. The Spanish maid (Ava insists she is royalty, "She follows me around because she digs me") closes the door and shuffles off into another room.

"You *do* drink—right, baby? The last bugger who came to see me had the gout and wouldn't touch a drop." She roars a cheetah roar that sounds suspiciously like Geraldine Page playing Alexandra Del Lago and mixes drinks from her portable bar: Scotch and soda for me, and for herself a champagne glass full of cognac with another champagne glass full of Dom Perignon, which she drinks successively, refills, and sips slowly like syrup through a straw. The Ava legs dangle limply from the arm of a lavender chair while the Ava neck, pale and tall as a milkwood vase, rises above the

74

room like a Southern landowner inspecting a cotton field. At forty-four, she is still one of the most beautiful women in the world.

"Don't look at me. I was up until four A.M. at that goddam premiere of *The Bible*. Premieres! I will personally kill that John Huston if he ever drags me into another mess like that. There must have been ten thousand people clawing at me. I get claustrophobia in crowds and I couldn't breathe. Christ, they started off by shoving a TV camera at me and yelling, 'Talk, Ava!' At intermission I got lost and couldn't find my goddam seat after the lights went out and I kept telling those little girls with the bubble hairdos and the flashlights, 'I'm with John Huston,' and they kept saying, 'We don't know no Mr. Huston, is he from Fox?' There I was fumbling around the aisles in the dark and when I finally found my seat somebody was sitting in it and there was a big scene getting this guy to give me my seat back. Let me tell you, baby, Metro used to throw much better circuses than that. On top of it all, I lost my goddam mantilla in the limousine. Hell, it was no souvenir, that mantilla. I'll never find another one like it. Then Johnny Huston takes me to this party where we had to stand around and smile at Artie Shaw, who I was married to, baby, for Chrissake, and his wife, Evelyn Keyes, who Johnny Huston was once married to, for Chrissake. And after it's all over, what have you got? The biggest headache in town. Nobody cares who the hell was there. Do you think for one minute the fact that Ava Gardner showed up at that circus will sell that picture? Christ, did you *see* it? I went through all that hell just so this morning Bosley Crowther could write I looked like I was posing for a monument. All the way through it I kept punching Johnny on the arm and saying, 'Christ, how could you let me do it?' Anyway, nobody cares what I wore or what I said. All they want to know anyway is was she drunk and did she stand up straight. This is the last circus. I am not a bitch! I am not temperamental! I am scared, baby. *Scared*. Can you possibly understand what it's like to feel scared?"

She rolls her sleeves higher than the elbows and pours two more champagne glasses full. There is nothing about the way she looks, up close, to suggest the life she has led: press conferences accompanied by dim lights and an orchestra; bullfighters writing poems about her in the press; rubbing Vaseline between her bosoms to emphasize the cleavage; roaming restlessly around Europe like a woman without a country, a Pandora with her suitcases full of cognac and Hershey bars ("for quick energy"). None of the ravaged, ruinous grape-colored lines to suggest the affairs or the brawls that bring the police in the middle of the night or the dancing on tabletops in Madrid cellars till dawn.

The doorbell rings and a pimply faced boy with a Beatle hairdo delivers one dozen Nathan's hot dogs, rushed from Coney Island in a limousine. "Eat," says Ava, sitting cross-legged on the floor, biting into a raw onion.

"You're looking at me again!" she says shyly, pulling short girlish wisps of hair behind the lobes of her Ava ears. I mention the fact that she looks like a Vassar co-ed in her mini-skirt. "Vassar?" she asks suspiciously. "Aren't they the ones who get in all the trouble?"

"That's Radcliffe."

She roars. Alexandra Del Lago again. "I took one look at myself in *The Bible* and went out this morning and got all my hair cut off. This is the way I used to wear it at MGM. It takes years off. What's *that?*" Eyes narrow, axing her guest in half, burning holes in my notebook. "Don't tell me you're one of those people who always go around scribbling everything on little pieces of paper. Get rid of that. Don't take notes. Don't ask questions either because I probably won't answer any of them anyway. Just let Mama do all the talking. Mama knows best. You want to ask something, I can tell. Ask."

I ask if she hates all of her films as much as *The Bible.*

"Christ, what did I ever do worth talking about? Every time I tried to act, they stepped on me. That's why it's such a goddam shame, I've been a movie star for twenty-five years and I've got nothing, *nothing* to show for it. All I've got is three lousy ex-husbands, which reminds me, I've got to call Artie and ask him what his birthday is. I can't remember my own family's birthdays. Only reason I know my own is because I was born the same day as Christ. Well, almost. Christmas Eve, 1922. That's Capricorn, which means a lifetime of *hell,* baby. Anyway, I need Artie's birthday because I'm trying to get a new passport. I tramp around Europe, but I'm not giving up my citizenship, baby, for *anybody.* Did you ever try living in Europe and renewing your passport? They treat you like you're a goddam Communist or something. Hell, that's why I'm getting the hell out of Spain, because I hate Franco and I hate Communists. So now they want a list of all my divorces so I told them hell, call *The New York Times*—they know more about me than I do!"

But hadn't all those years at MGM been any fun at all? "Christ, after seventeen years of slavery, you can ask that question? I hated it, honey. I mean, I'm not exactly stupid or without feeling, and they tried to sell me like a prize hog.

They also tried to make me into something I was not then and never could be. They used to write in my studio bios that I was the daughter of a cotton farmer from Chapel Hill. Hell, baby, I was born on a tenant farm in Grabtown. How's that grab ya? Grabtown, North Carolina. And it looks exactly the way it sounds. I should have stayed there. The ones who never left home don't have a pot to pee in but they're happy. Me, look at me. What did it bring me?" She finishes off another round of cognac and pours a fresh one. "The only time I'm happy is when I'm doing absolutely nothing. When I work I vomit all the time. I know nothing about acting so I have one rule—trust the director and give him heart and soul. And nothing else." (Another cheetah roar.) "I get a lot of money so I can afford to loaf a lot. I don't trust many people, so I only work with Huston now. I used to trust Joe Mankiewicz, but one day on the set of *The Barefoot Contessa* he did the unforgivable thing. He insulted me. He said, 'You're the sittin'est goddam actress,' and I never liked him after that. What I really want to do is get married again. Go ahead and laugh, everybody laughs, but how great it must be to tromp around barefoot and cook for some great goddam son of a bitch who loves you the rest of your life. I've never had a good man."

What about Mickey Rooney? (A glorious shriek.) "Love comes to Andy Hardy."

Sinatra? "No comment," she says to her glass.

A slow count to ten, while she sips her drink. Then, "And Mia Farrow?" The Ava eyes brighten to a soft clubhouse green. The answer comes like so many cats lapping so many saucers of cream. "Hah! I always knew Frank would end up in bed with a boy."

Like a phonograph dropping a new LP, she changes the subject. "I only want to do the things that don't make me suffer. My friends are more important to me than anything. I know all kinds of people—bums, hangers-on, intellectuals, a few phonies. I'm going to see a college boy at Princeton tomorrow and we're going to a ballgame. Writers. I love writers. Henry Miller sends me books to improve my mind. Hell, did you read *Plexus*? I couldn't get through it. I'm not an intellectual, although when I was married to Artie Shaw I took a lot of courses at U.C.L.A. and got A's and B's in psychology and literature. I have a mind, but I never got a chance to use it doing every goddam lousy part in every goddam lousy picture Metro turned out. I *feel* a lot, though. God, I'm sorry I wasted those twenty-five years. My sister Dee Dee, can't understand why after all these years I can't bear to face a camera. But I never brought anything to this business and I have no respect for acting. Maybe if I had learned something it would be different. But I never did anything to be proud of. Out of all those movies, what can I claim to have done?"

"*Mogambo, The Hucksters*—"

"Hell, baby, after twenty-five years in this business, if all you've got to show for it is *Mogambo* and *The Hucksters* you might as well give up. Name me one actress who survived all that crap at MGM. Maybe Lana Turner. Certainly Liz Taylor. But they all hate acting as much as I do. All except for Elizabeth. She used to come up to me on the set and say, 'If only I could learn to be good,' and by God, she made it. I haven't seen *Virginia Woolf*—hell, I *never* go to movies—but I hear she is good. I never cared much about myself. I didn't have the emotional makeup for acting and I hate exhibitionists anyway. And who the hell was there to help me or teach me acting was anything else? I really tried in *Show Boat* but that was MGM crap. Typical of what they did to me there. I wanted to sing those songs—hell, I've still got a Southern accent—and I really thought Julie should sound a little like a Negro since she's supposed to have Negro blood. Christ, those songs like "Bill" shouldn't sound like an opera. So, what did they say? 'Ava, baby, you can't sing, you'll hit the wrong keys, you're up against real pros in this film, so don't make a fool of yourself.' *Pros!* Howard Keel? And Kathryn Grayson, who had the biggest boobs in Hollywood? I mean I like Graysie, she's a sweet girl, but with her they didn't even need 3-D! Lena Horne told me to go to Phil Moore, who was her pianist and had coached Dorothy Dandridge, and he'd teach me. I made a damn good track of the songs and they said, 'Ava, are you outta your head?' Then they got Eileen Wilson, this gal who used to do a lot of my singing on screen, and *she* recorded a track with the same background arrangement taken off *my* track. They substituted her voice for mine, and now in the movie my Southern twang stops talking and her soprano starts singing—hell what a mess. They wasted God knows how many thousands of dollars and ended up with crap. I still get royalties on the goddam records I did."

The doorbell rings and in bounces a little man named Larry. Larry has silver hair, silver eyebrows, and smiles a lot. He works for a New York camera shop. "Larry used to be married to my sister Bea. If you think I'm something you ought to see Bea. When I was eighteen I came to New York to visit them and Larry took that picture of me that started this whole megilah. He's a sonuvabitch, but I love him."

78

"Ava, I sure loved you last night in *The Bible*. You were really terrific, darlin'."

"Crap!" Ava pours another cognac. "I don't want to hear another word about that goddam *Bible*. I didn't believe *it* and I didn't believe that Sarah bit I played for a minute. How could anybody stay married for a hundred years to *Abraham*, who was one of the biggest bastards who ever lived?"

"Oh, darlin', she was a wonderful woman, that Sarah."

"She was a jerk!"

"Oh, darlin', ya shouldn' talk like that. God will hear ya. Don'tcha believe in God?" Larry joins us on the floor and bites into a hot dog, spilling mustard on his tie.

"Hell, no." The Ava eyes flash.

"I pray to him every night, darlin'. Sometimes he answers, too."

"He never answered me, baby. He was never around when I needed him. He did nothing but screw up my whole life since the day I was born. Don't tell *me* about *God!* I know all about that bugger!"

The doorbell again. This time a cloak-and-dagger type comes in; he's wearing an ironed raincoat, has seventeen pounds of hair, and looks like he has been living on plastic vegetables. He says he is a student at New York University Law School. He also says he is twenty-six years old. *"What?"* Ava takes off her glasses for a closer look. "Your father told me you were twenty-seven. Somebody's lying!" The Ava eyes narrow and the palms of her hands are wet.

"Let's get some air, fellas." Ava leaps into the bedroom and comes out wearing a Navy pea jacket with a Woolworth scarf around her head. Vassar again.

"I thought you were gonna cook tonight, darlin'," says Larry, throwing his fist into a coat sleeve.

"I want spaghetti. Let's go to the Supreme Macaroni Company. They let me in the back door there and nobody ever recognizes *any*body there. Spaghetti, baby. I'm starved."

Ava slams the door shut, leaving all the lights on. "Fox is paying, baby." We all link arms and follow the leader. Ava skips ahead of us like Dorothy on her way to Oz. *Lions and tigers and bears, oh my!* Moving like a tiger through Regency halls, melting with hot pink, like the inside of a womb.

"Are those creeps still downstairs?" she asked. "Follow me."

She knows all the exits. We go down on the service elevator. About twenty autograph hunters crowd the lobby. Celia, queen of the autograph bums, who leaves her post on the door at Sardi's only on special occasions, has deserted her station for this. *Ava's in town this week.* She sits behind a potted palm wearing a purple coat and green beret, arms full of self-addressed postcards.

Cool.

Ava gags, pushes the horn-rims flat against her nose, and pulls us through the lobby. Nobody recognizes her. "Drink time, baby!" she whispers, shoving me toward a side stairway that leads down to the Regency bar.

"Do you know who *that* was?" asks an Iris Adrian type with a mink-dyed fox on her arm as Ava heads for the bar. We check coats and umbrellas and suddenly we hear the soundtrack voice, hitting E-flat.

"You *sonuvabitch!* I could buy and sell you. How *dare* you insult my friends? Get me the manager!"

Larry is at her side. Two waiters are shushing Ava and leading us all to a corner booth. Hidden. Darker than the Polo Lounge. Hide the star. This is New York, not Beverly Hills.

"It's that turtleneck sweater you're wearing," whispers Larry to me as the waiter seats me with my back to the room.

"They don't like me here, the bastards. I never stay in this hotel, but Fox is paying, so what the hell? I wouldn't come otherwise. They don't even have a jukebox, for Chrissake." Ava flashes a smile in Metrocolor and orders a large ice-tea glass filled with straight tequila. "No salt on the side. Don't need it."

"Sorry about the sweater—" I begin.

"You're beautiful. Gr-r-r!" She laughs her Ava laugh and the head rolls back and the little blue vein bulges on her neck like a delicate pencil mark.

Two tequilas later ("I *said* no salt!") she is nodding grandly, surveying the bar like the Dowager Empress in the Recognition Scene. Talk buzzes around her like hummingbird wings and she hears nothing. Larry is telling about the time he got arrested in Madrid and Ava had to get him out of jail and the student is telling me about N.Y.U. Law School and Ava is telling *him* she doesn't believe he's only twenty-six years old and can he prove it, and suddenly he looks at his watch and says Sandy Koufax is playing in St. Louis.

"You're kidding!" Ava's eyes light up like cherries on a cake. "Let's go! Goddamit we're going to St. Louis!"

"Ava, darlin', I gotta go to work tomorrow." Larry takes a heavy sip of his Grasshopper.

"Shut up, you bugger. If I pay for us all to go to St. Louis we go to St. Louis! Can I get a phone brought to this table? Someone call Kennedy airport and find out what time the next plane leaves. I *love* Sandy Koufax! I *love* Jews! God, sometimes I think I'm Jewish myself. A Spanish Jew from North Carolina. *Waiter!*"

The student convinces her that by the time we got to St. Louis they'd be halfway through the seventh inning. Ava's face falls and she goes back to her straight tequila.

"Look at 'em, Larry," she says. "They're such babies. Please don't go to Vietnam." Her face turns ashen. Julie leaving the showboat with William Warfield singing "Ol' Man River" in the fog on the levee. "We gotta do it. . . ."

"What are you talkin' about, darlin'?" Larry shoots a look at the law student who assures Ava he has no intention of going to Vietnam.

". . . didn't ask for this world, the buggers made us do it. . . ." A tiny bubble bath of sweat breaks out on her forehead and she leaps up from the table. "My God, I'm suffocating! Gotta get some air!" She turns over the glass of tequila and three waiters are flying at us like bats, dabbing and patting and making great breathing noises.

Action!

The N.Y.U. student, playing Chance Wayne to her Alexandra Del Lago, is all over the place like a trained nurse. Coats fly out of the checkroom. Bills and quarters roll across the wet tablecloth. Ava is on the other side of the bar and out the door. On cue, the other customers, who have been making elaborate excuses for passing our table on their way to the bathroom, suddenly give great breathy choruses of "Ava" and we are through the side door and out in the rain.

Then as quickly as it started it's over. Ava is in the middle of Park Avenue, the scarf falling around her neck and her hair blowing wildly around the Ava eyes. Lady Brett in the traffic, with a downtown bus as the bull. Three cars stop on a green light and every taxi driver on Park Avenue begins to honk. The autograph hunters leap through the polished doors of the Regency and begin to scream. Inside, still waiting coolly behind the potted palm, is Celia, oblivious to the noise, facing the elevators, firmly clutching her postcards. No need to risk missing Ava because of a minor commotion on the street. Probably Jack E. Leonard or Edie Adams. Catch them next week at Danny's.

Outside, Ava is inside the taxi flanked by the N.Y.U. student and Larry, blowing kisses to the new chum, who will never grow to be an old one. They are already turning the corner into Fifty-seventh Street, fading into the kind of night, the color of tomato juice in the headlights, that only exists in New York when it rains.

"Who was it?" asks a woman walking a poodle.

"Jackie Kennedy," answers a man from his bus window.

Sandy Dennis

JUNE 19, 1966.

SANDY DENNIS CAME FLAPPING into the room like a Volkswagen with both doors open. The dress (no makeup, barefoot, an old unstylish blue muumuu), the voice (a cross between Jimmy Stewart and Baby Snooks), and the manner (frowns and giggles interspersed with fingers on the eyelids when she's thinking and what-the-hell shrugs when she isn't) gave an airy support to her refusal to act like a star or look like one. She angled in for a crash landing on a flowered sofa, crossed her legs under her bottom like a Yogi contemplating the road to Mecca, and said, "About *Virginia Woolf*—"

Then, faster than it takes Clark Kent to duck into a phone booth, she was up and gone. Flapping again. And followed at her heels by five cats and two mongrel dogs who live with her and her husband, Gerry Mulligan. "Blow the cat hairs off the coffee table and I'll bring in some food," she yelled from the kitchen. Could this be the girl who just returned from making a movie with Elizabeth Taylor and Richard Burton under the bottled sun and plastic palms of Hollywood? There had been some mention of smoked oysters. And there *was* a view, sort of. You can see part of the Hudson River from up there on the 16th floor on West End Avenue. But there ends the resemblance to any movie star, living or dead.

The apartment is sunny and roomy, like maybe a girl from Nebraska lived there. The living room is all white, except for Gerry's grand piano. The walls are lined with bookcases containing jazz books, a bugle, a chess set, a watering can, a prune-juice carton, master tapes of assorted Mulligan concerts, and a collection of Billie Holiday records. The other rooms are filled with china ("I'm a fiend for dishes, some of it is Delft, some not, but all good"), an old toilet seat, rocking chairs, framed drawings of colored flowers, children's illustrations from an old volume of Stevenson's *A Child's Garden of Verses,* bowls of various sizes and descriptions which Sandy's animal friends eat from, and two very peculiar king-sized mattresses which line the hallway. "Everybody asks about those. They belonged to a bed we ordered from Altman's, but we didn't like it so we sent it back. Only they wouldn't take the mattresses. The cats like to climb them and sit on top. Know anybody who wants a couple of practically brand-new mattresses we only slept on twice?"

She flew into the room again, sliding across the carpet the color of lime Jello, offering a cold chicken leg, a mound of potato salad, and a tall wine glass filled with ginger ale. Lunch was served. She hopped onto the sofa again, eating cold sauerkraut from a Mason jar. "I guess you want to know about *it*—"

I guess so. Seven and a half million dollars, with $70,000 a day for three weeks over the schedule, for a movie which only employed four actors and one set? In black and white? Wasn't she excited? "No. When I heard I had the role of Honey and was going to make a movie with the Burtons, it wasn't such a big day. Lotta things I've wanted more and didn't get." But what about *him* and *her*? Exciting, right? "Well, I wouldn't know, really. I don't really like people much. I mean, I know I should like develop this passion for other people and like get to know them, but I couldn't care less. They were just people you work with and then you go home and forget them. Everybody was nice at Warner Brothers, I mean they should have hated us because we cost them so much money going overtime and all. It took us five and a half months. But friends? No. I've only had three friends in my life. Elizabeth was very sweet. She gave me a baby shower before I lost my baby and presented me with an old-fashioned wicker bassinet and Richard gave us a lot of expensive books. There was no big-star treatment. I can understand how when you get famous and make lots of money how you'd ask for things like air-conditioned cars, things I'd be too embarrassed to ask for. But they don't have to ask. People just give them things. On the set, Elizabeth didn't really get anything more than anybody else. Richard had a big dressing room and she had one two feet bigger in lavender. Big deal. All the studio did for me was send a car for me every morning. It wasn't anything fancy. Sometimes it was just a shirt-sleeved old man in an old Chevrolet. But I appreciated it.

"It never occurred to me that they were like stars. I wouldn't know anyway, because I don't know any stars. I never even saw any stars in Hollywood. Elizabeth is a very ordinary woman, really. And I liked Mike Nichols. Before Mike, I never worked with a good director in my life. Except Kazan. But my part in *Splendor in the Grass* was so tiny and I was such a kid then, he never paid any attention to me. In *Any Wednesday* we had five (or was it three?) directors and I can't even remember their faces. Mike works simply. I'd say, 'That's not right!' 'Do it anyway,' he'd say. Then I'd do it and he'd say, 'O.K., you were right. It's not right.'"

Is she satisfied with the picture? "I don't know. I haven't seen it. I've called Warners three times and asked if they would show it to me but I keep getting these nasty men on the phone who say no. I think it'll be good, but apparently the movie people don't know enough about movies to know if it is good or not, so they just hide it in a can and take it out now and then to show to priests and lawyers and things. I don't care. I'm never terribly moved by myself anyway, so I don't need to see myself on the screen. Like actors. It's not necessary to know them personally just because you work with them all day. When I was in *Any Wednesday* Gene Hackman and I didn't speak for a month, but we worked well onstage. In Hollywood, when I finished at night I was so tired I just went home, took a bath, and couldn't move. The Burtons gave a big bash with canapés and champagne when the movie was finished—you know, the bit—but Gerry and I were leaving for New York the next day so we didn't even go."

Gerry Mulligan came in and started playing the piano. "Here comes Elizabeth—that's the cat Elizabeth gave us." Elizabeth, a healthy Abyssinian, sauntered in and finished off the lunch, followed by another cat named Blaze Starr. "We saw her on the street one day draped over a man's shoulder. I bought her on the spot for two dollars. 'Look how big and fat she is,' I told Gerry. The next morning she had six kittens." The phone rang. "That's our kitchen phone, the one we answer," cried Gerry, but Sandy had beat him to the door. "Coming," she yelled at the phone.

Mulligan returned to the piano. "I don't go on the road much anymore. The marriage is working. Of course you have to like cats. She still doesn't know a damn thing about jazz. Sandy's a kid who had a fear of music laid on her as a child. She's just now learning to relax."

"It was my mother calling from Nebraska. She wanted to know if we had the cats wormed yet." Sandy plopped on the sofa again, looking like a girl who, in the next few months, will need a little relaxing. She'll make *Up the Down Staircase* for Warners (shot in New York), star in a Broadway play in October, *Daphne in Cottage D*, a black comedy in which she commits suicide onstage. "I get tired of being an actress, tired of work, tired of all the big fights with people all the time, but it's all I can do. Back in Nebraska, I dreamed all my life of being Margaret O'Brien. We lived across the street from the firehouse and one day I turned in a fire—after letting it burn awhile to make sure it was a good one—and got my name in the paper. After that, I thought it was so unfair that I didn't have parents like Margaret O'Brien's who would take me to Hollywood. Now that I've been there, I don't know. I hated the weather. We had a little house with a swimming pool and we could let the dogs out without having to walk them. I still have dreams of dancing through Central Park like Jane Powell, but I can't sing or dance at all. Mostly I just don't like moviemaking. Broadway makes sense. You rehearse, go out of town, and open. Movies are boring. You sit around and do nothing all day so that by the time your scene comes you couldn't care less."

Now that she's made it, she insists she knows nothing about the business side of her career. "I have less money than ever. I can't hold on to it. God, it costs thirty dollars a week to feed the cats. I've got two Tonys, but I don't know where they are. I mean, they're nice" (rummaging through drawers, searching, coming up with an empty box) "but you can't really *do* anything with them. I'm always making mistakes. I know nothing about managing things. Like the trip to London with *Three Sisters*. Usually if you're terrible or even mediocre, people are polite. Not the British. Their blatant rudeness was a nightmare. They booed and yelled, 'Yankees, go home!' Of course we deserved some of it. We never got onstage together until opening night, the stage was tilted and raised three feet, so all the props fell off the tables. I was wrong for the part. I'm not a classic actress. We were a lot of good people who got together and made a mistake.

"I was wrong for *Any Wednesday*, too. Everybody said 'Isn't she adorable?' but I did much better work in *A Thousand Clowns*. I was sick of *Wednesday* before it even opened. I stuck with it for over a year by the skin of my teeth, and was lucky to get out alive. I saw it only once after I left—in

Hollywood. Gerry got violently ill and we left after the first act."

Her biggest mistake, she claims, occurred when she was still in *Clowns*. "I was just a kid, so I signed a contract to make films for Seven Arts, for $15,000 a picture. It sounded like a lousy deal, but I had an agent who said, 'Oh, honey, you better grab it,' so I did. I don't know how to say no to people. They never offered me a film, but they won't let me out of that stupid contract. Now I have to get their permission to go to the bathroom. I hadn't heard from them in years, so I made a film with Kim Stanley of *Three Sisters* and now every day I get telegrams from Cheryl Crawford and the Actor's Studio wanting to know when they can release the movie. They need the money. But Seven Arts won't let it be released because they say I did it without their permission and it will be bad for my career. What do they know? People I never laid eyes on telling me how to run my life. Of course they let me do *Virginia Woolf* for a lot more money because they know it will mean a lot of publicity and then they'll cash in on it and still pay me only $15,000. Boy, I can hardly wait to make my first movie for Seven Arts. I'll be so bad in it they'll wish they never heard of me. I'm only kidding. Don't print that. No, go ahead. I don't care. It proves a point. You lose perspective when you become a name. All I want to do is act, so what do I do? I get involved with contracts and lawyers and money and that's not what acting is all about. It's over my head.

"I preserve my sanity by staying at home. We never entertain because it's such an effort and the animals are into the food before you get it on the table. After a few glasses of wine, I get sleepy and start yawning in the guests' faces and then they all smile painfully and tell you what a nice time they had while they pick the cat hairs off their clothes on the way out. They never come back. It's easier not to bother. I'm a slob. I'll just never get the hang of being a star. It embarrasses me. Look at my teeth. My father paid $5,000 to have them fixed and they still stick out. I get up at eight A.M., read, take care of the pets. We just got this green rug laid and they think it's grass, so I go around all day cleaning up the cat pee. I like it. I have to be in my own house with things I know around me. Then I feel safe."

So, don't expect Sandy Dennis to show up at the opening night of *Who's Afraid of Virginia Woolf?* in borrowed false eyelashes and an evening dress sent over from studio wardrobe. She'll be much too busy up there on the sixteenth floor, where things are never black and white, but baby blue. She likes it that way. And she's got the cat hairs to prove it.

Lotte Lenya

SHE WAS FULL OF BEANS IN BOSTON.

Outside the Shubert Theatre, orange leaves blew through the street as an autumn chill licked the frosty New England night. Inside, a well-dressed audience rustled its programs nervously through the first public preview of Harold Prince's Broadway-bound musical, *Cabaret*. Everything was going wrong. The sets refused to fall into place. The microphones hummed with feedbacks. The actors missed their cues. Typical tryout-in-Boston problems. Then, suddenly, before the first act was three scenes old, a whisper rose through the crowd that started like the rustle of taffeta and ended like the sound of water through a hose.

Lenya!

And there, up on the stage, glowing like a Halloween pumpkin under the hot lights of honky-tonk Berlin was the legend herself: face like a clock without a second hand, a red slash of lipstick across the mouth, dressed in a tacky maroon wrapper with big yellow flowers, a gold medallion on a black velvet ribbon around her neck, one hand on her hip and the other waving gently toward imaginary stars, singing in that voice like a musical mixmaster:

> *The sun will rise and the moon will set,*
> *And you learn how to settle for what you get,*
> *It'll all go on if we're here or not,*
> *So who cares, so what,*
> *So who cares, so what?*

Then and there, isolated from the reality of taxes and Vietnam, that audience in Boston knew it was hit between the eyes. The people came to see a musical about Germany in the Jazz Age, based on Christopher Isherwood's *Berlin Stories*, and they got the real thing. They also got a preview of an important new chapter in the life of one of the few genuine legends still left in show business. At 66—when most ladies her age are out buying cemetery plots or phoning up about Medicare—Lotte Lenya is embarking on a whole new musical-comedy career with enough energy to send the first missile to the moon and back. "For sixteen years," she says, smiling her crooked-tooth jack-o'-lantern grin, "I've been the widow of Kurt Weill. Now I'm *me!*"

Oh, the legend is still there, of course. You hear about her, if you're lucky, when you're still a kid. If not, you learn pretty fast while you're still fresh off the train in New York from wherever it is you came from. You hear about her in the booths at Downey's, late at night, listening to Those Who Know talk about Things That Matter, or in Sardi's when you have the price of a drink, or you see her name up on the posters at Carnegie Hall. And you listen, too, to her record collection of someone with taste, and like Scotch and avocados and most of the other things in life that are special, you learn to cultivate a taste for the way she sounds.

But today, after all those years of singing Kurt Weill's songs and playing Bertolt Brecht's women, the legend is letting its hair down. They still print pictures of her beautifully ravaged face leaning wistfully against vine-covered stone walls, or looking out sadly across the railroad tracks of war-torn Berlin. But those are the wrong legends. The real one sits in slacks with the chorus boys in *Cabaret* and laughs her warm, throaty croak and jokes about the past: "I've learned a lot since I arrived an immigrant from the Nazis in 1935. I went to Saks Fifth Avenue and bought a sweater and in my horrible English I asked the clerk, 'Would you rape it for me?' 'Sorry, miss,' he said, 'but it isn't my type.'"

That's Lenya. In *Cabaret* she dances with a trio of sailors and sings a song about a pineapple and brings the house down. She does it all, for the very first time in a musical, without the aid of Kurt Weill. Still, there seems to be a ghost in the wings. If the songs sound like Weill, as they often do when Lenya sings them, it is because she can sing them no other way. Under other circumstances, the comparison could be disastrous, but John Kander, a handsome, boyish young man who composed the music for the show, says: "A lot of people are comparing my music to Weill. The image Lenya brings to this show makes it hard to break out of the mold. She says kindly, 'No, it doesn't sound like Weill, it sounds like Germany,' but the feeling is still there." Lenya pooh-poohs the idea. "I feel comfortable in this show. After all, it is about the world I knew with Weill. Everyone is influenced by

88

somebody else in this world. Weill himself was influenced by Stravinsky and a Philadelphia critic once called him a tired Puccini. 'Puccini,' he said, 'so what? He wasn't such a bad composer, was he?' So if people say the songs written for me now sound like Weill, I just say, so what? Is it so bad to be influenced by someone so wonderful?"

Like most legends, she creates her own special aura. Joe Masteroff, author of the book for *Cabaret,* hit the nail on the head when he admitted that "the role she plays was written for Lenya, the songs were composed for Lenya, there was never anybody under consideration but Lenya. We are trying to re-create the Berlin of 1930, and when you think of that era, you think of Kurt Weill and Lotte Lenya. Weill is dead but Lenya is still with us. When she walks onstage she brings it all with her."

Offstage, too. For three days before the Boston opening, through the rehearsals and the miserable hotel food and the running out for cold coffee and stale sandwiches and the nerves exploding on the air, she brought to it all an air of another time, another place. Relaxing after the show in black leotards and a little pink shirt, she reached out for a tall, iced drink in a suite at the Ritz Carlton looking like a shining Teutonic sun, and memories flashed by. "It was this same hotel that we were sitting in—Ira Gershwin, Gertrude Lawrence, and Moss Hart were with us—when Sam Harris came in after the opening of *Lady in the Dark.* Harris never made contracts. A handshake was the deal. Everyone was busily talking and Sam came in and over the roar said, 'Gentlemen, I'm leaving. The show is half an hour too long. Good night.' What a producer. Those were the good times. People really cared in those days. The theater was more than just a business."

But she was getting ahead of her story. According to *Who's Who,* Lenya (nobody ever calls her Lotte) was born in 1900 in a working-class section of Vienna called Hitzing. Her mother was a laundress, her father a coachman, and she was one of four hungry children. It seems she could always dance. When she was only a baby her father would often summon her from the coal bin where she slept and make her dance for him. By the age of four, she had learned to stand on her head and walk a tightrope with an umbrella in a tiny neighborhood circus where she also danced the czardas. During World War I she studied ballet in Zurich and later left home and toured the suburbs of Berlin. "I lived with another dancer and we worked out a ballet evening—made all our own costumes, printed our own programs. We were only teen-agers but we were sure we'd take Berlin by storm. Nobody came, no agents signed us. My friend left, but I stayed on." She was earning an inflationary three-billion marks a week (about $5) as an actress in Shakespeare and Molière plays when playwright Georg Kaiser took pity on her and invited her to live with his family on a lake near Berlin. One Sunday, the family told her they were expecting a young composer to drop by. Would she take the boat across the lake and meet him? Her eyes cloud with mist when she tells the story: "I took the rowboat and went to the station and there was this funny-looking little man in great thick glasses and a little blue suit. 'Would you mind entering our transportation?' I asked him. Our eyes met. We lived together for two years and then I married Kurt Weill."

Although she now insists they "did not live in an ivory tower," that period in music has nevertheless become romantic history. Weill and Lenya were leaders in a movement to revolutionize the German theater. It was an era of black satin and dancing gorillas and female impersonators and black-market cigarettes and jazz and they used it all. Weill was a composer with a strictly highbrow compositional style and strongly atonal tendencies. Bertolt Brecht was a poet who was writing for the German theater the sort of black, smoky pieces Kafka wrote in books. They met and collaborated on a short song sketch called *Little Mahagonny,* and Weill's music began to take on the jazz influences that affected him the rest of his life. The work was premiered in Baden-Baden in 1927. "Never," recalls Lenya, "will I forget the riot it caused. The entire audience stood to cheer and boo and whistle all at the same time. Brecht had provided all of us with little whistles of our own and we just whistled right back." This marked the singing debut of Lenya. To this day she still cannot read music.

Back from Baden-Baden, they all lived in Berlin in near poverty. The first time Brecht came to visit the Weills in their pension, he was so shabby the landlady slammed the door in his face. Undaunted, they set about enlarging *Little Mahagonny* into a full-scale work, taking time out in 1928 to polish off a "trifle" commissioned by a rich avant-garde producer named Ernst-Josef Aufricht. They didn't want to waste badly needed time, but they were broke and Aufricht was offering them real money, so they took the job. The trifle was *The Threepenny Opera.* "Weill was twenty-four and we had a small theater at the end of a dark alley. To get to it, you had to cross a canal and there it was, hidden away so nobody could see it. Today that spot lies across the wall in

East Berlin. All the big Berlin producers said it would be a 'smash flop.' Even our friends warned us not to get involved in such a disaster. The dress rehearsal lasted until five A.M. and we opened cold the same night. They nearly stoned us because we broke all the rules of musicals up to that point. Nobody knew me. When Weill suggested me for the role of Jenny the prostitute they didn't want me. I was nobody. The producer said, 'We'll give her three days out of courtesy to the composer, then fire her.' On opening night they even forgot to put my name on the program. This was before the days of press agents. That's an American invention. 'I won't let you go on,' Weill said. 'Dalink,' I said, 'I've waited so long for this break they'll know who I am tomorrow.' And they did, they did." The next morning a top Berlin critic wrote in headlines: "Who was she? She was good. She was very good. Soon she'll be on the top." That discovery was the most exciting moment in Lenya's life. The show ran for several years before the Nazis took over and turned the glittering theater capital into an ash heap.

Success followed success as Weill and Lenya and Brecht turned out vintage rotgut about whores and pimps and Alabama mamas in songs full of the yeast and desperate barroom gaiety that made the last days of the Weimar Republic a corrosive commentary on human corruption. In 1930 they produced *The Rise and Fall of the City of Mahagonny*, a jazz opera about a legendary town where trains never stop, set on the gold coast of Florida. None of them had ever been to America and hadn't the slightest idea where anything was, but they turned out a masterpiece that was half beer-cellar Berlin, half New Orleans Dixieland. Its anti-Nazi sentiments, its decidedly Left Wing theme, and a growing hatred for its Jewish composer (Weill's father was a cantor) caused one of the bloodiest riots in the history of the German theater the night it premiered in Leipzig.

Sitting on the sofa in the Ritz, declining a slice of cantaloupe, and puffing on ragged menthol cigarettes from a well-mashed package, Lenya remembered it all: "All of us were fascinated by America as we knew it from books, movies, popular songs, headlines. Weill loved Sophie Tucker's records. This was the America of the garish Twenties with its Capones, Texas Guinans, Aimee Semple MacPhersons, Ponzis, the Florida boom, and the stock-market crash. Also the disastrous Florida hurricane, which we used in *Mahagonny*, and a ghastly photograph reproduced in every German newspaper of murderess Ruth Snyder in the electric chair, Hollywood films about the Wild West and the Yukon, Tin Pan Alley songs. We all dreamed of going there."

Lenya sat in the audience that night with Weill's parents as the brownshirts filled the square around the theater carrying placards. By the final curtain, when God appears to tell the sinners He cannot send them to hell because, "we were *always* in hell," fist fights had already started in the aisles, the audience was screaming and the turmoil overflowed onto the stage. The next night it played with all the houselights on. Lenya appeared in it when it played Berlin for the first time in 1931 in Max Reinhardt's theater on the Kurfurstendamm. It became the first opera in history presented for a continuous run in a commercial theater. "Even today I have but to meet a true Berliner of that time, a survivor of that truly glorious public, to hear him say 'Yes, yes, *Threepenny Opera* was wonderful of course, but *Mahagonny....*'"

Also in 1930, two years after sound came in, the great German film director G. W. Pabst asked Lenya to re-create her Jenny Diver role for his film of *Threepenny Opera*. Singing the "Pirate Jenny" song in her lachrymose style, she became the rage of the German intellectuals. But things were happening behind the scenes. Brecht had gotten involved with Karl Marx. Weill was interested in music, not politics. One night in 1933 word arrived from a publisher friend who had infiltrated into the Nazi party that Weill and Lenya were on the Nazi blacklist. "When we learned we were to be arrested, we left Berlin the very same night. One more day and we would have been in a concentration camp and I would not be appearing in *Cabaret* today. Still, you must understand that it was not because Weill was Jewish. In '33 it had not come to that yet. Hitler was attacking originality. Composers, actors, writers, anyone who had the nerve to speak out against the inflation and bigotry. We were called *culture bolsheviks*. It was because of the art, not anti-Semitism. That came after we were gone."

They fled to Paris, met Brecht there, and the three of them sat around gloomily in the sidewalk cafés, sipping Moselle, worrying about Berlin, and—worse—speaking no French. But they produced, too. Weill wrote a ballet called *Seven Deadly Sins* about a haunted girl named Anna, sung and danced by her split personality. The role was acted by Lenya, danced by the great Tillie Losch, and choreographed by a young newcomer named George Balanchine. "Everybody spoke a different language," says Lenya. "Years later Balanchine said to me, 'Lenya, if I'd understood it at the time I'd never have done it.'" But he did, and Anna has become almost as famous a Weill-Brecht character as Mack the Knife.

After that, an American producer approached the Weills to do a Biblical musical called *The Eternal Road* with Lenya playing both Miriam, the sister of Moses, and the Witch of Endor, and Max Reinhardt directing. *The Eternal Road* almost collapsed four times before they even got on the ship. It had an enormous cast and was a dismal failure, but it didn't matter. They were really in America, and as starry-eyed as chorus girls. "We were not afraid," says Lenya, eyes shining. "The New York skyline was as familiar as Berlin. We'd seen it so many times in the movies. Riding up in our first elevator at the St. Moritz Hotel was the biggest thrill of our lives. There were no skyscrapers with elevators in Germany. We dropped our bags and headed straight for the movies. It was *The Dark Angel* and I think it starred Ronald Colman and Vilma Banky. I'll never forget my first bus ride. I was a penniless immigrant and spoke practically no English, so every dollar counted. I handed the driver a dollar bill and he had no change. I rode all the way down Sixth Avenue terrified he wouldn't give it back. 'How courteous Americans are,' I said to myself when he actually gave me my change at the end of my trip. We learned English fast and never spoke German again. Do you know," she said, staring out of the window, "the last words he said to me before he died were not in German at all, but in English."

From the beginning, they were accepted. *Johnny Johnson*, Weill's second show, got a rave from Brooks Atkinson and Lenya has never forgotten it. George Gershwin invited them as his guests to the opening night of *Porgy and Bess*. "It was a terrible flop, only ran six weeks. Heartbroken, Gershwin came to our tiny apartment on 72nd Street and Kurt Weill told him, 'It will survive.' He was right. Gershwin always said, 'Lenya sing' and after I sang he would tell me, 'You sing like a hillbilly.' I didn't even know what that was until years later. Ira Gershwin was another friend. Still is, though he never moves out of his red chair in California anymore."

The greats came and went: Moss Hart and Maxwell Anderson and Larry Hart and Walter Huston and Gertrude Lawrence and Marc Blitzstein. All of them gone today but Lenya. And the shows came and went, too: *Knickerbocker Holiday, Lady in the Dark, One Touch of Venus, Down in the Valley,* and *The Firebrand of Florence,* a major disaster that starred Lenya. Tired of performing, she decided to retire and turn the spotlight over to her husband. With the money

93

from *Lady in the Dark* they bought an old farmhouse on the South Mountain Road in New City, where Lenya still lives today. "It looks upside down. You can sit in the field in the back and it looks like the front. The entrance is on the side. It's a crazy house, very old. The year 1878 is carved on one of the stones." Brecht visited them there in 1946, before he locked himself behind the Iron Curtain forever.

In that little farmhouse, Weill turned out *Street Scene* (1947) and his last work, *Lost in the Stars* (1949). His mood turned to nostalgia and he was accused of writing cotton-candy music that was soft, sentimental, and—worst of all—sophisticated. But life was happier in Rockland County, softer—and more sophisticated. On April 3, 1950, Kurt Weill died of a heart attack and Lenya's world collapsed. "When he died I wanted to crawl into a hole and never come out." She buried him in his favorite white turtle-neck sweater and a simple pair of slacks, explaining, "He's going to be very busy up there and I want him to be comfortable."

In 1951, happiness came briefly back in the form of her second husband, George Davis, a former *Harper's Bazaar* editor who had photographed the Weills as immigrants years before and had remained close to Lenya through her grief. "Davis," she says now, "taught me like you teach a child to walk again. 'Lenya,' he would say, 'there are thousands of people who want you back. Establish your own name as Lotte Lenya, not just the 'widow of Kurt Weill.' I remembered our past and Berlin and Brecht and Georg Kaiser and I knew what I had to do. Except to a few, Weill was known only for what he had done in America. But what of his youth and the way he had captured the bitter, insecure Germany of the Twenties? I wanted to make people know about that, too."

Together they set upon a campaign to revive Weill's music the way he always meant for it to be sung—by Lenya herself. ("I hear all my melodies," Weill always said, "sung in my inner ear by Lenya.") About this time Ernst-Josef Aufricht, the original producer of *Threepenny Opera* in Berlin, asked Lenya to appear in Town Hall. She was terrified. She hadn't appeared on a stage in six years, but somehow George Davis managed to get her there. "I felt like I was strangling. At eight o'clock I could not go on. I was very emotional, shaking all over. Then I looked out at that packed house and I thought, 'This is what *he* would've wanted!' " The applause lasted fifteen minutes. It was the beginning of a new career.

Everyone wanted Lenya. In 1953, Leonard Bernstein conducted her in an outdoor concert version of *Threepenny* at Brandeis University before 4,000 screaming fans. "They all knew the music and sat in their seats whistling it before we even started." What was the applause like? Deafening? "I don't know. I couldn't hear it because a train went by." In 1954, Marc Blitzstein's off-Broadway version in English opened at the Theatre de Lys in Greenwich Village. Every note was supervised by Lenya, who wouldn't allow a single change. It ran for six years and 2,611 performances. Even after she left the show, she would go back and help sharpen it up. "I would go backstage and tell the cast how good they were and they would say, 'But Lenya, it's because we knew you were in the audience.' I couldn't go back every night— no show is that good."

Through Davis' help, she began slowly to record Weill's music—the Berlin theater songs, the American theater songs, and many of his early works. A new religion was springing up and Lenya was its high priestess. College kids from all over the world wrote her fan letters. In 1955 she returned to Berlin for the first time in twenty-two years in search of biographical material on Kurt Weill. "I didn't want to go. I stood on the train and looked out over Berlin and I didn't recognize it. The war destruction was devastating. I felt weak. I didn't go out of the hotel. I wanted to leave right away." But she did stay and people mobbed her in the streets. At the first German performance of *Street Scene* in Dusseldorf she was given a standing ovation.

In 1957 she returned again. While she was in Hamburg recording Weill's *Mahagonny* score, George Davis suffered a heart attack, but recovered in time to accompany her to Berlin to handpick and train singers and direct a 30th-anniversary recording of the complete *Threepenny Opera* for the first time in German. They were collaborating on a biography of Weill to be called *September Song* and Davis was eating nitroglycerine pills like popcorn. She telephoned the widow of her old friend Georg Kaiser to come and live with them in their sublet apartment in Berlin. The day Lenya received West Berlin's "Freedom Bell" award for peace, Davis entered the hospital for a week's rest. He never came home.

With two husbands dead of the identical disease, Lenya collapsed totally. Friends, however, persuaded her that George would have wanted her to carry through the plans that had brought them to Berlin. A week after his death, sighing "This I must do for him," she supervised in Berlin the

95

recording of *Threepenny Opera* which today is considered a collector's item.

She returned from Germany in March, 1959, to a new life. She starred in an off-Broadway production of *Brecht on Brecht* (which she doesn't even like to discuss) and the movies discovered her again after twenty-seven years. In Tennessee Williams' *The Roman Spring of Mrs. Stone* she played a barracuda called La Contessa Magda Terribili-Gonzales, who procures boys for crumbling older women, and in *From Russia With Love* she was a homicidal lesbian charlady who tried to murder James Bond by kicking him in the shins with a poisoned dagger planted in the toe of her shoes. (A trick that she ably demonstrated in the Ritz, taking care not to damage the carpet.) A whole new generation claimed Lenya for its own and even bought her records, too. "One night," she recalls, "I was at the ballet and these two kids came up to me looking so sad. The boy was about seventeen and his little girl friend couldn't have been more than fifteen. 'Oh, Miss Lenya,' they said, 'we're so worried.' 'Why?' I asked. 'We don't know who's gonna sing these songs you sing so beautifully ten years from now.' 'Please, darlings,' I said, 'I'm not dead yet.' That was 1959 and I'm still kicking!"

Indeed she is. Today she is married to an American painter named Russ Detwiler, who is only slightly more than half her age. ("When you are in love," she confides wisely, "age just becomes something stamped on your passport.") They live in the old house in New City and in a tiny apartment on East 55th Street in the same building as Van Johnson and Noel Coward. They still print those sad photographs, but the real Lenya is more fun than most girls who are young enough to be her grandchildren. She doesn't need the lights of a Broadway stage to get her message across, either. The day after the preview in Boston, she leaned against a drugstore chair in pants and an old sweater, on a drafty stage in an empty theater. No lights. No violins. She just sang. Even the man in the box office out front came in to applaud. Then she sat down in a coffee shop across the alley and told everybody jokes.

Today most of the sadness is gone, and she can talk about her life with the joy of a woman who is proud of the way she lived it. "I'm overjoyed about the way people finally accept Weill for the genius he was. *Threepenny Opera* will be good a hundred years from now. Corruption and poverty don't go out of fashion. I think he had a tremendous influence on American music, too. On the opening night of *Knickerbocker*

Holiday in New York Larry Hart sat in front of us in the third row and at intermission he turned around and said, 'Kurt, because of you we're gonna have to write better books from now on.' That was 1938. Musicals got better after that. *Pal Joey* was Weill's favorite. Irving Berlin told him, 'You're new in this country. Just remember one thing—you're only as good as your last success!' But he was wrong. Weill was timeless. He had the capacity to appeal to all ages. He had only fifteen years in this country, but he absorbed it all."

She doesn't mind the way everybody distorts Weill's songs and tells a funny anecdote about the day she came across a recording of "September Song" by Stan Kenton and took it home. "I put the record on and said, 'Kurt, I want you to hear something.' 'That was very interesting,' he said when the record stopped, 'what was it?' After that we both followed the German saying, *Es Geht Auch Anders Doch So Geht Es Auch*—'It's possible this way, but it's also possible another way.'"

And Brecht? "Brecht was my mother's milk. Today his future lies with the college kids. I toured 25 colleges with *Brecht on Brecht* and those students had read everything. They're full of the same defiance he had in himself. Also, he wrote about things which Broadway audiences are not educated to understand. *Mother Courage* is about the Thirty Years' War. Who knows anything about that in America except college students? If you did a play about Daniel Boone in Berlin you'd have to explain it to the Germans. It's the same thing. Still, Brecht will never die. The very day after Weill died, he sent me a telegram saying 'Come immediately to East Berlin and work with me' but I couldn't. America was my home and I was still bitter. I feel different now about Germany. Last year when I played Mother Courage there I met the young people and they are very hip. They are ashamed of what happened in the war. They don't want to hear about past disasters, they want to look into the future positively. Also, in Germany today there is very little to attack. At the time of Brecht and Weill it was the zero hour. They do not put Brecht into a category by saying his work was an expression of Communism. Anyway, I don't think he took his work too seriously. He was very religious. He loved Christmas and always had two trees, one for his children and one for himself.

"I went into the eastern zone to see Brecht before he died in 1956. I hadn't seen him in ten years. He had an endearing quality, he could really blush. He sat in a huge Gothic chair and asked me to sing. I sang 'Surabaya Johnny' with no piano.

Halfway through, I stopped because the setting was too simple and I was afraid it was not epic enough, the way he had remembered it. He patted my cheek and said, 'Lenya darling, whatever you do is epic enough for me.' The next day I recorded a song for his acting class at the Berliner Ensemble and I remember he couldn't raise the asbestos curtain on the stage. He tried and finally I said, 'Brecht, after all you *are* behind the Iron Curtain!' He broke into a wide smile, then he looked around quickly to make sure nobody had seen him. I never saw him again.''

Today Lenya has enough money to do as she likes. She never has to work again out of necessity. Her one regret is that she has so few tangible remembrances of Weill's work. "Dalink, when you have to scram from the Nazis in the middle of the night you can't take paintings. We took two scores—*Carmen* and *The Magic Flute*. Years later Weill gave everything away, saying 'What do I need with my own scores? I have them in my ears.' ''

She never cooks ("I'd rather go to Riker's and eat beans"), is terrible at gardening ("Some people have a green thumb, I have a black one—everything wilts"), refuses to employ servants ("I won't live by their rules, especially in the country—they're so spoiled"). She runs a "loose household" and loves quiet evenings with friends like Milton Caniff (who draws Steve Canyon in the comics) or Al Andriola (who draws Kerry Drake). "No actresses—heavens! I'd rather talk to my doorman—my Irish Jimmy—than actresses!" When she entertains, she sends out for Chinese food. She recently traded in her Thunderbird for a new Jaguar and loves to race around the countryside. ("I can't speed much since they put in that 45-mile speed limit in Rockland County," she grumbles.) She still loves music, but regrets that not enough good songs are being sung today. Who does she like in the way of singers? "Barbra Streisand excites me, Judy Garland makes me cry. Otherwise nobody."

On the opening night of *Cabaret* in Boston, Lenya showed up after the show at Harold Prince's party at the Playboy Club, eyes glistening like sequins on a garter. The first reviews arrived. "I never read critics. I don't want to hear them. What do they say?" Harold Prince read the first rave through a microphone and everyone applauded and hugged each other. "Still," she said. "I've seen shows with grand notices in Boston fall on their noses in New York. I must continue to work." She danced a jitterbug with one of her sailors from the show, kissed all the chorus boys for luck, and at two A.M. stood surrounded by bunnies, saying good-bye in the door of the Playboy Club. It had been thirty-three years since she stood on the Kurfurstendamm and waved good-bye to Berlin. Now she was waving good-bye again, on her way to Broadway. And now, as before, good-bye was only the beginning.

The Living Theatre in Berlin

SUMMER, 1965.

"AMERICA STINKS," said the bearded young man with the dirty toenails peering out from his broken sandals, as he watched the morning crowds strolling along in front of West Berlin's sagging old Café Mozart. He spoke as well for the rest of the ragged coffee klatch seated around him—all members of New York's Living Theatre, which in case anyone has been wondering, is still living in spite of the financial setbacks that forced its members out of their theater in New York, in spite of all the unfavorable newspaper headlines ("Living Theatre Stages Sit In on Steps of Criminal Court Bldg," etc.) and in spite of the prison sentences served by the group's gurus, Julian Beck and his wife, Judith Malina, for failure to pay taxes on the theater's property in Greenwich Village.

They've survived it all, though not without considerable bitterness toward America and its judicial courts, deserting New York's Seventh Avenue for Berlin's three-kilometer-long Kurfurstendamm, forsaking their now shuttered attic playhouse for "a stage, a ball park, an open space in the woods—anyplace we can put on our plays without fear of persecution." The Living Theatre is, in short, existing in a self-imposed European exile with no plans of ever returning to the United States, where actors have to pay their taxes and wash behind their ears, just like everybody else.

"Man, like we've walked through hell to get this far. We're not giving up now," said a long-haired Jesus type from Los Angeles.

"Yeah, man," echoed the rest of the company.

They were having coffee a few doors down the street from

99

the tiny theater Berlin has given them free of charge, where half the company is performing a nightly all-male version of Genet's *The Maids* in drag. Another part of the group was in Munich with the Becks, setting up an improvised production of its own called, simply, *Mysteries*. A few others were off trying to buy visas to travel through the Communist zone of East Germany to rehearse with the group in Munich. For a group with big ambitions and no money, they were very busy.

"It's this way, baby," said Henry Howard, a hairy Al Capone type with a broken nose, who says he joined the group because he was tired of playing gangster roles in bad Hollywood movies. "It's been like a bad scene, man. We were really swingin', see, when it all happened. We had been invited to Paris to put on our production of *The Brig*. Well, two weeks after we got to Europe, the Becks got a telegram from the District Attorney in New York. Man, it was Jailsville, U.S.A. We lost the Paris gig because they chickened out when our directors went to jail. Man, we didn't know what to do. We were broke and hungry and nobody cared. So we all sat down on the sidewalk in Brussels and thought about our two choices: either give up the Living Theatre as a bad scene and go back home to the land of soap operas and David Susskind, or stay in Europe and pull the pieces together. We stayed. That's what theater means to us."

"Yeah, man," somebody said.

The ones who were left of the once-thriving Living Theatre, the controversial mainspring of the off-Broadway time clock, which once had such productions as *The Connection* and *In the Jungle of Cities*, the stomping ground of Brecht and Gelber and William Carlos Williams, pulled themselves together and retired to an old farmhouse in Heist-sur-Mer, on the Belgian seacoast, to lick their wounds. "Thirty people, man, twenty Americans, two Dutch, two Germans, and some Belgians we picked up along the way—shut up in seven rooms with only three coal stoves for heat."

For three freezing months in the winter of 1964 they lived there, all huddled together for warmth with not enough money even for adequate food. "We lived on nerve, man, but we didn't sit on our cans. During the winter months, while one group rehearsed its all-male version of *The Maids*, another group was busy improvising an evening of disconnected pop art scenes.

"Then this cat in Brussels knocked on the door one day and offered his theater, like free, man. People cared, you know?" It was Diane Gregory, a dark-haired Joan Baez type from New Jersey talking now. "In the afternoons the guys'd be welding out the set for *The Maids* in one room, the chicks would be cooking in another room. We opened *Mysteries* at this cat's theater, man, and the audience went wild. There's no language problem, because there's no dialogue, dig? We just act out whatever we feel like. Like what we did in New York, only more advanced. It's really theater."

"Yeah, man," the others echoed.

While they performed *Mysteries,* the set for *The Maids* was being designed in Julian Beck's jail cell in America. Judith Malina directed the play by mail in New York, arriving ten days before it opened to give the group her final stamp of approval. After the Becks completed their sentences, the membership split into two hybrid companies—one toured with *Mysteries* and *The Brig;* the rest went to Berlin, where *The Maids* opened July 12, 1965.

"They love us over here," said Rufus Collins, a Negro actor who claims he couldn't get a job in New York because of his color. "Man, you couldn't pay me to go back there. Here they judge you only because of what you are, not how you look. Every night someone takes us out after the show and buys us free booze. That never happens in America. There's no barrier here, no closed society. They dig what we're doing."

"Except in Trieste," said a tall girl in dark glasses who had been sitting quietly chewing on the ends of her hair. "Don't forget Trieste."

"What happened in Trieste?"

"There was a riot, man, like the *end!* Just because we decided to come out nude on the stage, these police cats started closing the show. The Becks were arrested and held for half an hour, then let go. The audience yelled NO! to the police and everybody threw things and we just kept on playing around the flying bottles—it was *beau*tiful, man, *beau*tiful! That's theater!"

"Yeah," said the chorus.

Nobody gets a salary. When business is good, there is enough to eat. One week the group split a $300 take after expenses. Another week, they went without food for five days. In Berlin, they are revered by the young German students, but the money isn't good. The Becks give them fifty cents a day and a pack of German cigarettes. "We sometimes hike out to the woods and eat wild cherries and nuts. It is very primitive and beautiful," said Collins. "We live in barracks, youth hostels, apartments of friends, lovers, anyone

101

who will take us in. We lived for two months once in a fourteenth-century castle in Rieti; but for the past six months there's been no money."

"It's been rough," said Peter Hartman, a young actor from Hollywood. "But somebody always comes through. In Brussels, when we didn't even have enough money for black bread, a $250 check arrived from Elia Kazan. It enabled us to open *Mysteries*. Others have helped. Jerome Hill, people like that. In Rome, the Italian artists had an auction and raised $4,000 for us. Nobody in America ever did that. They just laughed at us when we were in trouble. The Berlin Senate has offered us a house free of rent. John Huston paid some of us to be in the Sodom and Gomorrah sequence in *The Bible*, and Marcello Mastroianni got us bit parts in his new movie, *Io, Io, Io*. We'll survive."

"With no help from America," said a long-haired actor with a thick Southern drawl. "We turned down an offer from Stanford University for a lotta bread, man, because they would have censored our work. We're beyond that, now. We asked the Ford Foundation for money. You know what they said? We don't pay our actors $125 a week, and our work is not consistent with their aims, some crap like that. So they give money instead to ballet companies to keep alive dead ballets. We're the only repertory company in the world producing new stuff, man. The Old Vic does the classics. I saw Olivier in *Othello*. It was bad news. The Lincoln Center? A laugh. Even the Berliner Ensemble in East Berlin. Took us two hours to get through the wall, but we went. Man, they're doing the same shows they did thirty years ago, the same way they did them then. If we only had their money. We're a real rep company. One night the guys wear billy clubs in *The Brig*, the next night we've got on bras for *The Maids*. Our trouble is, we're ahead of our time, man."

The group's new masterpiece, *Frankenstein*, will be unveiled September 27 at the Biennale in Venice. Howard describes it as a "Zefferelli-type spectacular based on Mary Shelley's book, only updated to represent the universal monster in society. We'll have monsters in drag, people behind monkey bars, film clips from Boris Karloff movies, even musical numbers—it's our wildest project! Like what you'd expect at Jones Beach or Radio City Music Hall."

"Yeah, man," said the boy with the Jesus hairdo.

To help pay expenses for such an elaborate project, several members of the company have been playing jazz with West Berlin musicians in after-hours nightclubs. ("No need to speak the language, man, you just bring your sax, pull up a chair, and everybody starts blowin' Monk's 'Straight No Chasers' like you was in Birdland," says Luke Theodore, a San Diego actor-musician.) Some of the others have recorded their troubles with the U.S. government in a new film called *Who's Crazy?*, which will be premiered this summer at the Locarno Film Festival. On West German television they recently performed a "live" government-invited production of *The Brig* in English. Alberto Moravia's wife, Elsa Morante, is writing a novel about their hardships, which they hope will sell.

After *Frankenstein*, there are even bigger plans. Bertolt Brecht's widow, Helena Wiegel, who operates the Berliner Ensemble, is negotiating with Judith Malina for her English translation of Brecht's *Antigone*, with talk of dual premieres— a German company in East Berlin and the English-speaking Living Theatre in West Berlin. There's the possibility of a Czechoslovakian tour if the visas can be drawn up. There has been an offer from Sol Hurok to tour several American universities, which the group will probably decline, since they'd have to return to America to accept it.

Somebody returned from the border control office at Checkpoint Charlie and there was a bit of commotion. "They won't let us all through in Peter's Volkswagen, man. Esther's gotta go through the wall on the train."

A girl named Esther protested loudly, and the others laughed. "She's too much, man. Here she is surrounded by Communist machine guns and she won't go on the train to Munich. She's still an American, man! Fight 'em to the end!"

"It's gonna cost twenty marks for visas."

"Where we gonna get twenty marks, man?"

"Do I have time to go to American Express to check my mail?" somebody asked.

"If we're going to drive to Munich, I refuse to eat in East Germany. I believe in ideal Communism, but not practical Communism."

"We'll pick up some stout and animal crackers and eat in the car."

"This goes on every day, man," said Howard. "But sooner or later our problems get solved. We're on our own over here. Sometimes our biggest problem is just figuring out how not to get gypped. Half the company are green apples, never been on a stage before in their lives, man. But we're not amateurs. In Europe they respect us for what we're doing— in America, they'd laugh at us or call us beatniks." The Becks plan to remain in Europe for the next five years, after which

103

the probationary period of their jail sentences will be over. They have no plans for returning to America even then, but if the group ever does make it past the Statue of Liberty again, it will not be housed in a permanent theater as before.

"Who needs America? They're much hippier in Europe," said the boy with the Southern drawl.

"Except Trieste," reminded the girl chewing on her hair.

"But that's the theater, baby," said the boy with the Jesus hairdo.

"Yeah, man," echoed the chorus, staring at the cold coffee rings in the bottoms of their empty cups. And being very sensitive and wise. And wishing, no doubt, that one of the wonderful people out there walking briskly in the Berlin sunshine would come inside and pay the check.

Shirley Knight

ON THE EXTERIOR she is right out of Louisa May Alcott: fragile, dreamlike, Beth coughing her way through another snowy winter. Then *sock!* Get to know her, and underneath the little-girl dresses and the daisy-yellow hair and the big round-rim glasses Shirley Knight is tough, alert, fiercely intelligent, and dedicated to her craft like few actresses since Duse. It is almost impossible to write about her, in fact, without sounding corny. "Big movie star gives up big Hollywood money to go on the stage, ends up in low-budget films for noncommercial markets. . . . I mean, everybody knows actresses like that don't really exist. Stage actresses are all dying to rub elbows with those California palm trees. Reality is the other way around, right?

Well, not with Shirley. I am sitting in this dainty little doll's house chair in this great big living room with a grand piano and lots of shutters, trying not to think of the filthy snow melting into black puddles down below in Central Park, and we are drinking the English breakfast tea she bought in London when she was there filming *Dutchman*. *Dutchman*, in fact, is what I'm here to talk about, but with Shirley it is not possible to dwell on current triumphs without bringing up the past. From such humble beginnings as a childhood in Goessel, Kansas, and schooling in Enid, Oklahoma, she left the wheatfields and moved to Hollywood to become a movie star. She became one when an agent came to a Little Theater production of *Look Back in Anger* to rediscover child stars Dean Stockwell and Little Beaver, instead discovered Shirley. Five years of living at the Hollywood Studio Club, six films and two Academy Award nominations (*Dark at the Top of the Stairs* and *Sweet Bird of Youth*) later, the strange wispy girl who didn't like smog packed her bags and headed for the soot of New York. "I just hated it. I kept trying to tell myself it was what I wanted, but I was only kidding. I was working with big names who didn't have sense enough to come in out of the rain. I had no respect for anyone, least of all myself. I guess I just didn't want to be Natalie Wood."

Today she is recognized as one of Broadway's finest actresses and looks back on the entire movie-star experience with horror. "The Oscar nominations? Listen, they give Oscars to people like Charlton Heston. All the clichés about Hollywood are true. It's silly to knock it, because it is so obviously stupid. The movie business is run by blockheads who sit around long tables and pay out all the money to *people,* instead of putting it into their product. They're learning they can't spend thirty million dollars for a movie, because they can't get their money back, but they're doing it at the expense of a lot of talent."

Shirley is now a member of the Actor's Studio. She played Irina in their production of *Three Sisters,* performs scenes there almost every week, is now learning the entire score of *Così fan tutte.* Her next stop is opera. ("If I were a composer, I'd want to be as good as Mozart. That's what I'm all about.") She made one film, *The Group,* in New York. She hates it. She finally went back to Hollywood two years ago to star in a stage production of *Dutchman,* produced by her husband, Gene Persson. "That was the end for me. The John Birch Society threatened our lives, we couldn't advertise in the papers. We knew that place was in trouble. Three weeks later the riots broke out in Watts. I mean it's spooky out there—any state that elects George Murphy to Congress and Ronald Reagan as governor, well, you *know* they're in trouble!"

Time and time again Hollywood phones. Shirley keeps on hanging up. "It's not the money; I don't care about that. Each person has to take care of his own little corner of the

105

business, do what he believes is right. I have no respect for people like Marlon Brando. People say, 'He wants to give up making trashy movies, get back to acting, do a play, but he can't afford it.' Bunk! When you've got that much money, you can afford anything, especially your own self-respect. I don't want to wake up some day and be forty and not have done the things I became an actress for. The greatest success of my life was not those Oscar nominations, but playing Julie for Negro schoolchildren in Delaware for seventy-five dollars a week. It gave me more joy than making some silly movie with Yul Brynner in Japan, for which I made fifty times as much. It makes me sick to see actors prostitute themselves for money. Can you imagine the pride a man like Laurence Olivier has to swallow to make a movie for a man like Otto Preminger?"

Shirley is so outspoken she once hit a director she didn't respect over the head with a broom, and when a press party was thrown to introduce the girls in *The Group* she ended up on the front page of *Variety* after dressing down a United Artists executive for calling her an "unknown." "I've worked hard to get where I am today, and I am losing patience daily with people who make stupid remarks. When *Three Sisters* opened, Geraldine Page, Kim Stanley, and I did a Barry Gray radio show with the critic from *Newsweek* and Judith Crist. They made such inane remarks, without even understanding what we were trying to do onstage, that I spent nearly half an hour telling everybody off, then I walked off the show. Kim kept yelling at me, 'Don't be a sore ass!' but I just couldn't help it. I have a terrible temper."

Show people love labels and such behavior has developed for Shirley a reputation as a kook in some circles. Temperamental. Difficult to work with. The truth is that she is an idealist, a dedicated innocent who has landed kerplop in the middle of a quagmire of professional jealousy, viciousness, and distrust called show business. She doesn't care. "I have a friend who says, 'Shirley, you're one of the most normal people I know, but you're still a bit nutsy.' Well, I have relatives in Oklahoma I think are nuts. Everybody is a little crazy, but if you reach the point where you have no sense of honor, everything goes." She gives to each project total concentration and she expects nothing less from everyone else around her. She detests mediocrity, but she is surrounded by it and that is a tragedy she cannot bear.

For example, her stardom in the recent Broadway adaptation of Shirley Jackson's *We Have Always Lived in the Castle* has left scars that may never be erased. The night before the

lay died an agonized death, victim of the critic's axes, Shirley
vent berserk onstage, broke whatever she found in sight, and
prought down the wrath of Actor's Equity. Those Who Know
eaped to their phones to burn her in effigy as a lunatic
Method actress on the loose. But, as usual, Those Who Know
didn't know a thing. "Let me tell you about that, because it's
important. It's also a good example of the crap that goes on
on Broadway. First, it was badly produced, also Garson
Kanin was the worst director I've ever worked with in my
ife. For five performances in Washington, when we needed
him most to reshape the play, he didn't even see the show!
Can you imagine that? Also, it was totally miscast, the
company was right out of summer stock, it was under-
rehearsed. Not one single night during the entire run did the
technical things work, which is incredible considering what
the union technicians get paid! One night we did the third act
in total blackness with literally only candles to see by—and
Broadway is supposed to be the epitome of perfection! They
fired people every day, but I never blew up once. Everybody
knew we were closing, but David Merrick and Kanin didn't
give a damn about the play, so they let it die. In spite of
that, I continued to work. I had gone through four months of
work on that part and two months of inadequacy in rehearsal and yet I was still working sixteen hours a day on that
play, but nobody gave a damn but me. Do you know what
the union men did when they heard it was going to close?
They went over to other shows they knew were going to run
and got themselves replaced by second-rate technicians who
were out of jobs and who didn't know any of the light or
sound cues in a complicated show which depended strongly on
them. For instance, I was supposed to hear voices in the play
and half the time the voices weren't even there, so the
audience would just roar with laughter. I had to check every
prop myself or they wouldn't be there. Finally all the sound
cues failed and all the lights went out and I went nuts. I
should have lost my temper the first day of rehearsal, then
maybe things would've worked better. I've done things in stock
and Little Theater where the people worked more professionally than in this 'Broadway show' that cost thousands of
dollars. I will never do another play on Broadway without
a clause in my contract that will allow me to demand a
complete technical rehearsal if something goes wrong. I will
not go through that again. I want to work in the damn New
York theater, Gene and I even want to own our *own* theater
—but not when I have to sacrifice my own art to worry

107

about whether the lights are going to go on. Who needs that kind of pain?"

Shirley feels her best work as an actress is in the movie version of *Dutchman*. She plays a mentally ill slut who tries to seduce a Negro man on a subway—hardly the embodiment of what she is like in real life, but she spent years working on the part and the work shows. She knows the film's hatred for the white man will offend many people, but "So what? If we make people angry, that's good. People are so blasé about everything they need to get stirred up about *some*thing!" The film was shot in London after the Perssons were refused permission to film it in New York. Lindsay was in office, but the transit strike was on and the Transit Authority wasn't about to do him any favors. So Shirley and Gene went to London, made it for only $65,000 in six days on a set constructed from photographs by a British crew that had never seen a New York subway.

The warmth with which their work was encouraged in England was overwhelming. "Bryan Forbes loaned us his entire crew. John Barry, one of the hottest composers in the movie business, saw a screening and although we weren't originally planning to use music, said, 'I want to be involved, to contribute something. I don't want to be paid anything and if you don't want to use it you don't have to.' Incredible! I don't think anyone in America would do that. We shot it in ten-minute takes. We'd put film in three cameras and do the scenes until the film literally ran out of the cameras and then shoot again. Hollywood films are usually shot so stupidly, one minute at a time, it's no wonder nobody ever has time to do good work."

Everyone worked for a percentage. Shirley made about $135 for the entire film. Then they came back to New York, sneaked onto the subway platforms at 4 A.M. on a Sunday with hand-held cameras hidden in paper sacks and shot the exteriors. "We are very proud," says Shirley, "because it was something we believed in and wanted to do, so we went out and did it against total opposition. Every time we tried to raise money, people said, 'Only two people in the cast, only one set, the language'll never get past the censor, it'll never go over.' Well, as a result every major company in America wants to distribute it. It is the official British entry in the Cannes Film Festival. Because of the deal we made we've practically already made our money back. Anyone who says it is dirty is crazy. Have you seen *The Game Is Over*? That is an obscene film. So far removed from any creative process that it makes me sick. When you say, 'I'm going to photograph *this* girl in the nude in front of *this* mirror' just because t's going to titillate someone, *that* is sick."

Shirley and Gene want to make more films together, but hey hope to do them in London, where they can work inhampered by all the insanities of the American unions. Shirley wants to move there, maybe work with Olivier's National Theatre ("They make sure your props are in the right place *there!*"). "If I couldn't do plays, I wouldn't even act. I find movies a big bore and very unfulfilling. I'm a slow worker, and it takes me an awfully long time to be any good at all. Harold Pinter and his wife, Vivien Merchant, saw *Dutchman* and wrote me a six-page letter saying they'd love to meet and talk, so we all went out to dinner the other night and she—this brilliant actress—said 'I just made my second film and it's my last. Movies are stupid and have nothing to do with acting.' It was like hearing myself talk, but it's true. Any actor who tells me he is fulfilled artistically by working n movies is full of it."

Which leaves Shirley Knight on the horns of a dilemma. She knows the theater is dying of cancer, but she wants to work in it. She knows movies are unrewarding but she wants to do those, too. Meanwhile, there was just enough time to pick up spilled raisins from the rug, tuck her daughter Kaitlin into bed for her afternoon nap, and head for a rehearsal of *The Rivals* at the Actor's Studio. "The only answer seems to lie with producers with less money who are less gung-ho. I say, take chances, even if Oliver Smith doesn't do the sets." Shirley has taken chances. She is strongly admired by the hardworking, no-nonsense crowd. And she still does not want to be Natalie Wood.

Robert Anderson

"I CAN WRITE PLAYS, but I can't read a timetable," said Robert Anderson on the phone. But he was there, at the little station, to meet the Saturday train on time. Not looking very much like Hollywood's idea of a famous playwright. More

109

Jimmy Stewart than Reginald Gardner. Boots, little red hunting cap, big furry windbreaker, and soft, silvery hair falling boyishly over his forehead. Healthy, joyous, and raspberry-cheeked over the smash of his four new one-act plays called *You Know I Can't Hear You When the Water's Running.* "I haven't had a hit for fourteen years. Now it's nice not to be 'the man who wrote *Tea and Sympathy*' anymore," he beamed, steering the car toward home.

It had been a long time between tea, and as the Oldsmobile chugged along roads cleared by snowplows, past white-washed church steeples, evergreen trees and chestnut stallions running behind farmyard fences, Bob Anderson talked about it. "I was never really away. I wrote a lot of plays and a few movies. But it's great to have another hit, because more than just the money it means what you write makes sense to more people than yourself. When you've been stomped on it's hard to get back to that writing desk. After *Tea* I wrote a play called *All Summer Long,* which got great reviews, but never found an audience. Then *Silent Night, Lonely Night* disturbed me because I felt I might have written too personally about my own life. But I still love that play. It's listed in my works as a failure, but that's silly. It's performed all over the world, so it's not a failure to me. I understand if people didn't respond to those plays, but I don't denounce them. I'm very fond of all my plays. I go over to the theater and die laughing. People say, 'Christ, man, have you no shame?' The real tragedy lies in playwrights who really believe their plays are bad when people don't like them. Every play I've ever written is me. I am naked when I finish. Everything I write is full of my own beliefs. The new ones just have a wider appeal for a more general audience, that's all. Broadway today is the only criterion by which plays are judged successes or failures. That is wrong and that is why I gave my last play, *The Days Between,* to the American Playwrights Theater. Several people wanted to produce it on Broadway, but I was plagued by casting problems and I just got tired of waiting. It was performed all over America in fifty different productions and it was an enormous success, but because it hasn't been done in New York yet, people think that was a failure, too. In Ohio, they sat in bleachers under a stadium in a thunderstorm with rain pouring down their necks but they came to the theater to see my play. It was the most enormous compliment I've ever received. I wish there was a way to make a living in the theater and not just a killing."

We got off on the subject of his movie version of *Tea and Sympathy*, which had been banned by the Legion of Decency before its original release. "I'll never adapt a play of my own again for films. Once you conceive it onstage it's hard to reconceive it for films. We had to make concessions and I had a terrible row. They were afraid it would establish a precedent. If they let the woman commit adultery the next guy would come along and make a vulgar exploitation film and say, 'Look, you let MGM and Vincente Minnelli and Bob Anderson get away with it, why can't I?' But I still refused to pull the rug out from under the meaning of my play. I said 'Would you rather have the woman commit adultery or the boy commit suicide?' They changed their minds and the next day we opened at the Music Hall."

The 1825 New England farmhouse sparkled in the snow like a gingerbread house covered with powdered sugar. Mrs. Anderson was waiting in the kitchen doorway. Some people call her Teresa Wright, the movie star, but most of the folks in the nearby Connecticut town of Bridgewater know her only as "that nice Mrs. Anderson from down the road." She likes it that way. They are real people, unhampered by professional labels—sunflower people, warm and special, who love to sit by the fire and talk and learn things about life and their house looks just like them. It's a big gray farmhouse with a yellow door and last year's Christmas tree tilting on its side outside the dining-room window. Inside, antiques and pots of geraniums and walls of cheerful books and paintings and wooden beams holding up the white country ceilings. There's a big brass bed and farmhouse furniture and friendly fireplaces crunching on wooden logs and a kitchen that smells like cinnamon and nutmeg, where something wonderful is always about to pop out of the oven. A man could write plays in a house like that.

We sat in the den, where a funny hand-licking dog named Mam rubbed against our legs as we sipped Teresa's "ice box soup," made from leftovers and tasting like some gourmet-blend of Creole exotica, and talked about the city and children and dogs and plays and actors and what it's like to be Bob Anderson. "People think I'm from some distinguished Boston family or something," he said. "It's not true. I worked my way through Exeter as a janitor and waited on tables and I was a proctor in the dorm so I got my room free. I wanted to be a singer, but my father never understood that. He was a fascinating guy—a self-made Dead End Kid who later ran for mayor of New Rochelle. An old-world type who knew this country gave him a tremendous break, realized the obligation, and gave it back." His newest play, *I Never Sang for My Father*, is about a middle-aged son and an eighty-

111

year-old father. More of his own life. ("It's shattering," say Teresa.) "I acted in plays at Harvard and sang in the glee club and one day I tried out for a part in a girls' school play and met the director, a wonderful woman named Phyllis Stohl, who was about eight years older than me. She encouraged me to be a writer instead of an actor. She changed my life."

He married her in 1940, before he went into the Navy. She had made a man out of a boy and he worshiped her for it, even though he disappointed his father by leaving school (all he lacked toward his PhD was writing the thesis) to write. On a ship in 1945, while Navy seabees and riveters worked around him, he wrote a small play called *Come Marching Home*, which won a $100 prize. Between kamikaze attacks on the battleship *Texas* at Iwo Jima he turned out more plays and together with the first one, they won him a $2,000 National Theatre Conference grant. The money made it possible for him to live in New York, where Phyllis became a play reader and agent helping other playwrights and he taught at the American Theatre Wing. To make money, he adapted other people's plays for radio. In one year, he turned out twenty-five radio scripts. "That's how I learned to write. Writers think their every word is sacred, but I learned if a scene didn't work one way I took it home and batted out a new one."

After fifteen plays of his own, he wrote *Tea and Sympathy* and dedicated it to his wife with the inscription: "This is for Phyllis, whose spirit is everywhere in this play and in my life." "I guess it was autobiographical in spirit, if not in fact. Some of my problems with my father were reflected in the role of the husband. I had been very lonely at prep school, the way all people are lonely when they are young, and I had been in love with an older woman. I was afraid they'd never let me back into Exeter. I went there later to give a talk and said 'I hope this play hasn't caused you any embarrassment' and the housemaster's wife where I had lived said, 'Nobody has been so kind as to call me Laura.' What a wonderful thing to say."

The play made history but in his personal life success was overshadowed by tragedy. After ten years of marriage, Phyllis developed cancer. After her first operation he was told she had six months to live. He debated whether to tell her or not. He never did. She lived for five more years, died in 1956. The morning she died, when he brought her home from the hospital, there was a pad on her desk with a list of things still to be done for her playwrights. For a while he lost the will

112

to work and even the will to live. He went to Europe to get away and developed a long and understanding friendship with Ingrid Bergman, who starred in the Paris production of *Tea and Sympathy*. One of his prize possessions is a gray-wool scarf she knitted him onstage during the run. He wears it constantly and teases Teresa by not letting her put it in the washing machine. He also still owns the little house in Roxbury he shared with Phyllis before she died, where part of *Tea* was written, just up the hill from the house where Arthur Miller once lived with Marilyn Monroe.

Life is happier now with Teresa, who knows writers. (Her first husband, Niven Busch, wrote *Duel in the Sun* and countless movies.) "I never talk to anyone about my plays while I'm working on them. During *Tea* Phyllis finally said, 'For goodness sake tell me something about it' so I said it took place in a boys' school and she said, 'Oh my God, not another play about a boys' school!' I learned my lesson. But when a play is finished I show it to my 'kitchen cabinet'—my friend Elia Kazan, Audrey Wood, John Wharton—and of course Teresa."

Teresa beamed. "It's a very traumatic experience the day he asks me to read. A very special occasion. If it comes on a very mixed-up day when I'm under the hair dryer I postpone it. I like to read them in bed."

"I present the script to her and then I go away for the whole day. I always make her read it in one sitting because that's the way you see it onstage. She's scrupulously honest, tells me exactly what she thinks." He gave her a warm hug. There had been talk of her starring in *Days Between* but it never came off. "I directed her in *Tea* for three weeks once, but we don't really want to work together. If you do that the wife ends up saying 'Why doesn't he write better lines' and the husband 'Why doesn't she say them better.' She'd rather have the marriage than the part."

Lunch was served on a wooden table in front of a picture window overlooking the staggering white purity of snow drifting down from a purple Berkshire mountain range. "Gee," said Bob, "I should be interviewed every day. Usually I just get a jelly sandwich."

"He'd eat nothing but hamburgers if I let him," said Teresa. We talked about her two children, Mary-Kelly, a freshman at Bradford, and Terry, 22, a rhetoric major at Berkeley and a budding novelist himself. "He wanted to be an actor once," said Bob, "but I think we talked him out of that. The first play in this new batch is about all the poor actors I've seen. An actor once came up to me with tears running down his face and said, 'I heard you wouldn't cast me if I wore glasses, so I got contact lenses.' After Deborah Kerr left *Tea* all the girls who read for me wore pink blouses and red hair. It's tragic what actors will do for a part. I know in thirty seconds if they are even possible, but with my tender heart I sit and talk to them until I'm exhausted."

The dog barked at something in the snow. "She's ten years old," he said.

"No, she isn't, hon," corrected Teresa.

"Yes she is. My wife has a terrible memory. You know that fourth play? It's not about senile old people, it's about Teresa and me." "Oh, Bob—" "It's true. We make dates to meet for a movie and she turns up at the wrong theater, or if I'm supposed to meet her at 53rd and Fifth, she'll turn up at 63rd and Park. What can you tantalize us with for dessert?"

"I have some lovely sherbet." She left the room and he talked about his films. He doesn't really like the medium, because in movies a writer has no artistic control over his work once it is finished. "In the theater I get cast and director approval. I could go to the theater tomorrow and rewrite those plays if I wanted to. Not in a movie. I wrote *Nun's Story*, which was a lovely film, but with Fred Zinnemann I couldn't lose. But suppose Audrey Hepburn is walking down the aisle, you've got the cathedral and the choir and 500 nuns and she says, 'Forgive me, Mother, I have sinned ... bla ... bla ...' and I say 'Gee, Fred, I'd like to write that line again tonight after I think about it,' he'd say 'What are you, crazy? We got 500 nuns getting overtime.' So you see it's not the same." He also wrote *Until They Sail*, a good film that got buried in its release and *The Sand Pebbles*, for which he got no closer to China than Admiral Dewey's gunboat in the Philadelphia harbor. On *Night of the Generals* he spent time in East Berlin on a script that was never used and for his screenplay based on the life of Dr. Tom Dooley he followed him to Bangkok, got mixed up in the Laotian Revolution, and Hollywood said, "Where's the drama?" Bob says he was a man who "had a whole nation worshiping him but no personal relationships. I just wouldn't write in scenes where he got his foot bitten off by a crocodile or have him living with a nun. The script was never filmed." Still, his movie scripts have brought him pots of money and that's the stuff playwrights live on just like everybody else. "People say, 'Why don't you live in a garret?' Well, I've had my garrets. It's too late to go back to that. So I do movies in between my plays."

114

Teresa stood in the doorway blushing. "I'm glad I didn't deny what you said about me forgetting, because I don't have any sherbet." Everybody laughed and settled for fruit.

We talked the afternoon into dusk, took a drive up to the old cabin, which he plans to turn into a place for writing, and he expressed enthusiasm over regional theater. "People deserve the pleasure of seeing a play in their home town without the approval of New York, even if you can't get Deborah Kerr to star in it. There are many reasons why good plays don't get produced—somebody's tax structure is at stake or the star doesn't like the director. But the young playwrights can now take their plays on the road, get them seen by audiences who haven't been told to stay away by the New York critics . . . plays are no good on a shelf." He was mixing drinks in the kitchen. His "Jo Mielziner sunset" flooded the house with lemony yellows from the hills and Teresa was talking about the maple trees outside the window.

"What kind of maple trees are these, Bob?" No answer. "I said what kind of maple trees are these in our yard?"

"You know I can't hear you when the water's running!" he yelled from the kitchen sink. And that's where his title comes from. From our separate posts in the evening light, we burst into a laughter that sustained itself through an old-fashioned roast-beef dinner at a country inn in New Milford and on our way to the station for the late train back to Manhattan, snuggled under blankets in the car, Bob in his Ingrid Bergman scarf. Standing there in the country depot, with the snow crunching under their boots, hugging each other for warmth, they waved good-bye at the end of a story-book day. That's how they are. And years from now, when people talk about them—and they will—they'll be kind.

Angela Lansbury

> In time the Rockies may crumble,
> Gibraltar may tumble,
> They're only made of clay,
> But Angela Lansbury is here to stay.

Or so Gershwin might have whistled had he been in the audience at *Mame*. But of course he was nowhere around, so the audience did its own whistling. And when the people got tired of whistling and clapping like thunder, they stood on top of their newly refurbished seats in the Winter Garden and screamed.

And up on the stage, under those revolving rainbow lights that make you feel you're looking at the world through spun sugar, was something to scream about: Angela Lansbury blowing a trumpet in backless canary-yellow spangles on top of a grand piano. Angela Lansbury doing a slow Theda Bara burn across a speakeasy floor in silver lamé and monkey fur. Angela Lansbury leading an imaginary parade into theatrical history with a peppermint stick. Angela Lansbury bringing the Broadway stage about as close to an MGM musical as the Broadway stage is likely to get, singing about hot dogs and mustard and Ferris wheels while rebopping to a dazzling jitterbug. A happy caterpillar, turning, after years of being nose-thumbed by Hollywood in endless roles as baggy-faced frumps, into a gilt-edged butterfly.

Outside, in the traffic, people hummed under their umbrellas as they crowded around the stage door. People who, only last year, pointed at Broadway's new darling and said, "Look, there goes what's-her-name." Waiting now, with programs open and autograph books raised, for what's-her-name's suddenly valuable signature. The doorman had a time handling the mob that pushed backstage. And up the rickety stairs the noise sounded like the Fourth of July. Two flights and a sharp turn to the right and you're there—a tiny white room with a dark-blue carpet and no furniture. Framed caricatures, an Al Hirschfield cartoon showing Mame hanging precariously from a satin moon, and a refrigerator containing some crushed gardenias, a dozen bottles of seltzer water, a can of frozen orange juice, and a bottle of Scotch, from which Miss Lansbury's husband, Peter Shaw, pours cheer into a paper cup.

"Damnedest thing you ever saw," says Shaw, an MGM executive who looks like a Mississippi riverboat gambler in an old Tyrone Power movie. "Suddenly, after years of beating her brains out, Angie's really a star. Had to throw a guy out of Sardi's last night, it got so bad. He came up to our table, see, and said, 'Excuse me, but I'm a friend of Ida Lupino's.' Well, anyone who can deliver an opening line like that deserves to be heard, right? He turned out to be some drunk gypsy dancer Comden and Green had discovered in Hollywood. Couldn't even sit up straight, but it broke Angie's heart to get rid of him. She's all heart and no ego. She'll let the biggest bores in the world bend her ear all night and feel so sorry for them she'll invite them for breakfast the next morning. That's the kind of girl she is."

Suddenly the girl herself flew into the room, barefoot, peachy skin glowing, champagne hair bobbing, looking for all the world as though someone had just bottled the secret of daisies and dandelions and allowed her to impishly swallow the formula. "Albert!" she yelled, arms flying. A little man with a round bald head and a grandfatherly smile peered through the door, which, after a lot of kissing and promises for dinner, she closed against the onslaught. "That was Al Lewin, who directed me in *The Picture of Dorian Gray*. He sort of discovered me when I was fresh off the boat from London." Fighting tears in her Valentine-heart eyes. "Not long ago we had a little reception for Al at one of the museums. They showed *Dorian Gray* and I sang 'Little Yellow Bird' and the man who painted the portrait came out and Hurd Hatfield made a little speech and we all cried. Such a wonderful darling little man."

"See what I mean?" winked her husband, as the crowds came and went like smoke rings in a bar. An agent (was it GAC? William Morris?), Bea Arthur, who always kisses her good night before leaving the theater, and Gene Saks, the director, who is so happy with the show he kisses everybody good night.

In the street the mob surrounded her limousine, yelling "Angela! Angela!" Inside the car, with the windows rolled up and the air-conditioning icing up the windshield so you felt you were looking at the neon lights from the inside of a submarine, the star relaxed. "How can I tell you what a staggering victory *Mame* is for me? I always suspected I could reach everybody, but I never did until now. I've always done two types of things: first, things like *The Harvey Girls* and *Harlow*, which I could do competently but with my hands tied behind my back, but which appealed to huge masses of people. And second, roles which taxed me emotionally and physically and broke my heart with pride, but only appealed to a small, rather special audience. Roles like Annabel in *All Fall Down* and that heartbreaking woman in *Dark at the Top of the Stairs*. And of course my musical debut on Broadway in *Anyone Can Whistle*. The first breakthrough was the fiendish mother in *Manchurian Candidate*. Imagine! I was only thirty-seven and playing Larry Harvey's mother. I've played so many old hags most people think I'm sixty-five years old. I didn't want to play all those nasty ladies

117

but in Hollywood you're either a member of the working group or not, and if not you're very easily forgotten. I've had high spots, medium spots, and a couple of low spots, but I've always been in there pitching."

The crowd in front of Sardi's applauded as she made a sweeping entrance. The head waiter bowed and said he had said a prayer to St. Jude for her. "Let's face it. I've finally arrived," she giggled, diving into a dish of strawberries and cream. "I always knew I would hit on something that would unlock all the doors and hit all those people between the eyes. Don't get me wrong. My career has been very satisfying and a lot of wonderful people have dug what I've tried to do. When I did *Anyone Can Whistle*—a magnificent failure—the crowd yelled bravo, too. But that was the insy-poo New York crowd. They're marvelous, but they fizzle out after six weeks. I'm out to get the taxi drivers, shop ladies, and people on the street. Even teen-agers are paying $9.50 a seat to see *Mame*. They love this dame. I hope the way I play her she's more than just a song and dance. She's all the women I've played. I'm like a sponge. Everything I see is ducated away in my pores. I've known a lot of Mames in my day and underneath they all cry 'Need me.' It's taken me forty-one years, but I've finally found a role that is the sum total of everything I know and everybody's digging me for the first time."

Well, not exactly. For years she's been *the* actress who could do (and did) literally everything. People may not have applauded in the streets, but they could watch her on the screen and know they'd been had by a real pro. Nothing papier-mâché about this Mame. Her mother, British actress Moyna Macgill, was a mayoress and ambulance driver in her spare time, who taught little Angie to do precise imitations of Wagnerian contraltos and takeoffs on Bea Lillie at the age of eleven. At twelve, she sat through three performances of *Pygmalion* at London's Old Vic and vowed that, somehow, she had to get on a stage. By 1940, Hitler's bombs were falling on London's docks, so Angela's mother packed her up with her nine-year-old twin brothers and boarded a refugee boat with 600 other children bound for America. After floating around New York and Canada doing pantomimes in cabarets, the Lansburys ended up in Hollywood. In 1943, when she was eighteen, a boyfriend arranged an interview at MGM. They wanted a cockney girl to sing a song in *Dorian Gray*. Somewhere during the interview a man took her by the hand and led her down the hall to George Cukor's office to read for the cockney maid in *Gaslight*. She

118

ot both roles and two Oscar nominations. James Agee wrote that she reminded him of "the milkmaids in eighteenth-century pornographic prints" and the girl was on her way.

"One day I was making $18 a week at Bullock's department store and the next day I was up to $500 a week at MGM." Trouble was the MGM lot didn't know what to do with a teen-ager who could play anything. They already had Esther Williams to swim, Judy Garland to sing, June Allyson to jitterbug, and Lena Horne to lean sultrily against pink pillars with her mouth open. "All I wanted to be was Jean Arthur." Instead, Angela ended up in the roles nobody else could play (or wanted to play). Still, she remembers it all with a big heart. "Not a moment was wasted, because I still have the memories. I rode to work every day on the Asbury Park bus with Margaret O'Brien and her mother. There was a war on and nobody could afford gas. Louis B. Mayer and I got along like a house afire. He never chased me around his desk or tried anything with me. Of course, he never gave me any good parts, either. I'll never forget begging him to let me play Lady De Winter in *Three Musketeers* and watching the part go to Lana Turner while I had to play Queen Anne."

They were all about like that: Elizabeth Taylor's older sister in *National Velvet;* a mysterious woman who came out of panels in the wall while Van Johnson played the drums in *Remains to Be Seen*; a tough 45-year-old newspaper publisher in *State of the Union*; a villain who terrorized Ethel Barrymore in *Kind Lady;* a Western honky-tonk singer who made things tough for Judy Garland in *The Harvey Girls* ("People hissed me in public for being mean to Judy"); Hedy Lamarr's older sister who gets speared to the wall in *Samson and Delilah*. "People ask me to this day if it still hurts. With De Mille, everything was that real. I feel sorry for actors who never worked with him. He was an experience. Taught me how to throw a javelin. Twenty-five yards and I can still hit a bull's eye."

"The all-time low point for me was when Peter and I needed money so badly that I played a seamstress in a Tony Curtis film. The star was some girl who later married some man who was married to Betty Hutton. I don't remember her name or the picture, except it was about this guillotine. I can't even remember how many pictures I made. When we tried out *Mame* in Boston some man called and asked me to autograph his collection of film annuals and I discovered I had been in more than seventy films. I was even up for *Forever Amber*. Whatever would I have used for bosoms?" What's left? A Western? "Darling, I've done that too. I once

119

rode off into the sunset on a buckboard with Randolph Scott in *The Marshal of Medicine Bend*. Another low point. Well, I *told* you I've done everything!"

Today she is calm and sure. Her hands don't shake, she doesn't smoke, doesn't drink, and she is "absolutely militant" about getting eight hours of sleep a night. She doesn't act like a star marquees light up for. During her snack at Sardi's, she leaped to her feet five times to hug people's necks. She insists she is a slob, really, because she'd rather schlep around with Peter and her three kids (ages fourteen, fifteen, and twenty-three) than work. "I don't work at being an actress. I'm the lettuce type. Between parts I just sit in our house out at Malibu. Glass overlooking the beach, antiques, books, junk, and people. You can exist there and never do a damn thing. I get complacent and fat and I say I'm going to be a great wife and not an actress. Then something like *Mame* comes along. I don't know how I do what I do. I just sort of slide into it and then I'm working twelve hours a day. I find the energy somewhere."

Midnight supper over, she glided past the outstretched hands and paused next to the entrance, where, on the wall, stood a framed caricature drawn when she appeared in *A Taste of Honey*. She whispered into a bent ear: "See what I mean? They used to hide that thing way off in the back room where nobody could see it. Now they've moved me up to the front door. When you make it from the back room at Sardi's to the front door in one night, it must mean something!" A last look over the shoulder before pushing through the glass doors into the popping of flashbulbs. The wink said I told you so and the smile was pure Technicolor. Louis B. Mayer would have approved.

Buster Keaton

OCTOBER, 1965.

> (The last interview Buster
> Keaton ever gave.)

FEDERICO FELLINI WAS THERE. Jean-Luc Godard and Michelangelo Antonioni and Luchino Visconti and several hundred bikini-clad starlets were there. But just before the 1965 Venice Film Festival ended, a silent fellow from the silent era stole the limelight. Film buffs jammed the exits to get his autograph, the Italian photographers watched the pier night and day for a sign of his boat, and inside the Cinema Palais on the Lido a hardboiled audience of international critics waited with their pencils poised.

Then suddenly Buster Keaton was there, looking for all the world like the kind of man dogs kick. His pants were a little baggy in the seat and he had forgotten to bring a tux; his hat was a bit crushed around the edges and his floppy bow tie struggled crookedly for support on his Adam's apple. But it didn't matter. Keaton was there and that was understood in every language. He had come to show *Film*, an arty twenty-two-minute silent he made in New York in 1964, and when the projector stopped they stood and cheered for five minutes.

"This is the first time I've ever been invited to a film festival," he said, fighting back tears, "but I hope it won't be the last."

IT PROBABLY WON'T BE. On October 4, Buster Keaton reached his 70th birthday. At an age when most people are out buying graveyard plots, his career is taking on new life. In Europe he is almost as popular on the list of American exports as Coca-Cola. His films are shown at the Cinémathèque Française in Paris and the British Film Institute in London. In Berlin, there's a Buster Keaton Film Festival. In France funnyman Jacques Tati is such an admirer of his that

121

he has composed a new musical score for the old Keaton evergreen, *The Navigator,* which will be reissued this fall. "That picture was made forty-two years ago," Buster says, "and it still holds up. I said they could add music, but that's all. Best not to tamper with the old ones." He owns all of his old films and keeps them in a vault in Los Angeles. He's lost track of the exact number but says it's "more than a hundred."

In America, a whole new generation of teen-agers has "discovered" him on TV and in such real gone opuses as *Beach Blanket Bingo* and *How to Stuff a Wild Bikini.* And this winter, when eleven more of his film classics are revived throughout the world in a Buster Keaton package, new audiences will get a chance to see the still-fresh magic of hand-cranked cameras in such sad-sack history makers as *Steamboat Bill.*

Not that Keaton is relying on the old-timers to keep his flame going. This year alone he has completed six films ("I work more than Doris Day," he says). Recently, for nearly three months he was living in Rome, playing a wacky German general in *War Italian Style,* but now he has joined Zero Mostel and Phil Silvers in Madrid for the movie version of *A Funny Thing Happened on the Way to the Forum.*

One reason Keaton is so popular the world over is that in his work there has never been a language barrier. Most of the time there's been no language. "With a face like mine, I guess they figure who needs dialogue? When I was a baby my folks were in vaudeville. One day my Dad looked at me and said, 'Son, you better get into show business, 'cause with a face like that you'll never get a job anyplace else.' I got my first paycheck when I was four and made my first picture in 1917. They didn't let me talk for more than thirty years after that." Mike Todd let him say a few words in *Around the World in Eighty Days* but he figures his talkiest scene was the telephone conversation with Spencer Tracy in *Mad, Mad World.* He doesn't know about *Sunset Boulevard.* He never saw it.

Keaton doesn't like what's happened to comedy. "They'll do anything for a laugh today. But people aren't laughing. I think it's because the comics are all alike. There's no originality. In the old days, when Chaplin and I were great friends, Charlie would give me gags right out of his own pictures if they didn't seem right, and I'd do the same for him. They don't trade anymore. They just steal."

His taste for humor may have changed, but his sense of humor hasn't. In *Film* he shows his tragic side, but he still
122

had fun shooting it. "Heck, I'd be the last one in the world to comment, because I didn't know what those guys were doing half the time. The director, Alan Schneider, just told me to keep my back to the camera and be natural. Just try acting natural with a camera crew aiming at your back. And as for Samuel Beckett, I took one look at his script and asked him if he ate Welsh rarebit before he went to bed at night."

He admits he thinks about the old days sometimes, but not with sadness. "He cried like a baby when De Mille died," says his wife, Eleanor. "Yes, but I'm not sentimental by nature," he is quick to correct. "Sure I miss the Keystone Cops and Mack Sennett and Stan and Oliver and the rest, but I don't moon over the past. I don't have time."

When he's not working, he takes care of the garden on his acre and a half of farmland in Woodland Hills, California. His son owns a tourist lodge on Lake Tahoe and sometimes he gets in a bit of hunting there. He is an avid bridge player and stays up all night watching the late movies on television. "We're twenty-five miles from Hollywood, so we gave up driving into town to go to the movies. The only time I see my friends is on the late show."

Most of his old friends have either passed on or live in the Motion Picture Relief Home, about a mile and a half from his farm. "I drive by sometimes and talk to some of the old-timers, but it makes me so sad I don't do it often. They live in the past, I don't. One Easter Sunday I went to a party at Mary Pickford's house. Everybody from silent films was there. I tried to have fun, but I discovered we had nothing to talk about. Some of them had never heard a Beatles record. They haven't kept up with the times."

He stays young, he says, through hard work and nothing else. He doesn't eat nutburgers or drink spinach juice, has never read Gayelord Hauser, and refuses to take vitamin pills. He has so much energy, his wife says, that the neighborhood kids ring the doorbell constantly, wanting to know "Can Buster come out and play?"

Buster Keaton is already a legend in his own time, and shows no sign of slowing down. "I had four friends who retired at the age of sixty-five and they were all dead within a year. They simply had nothing to do, nothing to occupy their minds. I have so many projects coming up I don't have time to think about kicking the bucket. People are always telling me I'm immortal. I just might prove them right. Hell, the way I feel, I just might live forever."

Marianne Moore

AUTUMN, 1966.

FOR MANY YEARS the voice of the turtle in American poetry came from a modest little house on a run-down street in Brooklyn. Marianne Moore lived there. That was in the days when the Brooklyn Dodgers were the cat's pyjamas, people made movies about the *Brooklyn Eagle,* Betty Smith could still find a tree growing there, and Bill Bendix could break you up just pronouncing the word. Today no one laughs. Ebbetts Field is a nondescript housing project, the *Eagle* is dead, and Marianne Moore—terrified by hoodlums who rang her bell at three in the morning—has moved away.

The climate has changed, but the voice is still there. This autumn she will narrate the first New York concert performance of Stravinsky's *The Flood* at Philharmonic Hall. Although she has won every award for writing it is possible to imagine, including the Pulitzer Prize, and has been honored by enough fellowships and degrees to fill Fibber McGee's closet, the thought of appearing with the New York Philharmonic has her a bit muddled. "I hope I remember to come in in the right place," she said one morning recently as she busied herself in her new Greenwich Village apartment. "They took away my synopsis, so now I don't know what to do. I have a Stravinsky record here somewhere filed in my filing cabinet." She led the way past dusty Brillo boxes stacked to the ceiling containing her valuable letters from Eliot and Ezra Pound and Gertrude Stein, and the collections of rare books she has never uncrated since her move from Brooklyn. "I don't know music at all, but Mr. Stravinsky will be there, so he will surely let me know when to get up and when to sit down." She poked through file drawers bulging with manuscripts and postcards and overdue bills, past headings like "Beaton, Cecil," and "Musk ox" and "Invitations to the White House." "They wrote out my part on large sheets

124

of paper because you know my eyes are not what they used to be, but now I can't seem to find that either. I have to talk like a serpent and later I play Eve and Noah. Thank goodness, I'm not God."

She never did find the Stravinsky record. But it probably won't matter. At seventy-eight, when most ladies her age are watching the afternoon doctor shows on TV or phoning up about Medicare, Marianne Moore can do anything. She shows up at parties in her Napoleonic tricorn hat, with Frank Sinatra and Mrs. Ernest Hemingway, appears at respectable happenings (like a recent handout party for the *Paris Review*) looking like Beulah the Witch among the Navy pea jackets and St. Laurents, and ends up more often on the fashion pages than in the book sections. She prefers reading *Sports Illustrated* to stuffy literary quarterlies and loves to frustrate culture vultures by talking about Willie Mays instead of iambic pentameters. ("Poetry? I too dislike it; there are things that are important beyond all this fiddle.") As a result her poetry is a fiddle-free museum of observations, "written simply enough for dogs and cats to read," about everything under the sun: reindeer and paperweights, Negroes and quartz-crystal clocks. Juniper boughs and mud hens and baseball games and plumet basilisks. But don't be fooled: as she walks through parks looking like somebody's grandma, her mind is busily rearranging subjects and predicates the way the Japanese arrange flowers.

She once spent ten years translating the works of seventeenth-century French poet La Fontaine with only three years of high school French. She taught a business course to Jim Thorpe in a Pennsylvania Indian school long before he became an all-American athlete, and long before Burt Lancaster played him in the movies. She once got a medal blessed by the Pope for Floyd Patterson. In a black cape and a flowering white orchid she has munched chocolate cookies and played the snare drums for a thousand screaming teenagers in a crowded slum school. The Ford Motor Co. once asked her to name its new model, so she dreamed up some titles like "Mongoose Civique" and "Utopian Turtletop," before they decided on "Edsel." Her poem *To a Giraffe* inspired a Steuben glass display. She has picketed with Arthur Miller and E. E. Cummings to preserve Walt Whitman's printing shop on Cranberry Street, made bandages for the Red Cross and modeled Emilio Pucci hats on television. In an age when you need courage just to walk down the street, this snowy-haired old lady with quick, robin's-egg-blue

125

eyes has made the world a slightly happier place just by being around to read about.

Today, she shows no signs of running down. She offers a celery tonic in a jelly glass, saying "Now drink it all, because there's nothing more useless than a half-empty bottle of celery tonic," unaware of the impression she makes on the people around her. The grin is flawless, like her poems, and her twinkling eyes don't miss a move. "You're looking at the mess in my apartment. I call it classical disorder. Since I moved to Manhattan, I cannot find a thing. They tell me I am a fire hazard and they won't let me keep my papers and books in the basement, so I have them in crates. One of my favorite paintings has fallen down behind that bookcase and I haven't been able to dig it out. I've had to give things away, like my old *Country Lifes* and my Illustrated News Weeklies dating back to 1900. Yale asked me to write a tribute to Randall Jarrell, but I can't find any of his books—it's very disturbing. Especially since he has said such nice things about *me* in print, like I was Cassius Clay. I refuse to sell my lovely letters from Ezra Pound, but I must get rid of things somehow. I can't even get into my closets for all the boxes. Something has to be done."

She sighed, looking over the contents of her cluttered little home: walls filled with rare books, many so old the backs are falling off, bound manuscripts and unpublished poems, unopened Christmas packages, jade figurines, stacks of unanswered mail in brown manila envelopes, an old seventy-eight-rpm phonograph, citations, signed photos of practically every writer you ever heard of, plaques, lampshades, an E. E. Cummings watercolor of a yellow rose drawn on a shirt board, hammers, a Maurice Sendak ink sketch of Puss 'n' Boots carrying a sign reading "For Marianne Moore." "I suppose the reason I have so much junk is that I am interested in the most useless things. Pigs' tails and why they curl, things like that." She embarks on a fascinating story about why pigs' tails curl, then retrieves from the mantel her prize possession, a walrus tusk sent to her by an Eskimo. "I'm also fond of rodents, but I had to give up my mice, because I was spending all of my time with them and getting no work done."

She finished her most recent poem a month ago. "Let's see—oh yes, it was about the Brooklyn Bridge. Did you know the woven cables Roebling invented for that bridge are now copied everywhere? His wife studied calculus to finish the bridge when her husband died of gangrene after being hit by a ferry. My father was an engineer, so I inherited a love of

126

ridges. Especially the Brooklyn Bridge. Its catenary curve
akes my fancy. Catenary, dear. That's spelled c-a-t. . . ."

Her main occupation today, she says, is comforting other
writers, the ones who come to New York bottling up irrita-
ions, but producing no pearls. "It's an odd day's mail that
doesn't bring a letter from a desperate writer. Even my
doorman has a friend who wants to be a poet. But it's a
privilege to help, not a hindrance. When I was young, I was
o excited by poetry. Today it's all about marijuana cigarettes
and God is dead. If that doesn't wither up it'll be a pity. I
won't live to see it, but it has to happen. These poor young-
ters come to the city to write, and end up filling inkwells in
some publishing house. No wonder they are bitter. We live in
a world of tigers and tanks. I'd rather die myself than send a
boy to Vietnam. We're all pacifists in that. But I look to the
Book of Job for the answers. Physically and mentally, we
must bear the tortures of our times, or we're lost."

Has she ever written a novel? "Once I tried my hand, but
my editors said it was just too innocent to sell. It was called
The Way We Live Now, and it had nothing to do with the
way we live now. It had a death scene in a drawing room,
bears riding bicycles, everything. I saw it down in the basement a week ago, and I threw it in the incinerator, so that's
the end of that."

The thought of anyone tossing an unpublished Marianne
Moore into an incinerator is hard to conceive. Unless you
happen to be Marianne Moore. Where does she get the
strength of ten women half her age? "People are endlessly
kind to me. I get my strength from other smiles. I have
servants, but my niece who is a secretary looks in on me, and
the phone never stops ringing. Some folks just drop by to visit
without phoning first, which is going to drive me into a ward
at Bellevue. I can't get my work done. Still, I would not
survive if I told everyone to mind their own business. Also, I
read—I get strength from writers like Martin Buber, Floyd
Patterson, Roy Campanella, and my beloved Dodgers. I also
take one-a-day Unicap vitamins with apple-cider vinegar. I
knew a man once whose cow couldn't get up when she lay
down. So he gave the cow some grass where the vinegar had
been dumped that day. The cow got well. It works for me,
too. I also take a teaspoon of the best honey straight from
the hive after each meal. People worry that I might have a
stroke up here all alone some night. They also worry because
I never lock my door. 'Anyone could walk in on you,' my
brother warns. But I've never had an enemy—although I
never got along too well with Gertrude Stein's brother Leo—

and I'm too old to make enemies now. When my mother died in 1947 I thought nothing mattered. I gave up my interest in life, and I nearly died. Ezra Pound and others helped a lot. He used to write me after each of my poems was published. 'Get rid of your damn French syntax,' things like that. His letters were so profane and blasphemous I would go on strike and not write him for months. But I'm the only one he never told off."

The dressmaker had arrived to fit her gown for the concert. "I had a little velvet skirt already, and a friend gave me a piece of silk and we copied a lovely jacket from a fashion magazine and I wore it to a lecture at Wellesley in that auditorium they've got that's as big as Shea Stadium, and everyone thought it was so lovely. I have two Ben Zuckerman suits and two Irene hats—they cost thirty-five dollars apiece—but I thought it should be something special for Stravinsky."

Liberating everything around her, the way she has liberated modern poetry, the lady who knows nothing about music prepared herself to meet the New York Philharmonic head on. The mirror beamed back approvingly. So, it seems, will Mr. Stravinsky. With Marianne Moore, nothing less is possible.

James Mason

IN A ST. REGIS HOTEL SUITE best described as "early Kublai Khan" (Japanese murals showing water oxen waiting at the station, Victorian draperies, French-provincial furniture) James Neville Mason, fifty-eight, sat declining ginger ale, Napoleon brandy, and just plain ice water, preferring—he said—to talk. He likes to talk, and when he talks now, it is without the old Mason malice that once sent reporters cowering with fright. Freed from the shackles of being a Hollywood star, he says he is a new man, and most of the old Mason venom is aimed these days at Mason himself. He is his own severest critic, and his range of criticism includes his life, his marriage, his career, and just about everything else if you are lucky enough to get in on the conversation.

Just returned from a film festival in Acapulco ("I only went because my fare was paid"), he sported a healthy bronze glow on that famous drawing-room face. "It's not a tan," he grumbled. "I'm rather ruddy. I'm getting ruddier." Then he produced a handful of photos of three young girls in bathing suits: "This is Lynn Redgrave—wasn't she marvelous in *Georgy Girl?* I didn't mind being eclipsed in that one. In all my years of reading scripts I never read such a marvelous role for a girl. It's miraculous that the right girl and the right part came along together. Now this next girl is Rita Tushingham and this is my daughter, Portland, who is a kooky girl herself. One of the last films I made in Hollywood was a candidate for the incinerator called *Torpedo Bay*. At the same time Portland was making her first big one, *Great St. Trinian's Train Robbery*, and when I went to England to live, the two films opened together in London and I ended up on the bottom half of Portland's picture. Imagine how I felt. I'm a big second-feature actor."

Nothing second feature about his new film, Sidney Lumet's *The Deadly Affair*, in which he's top-billed over Simone Signoret, Maximilian Schell, Harriet Andersson—and Lynn Redgrave again. "It's one of my best films and that's something because there haven't been many good ones. Sidney is a marvelous director. I need direction. I want it and I expect it. I work better if a director will needle me, discipline me, help sharpen up my ideas. Sidney knows the value of rehearsing a film before shooting it. That enabled us to get all the director-cameraman conferences out of the way so no time was wasted when we got on the floor. I think it's a good film and I have to grab the good ones when they come my way or people have a tendency to forget me."

Fat chance. The son of a Yorkshire wool merchant, James Mason arrived in America in 1946, accompanied by twelve cats, a parroty new bride named Pamela, and such a spectacular reputation for breaking the bones of pretty girls in British films that when he tried a brief fling at Broadway the next year in a flop called *Bathsheba* Brooks Atkinson panned him because "neither the Bible nor the play permitted him to push Bathsheba in the face or even so much as twist her arm."

People forgot *Bathsheba* but not its star. The years that followed were so filled with popping flashbulbs and front-page scandals that he became the most publicized eccentric in Hollywood. In 1954 there was a one-million-dollar lawsuit against a fan magazine that insinuated his marriage was on the rocks. In 1955, another lawsuit against *Rave* magazine for accusing him of "immoral conduct." In 1958, a three million-dollar libel suit against a TV producer who accused him of "being disloyal to England." In between there was time to raise two children—a cigar-smoking daughter named Portland, now nineteen, and a precocious son named Morgan, thirteen—and time to turn out enough roles (everything from Field Marshal Rommel to Gustav Flaubert) to inspire the comment, "Gee, Mr. Mason, I *loved* your last two hundred movies."

Actually it was only a modest eighty at last count and he loves to talk about them all. "Did you see *Prince Valiant?* It's pop art now." Then he demonstrates the spectacle of Henry Hathaway trying to teach Robert Wagner how to say "TRAITOR!" as he's set upon by Vikings. The entire room breaks up. "It was a sour-grapes period during which I was often very cross. I wanted an identifiable Hollywood leading-man image, but it never worked. I tried to get away from heavy parts, where I had to terrorize some pretty young thing, because that's what I was offered most. The Hollywood period lasted sixteen years, but I haven't really worked there since I went to England to make *Lolita.* The last films I made in Hollywood were *Hero's Island,* with Rip Torn, which had a great success in private homes *before* it was released, and *Marriage-Go-Round* with Susan Hayward—another candidate for the incinerator.

"People always tried to find something wrong with me, but the only things they could draw on were the fact that Pamela's ex-husband lived over the garage and I was fond of cats. So they made things up. I used to buy the *Enquirer* every week at Farmer's Market just to see what new scandal I was involved in. They invariably had us in some sort of *ménage à trois.* All the publicity about the children was phony. We simply raised them in European style, where kids are treated like adults. Hollywood couldn't adjust to that. I remember Pamela and I were fans of Katherine Dunham, so once we sneaked Portland into Ciro's to see her perform and suddenly the columns had her going to nightclubs! My wife cut the pockets off an old mink coat and let her take them to bed with her and suddenly she was the only child in Hollywood with her own mink coat. That's how Hollywood gossip starts. The kids have shaped up now. I see them three times a year and I like them. Portland is quite lovely and bright. I think she could be a writer. Morgan played Elizabeth Taylor's son in *The Sandpiper* but I would never persuade him to
130

be an actor. He's too intelligent. I think he should go into a more taxing profession. Every time he sees one of my films he says 'I don't want to offend you, Dad, but. . . .' "

On the subject of ex-wife Pamela he is less enthusiastic. "Let's just say we're friendly without being cordial." No wonder. After twenty-three years of marriage, Pamela divorced him in 1964, asking more than one million dollars in property settlements and fourteen thousand dollars a month for child support. That, according to the wags, is why he made so many bad movies. True? "That divorce cost me quite a whack. I go on even now paying quite a lot. So I am not in the position to say 'This year I'll do nothing but make one marvelous film which I will also direct.' I have to make money. It's not something I'm complaining about. It's just a circumstance under which I am forced to live. I would like to direct, but I don't want to lay aside a healthy salary to start out at the bottom as a director. Looking back, I'd say I've wasted a lot of time. I haven't done as many interesting things as I'd like to have done. There were puny years when I did whatever was offered me. It wasn't very big money either, just money. I think the question people *should* ask actors is 'Of all your films, which is the one you'd like most to have destroyed?' "

A Star Is Born—his best role to some critics—is, surprisingly, one of his disappointments. "It was shot at ludicrous marathon lengths, with superfluous musical numbers thrown in at all the wrong times. Then it was cut unmercifully, and some of Judy Garland's best scenes were gone and some of her more dramatic ones—not all good—were kept. Also, we never really had a producer. Sid Luft was an amateur. There was nobody to check on or discipline Judy *or* George Cukor. As for Moss Hart, he just turned in the script, dealt very severely with anyone who criticized it, and packed up and went back to New York. Recently Portland and I were taking a long walk near my home in Switzerland and we came across a mountain café where it was playing on TV. There I was, dubbed in French, and I rather liked it. That long, disturbing 'Born in a Trunk' number had been cut and it seemed much better."

Mason has no respect for Oscars ("They don't mean anything unless you win one, then your salary goes up") or Hollywood comedies ("They've never come up with a replacement for Preston Sturges—frankly, they have no relation to what's going on in the world"), but he likes European films, especially Fellini's. "The way he uses his camera is thrilling, not gimmicky but fluid and to the point; if the circumstances were right I'd like to work for him." He seems confident of his own future, perhaps for the first time. "I learn something new about my potential all the time. I'm prepared to tackle anything in my physical range now. I have self-confidence I have only accumulated since leaving Hollywood. I like working in Europe—there's no displaced delusion of grandeur there, none of the phoniness. The whole business of status there is less important. I have a flat in Switzerland, near Vevey, where Chaplin lives. We're great friends. I don't own real estate although I just sold a castle in Spain. I needed publicity in Hollywood because I wanted people to remember I was still alive. Now the power of big studios and talent agencies and management companies I do without. I have two more unreleased films—*Player Pianos,* with Melina Mercouri, and *Stranger in the House,* with Geraldine Chaplin—and I have one or two no-account projects coming up. I was rather persona non grata for a while I suppose, but I'm not doing badly now. I just kind of play it by ear." He smiled his gentlemanly manor-house smile, and in the afternoon light streaming through the windows, looked very grata indeed.

Dame Edith Evans

SHE STEPPED OFF THE PLANE, England's greatest actress—maybe even the world's—carrying her own hatbox with her head held high. At the age of eighty, Dame Edith Evans has no need for things like walking sticks and porters. "Nobody looks upon me as an old trout yet," she says and lives up to it with the dedication of a Zen high priestess. Dressed in a beige suit and a prim blue linen coat with long white gloves, sensibly British shoes, a snappy red hat, and a baby tiger orchid pinned to her lapel, she wasn't about to stand around waiting for the limousine United Artists had sent along. By the time the car had located her, she was already through Customs, darting through back doors like a Sophia Loren and hustling a cab on the curb with the crisp

132

disapproval of an old-world duenna surveying a come-lately America.

Dame Edith was in town to discuss *The Whisperers,* a new film directed by Bryan Forbes in which she becomes a full-fledged movie star (above the title) for the very first time in her long and illustrious career. She had just returned from the Berlin Film Festival, where she won the Golden Bear for the best actress of the year. "I've got the bear in my luggage," she said, climbing into the car without assistance. "That's why it's so heavy. I didn't know how to pack it, so I wrapped it in tissue paper. I'm not going to let it out of my sight. It's very hot here. I think they said it was eighty-three."

She is difficult to interview, because more things interest her than her interviewers and one thing that does not interest her at all is Dame Edith Evans. Ask her about that wonderful rococo voice like Mahler played on a dulcimer and she'll say, "I don't really like it much myself. Ellen Terry told me many years ago, 'Just speak up girl so everyone can hear you,' and I've been doing it ever since." She is set in her ways (when she works, she allows nobody to stand in her direct line of vision at any time) and has a bit of a salty reputation among English reporters. "How can I talk to journalists and people during the day?" she has been known to say on movie sets, and once she told a leading Hollywood writer, "Go home and read your notes before you interview me—you are not prepared."

But on this cheerful sun-kissed day, looking out from the rolled-up windows of her limousine, surveying the world about her like a great dowager empress aware of the knowledge that she had outlived all her noble subjects but content with the fact that the survivors are still ready to bow, Dame Edith seemed happy and ready to talk. "People always ask me the most ridiculous questions. They want to know 'How do you approach a role?' Well, I don't know. I approach it by first saying yes, then getting on with the bloody thing. I read the script for *The Whisperers* and said yes in less than twenty-four hours. I don't do anything I don't like and this story moved me greatly. It is based on the theme of loneliness. Bryan Forbes had wanted to do a film about lonely old people living on welfare ever since his wife, Nanette Newman, told him about an old woman who had died in her apartment dwelling years before she was married. The poor old soul was dead several days before anyone even missed her. Isn't that sad?"

Like most of us, Dame Edith knows what it's like to be

133

lonely. "I have a secluded little flat right near Piccadilly Circus in London, which is very much like living near your own Times Square in New York, and I am alone most of the time. But there is a difference between loneliness and aloneness. You can be alone like I am and not lonely. Thirty years ago I lost my mother and my husband in the same year. The loss was inconsolable. I think of them often, especially my mother. I took her for granted, simply because she was my mother. I had so little conscious appreciation of the security and warmth they gave me. Now if I could only have them again. I want to say things to them. Share little triumphs with them. We never do enough for the people we love until they are gone. But I had to press on. Now I am not really lonely. I'm involved with many theatrical activities which fill my life, and I am very fortunate people come to see me. A woman ran after me in the street the other day, can you imagine that? It was a lovely feeling. I enjoy young people—aren't the Beatles marvelous"—she went into a rock chorus of "She loves me, yah-yah-yah" and blushed to a soft lilac glow—"but as Noel Coward said recently, 'If a person over fifty tries too hard to be *with* it they soon find they are *without* it.' I think our little film *The Whisperers* will find its friends. We filmed it with love because we believed in it. Not many projects are undertaken out of love in these times. We were good as gold all through it. We brought it in under budget and on time. I've been playing crusty old ladies and retired actresses saying smart things for so long I wanted to do some creative work. Now it's back to the grand old ladies, I'm afraid. I just finished another film with Dick Van Dyke called *Fitzwilly*. It's quite light and gay really. And I must return to London in a week to report for work again—another nice elegant part with Deborah Kerr in *Prudence and the Pill*. No, no, it's not about a child who is a pill, it's about *the* pill, my dear. All the wrong people take it and they all get pregnant and—well, you'll see. It'll be all right. I've had a nice rest in my country house and now I'm ready to work. All I did was sleep and pay bills. I won't tell you where I live, because I don't want it to appear in the papers. My private life must be private. I don't encourage fan mail. I don't want fans in my private life. If I can't earn me living without sending postcards, then I'd best do something else. They're very unsettling, you know—they'd just as soon turn away from you as come to you. Fans cannot be trusted."

We passed a truck with an enormous bear painted on its door. "Oh look, that's a good omen," she said, clapping her hands, not missing a thing. "What does it say? I can't read without my glasses." It said Green Bear Construction Co. of Long Island City. "How friendly, with my golden bear in the trunk tucked safely away. I won my bear last Thursday. Or was it Friday? I don't know where the days go. Is that the World's Fair we're passing now? I was here in '64 with John Gielgud and we saw it in the distance, but I never saw it first hand. What time is it? I'm a good traveler. The instant I leave the ground I think in American time. I must set my watch. Seven hours in the air and now I'm here and it's all the same—trams, buses, streetcars. Extraordinary! I shan't do any acting this trip, so I shall relax and be a very good girl and do all the telly they request. I don't mind publicity if it's all nice and friendly, but I'm a girl who likes her roots. They tell me I shall be resting at the Regency. Is that a good hotel?" It is mentioned that Ava Gardner stays there. "She was jolly good in that picture about the Bible—what was it called? I used to stay at the New Weston, but they tore it down. Once I stayed in a small hotel in Greenwich Village. I had no service and I couldn't get hot milk at night, but when you're paying for it yourself you don't want to spend all your money on a hotel, do you? In California I had a little bachelor flat on Sunset Boulevard. It had a nice stove but no service. I must be somewhere I can ring a bell. A man can come in soiled from a day on a movie set and just climb into a shower, but I'm an old lady who likes the comforts of being fussed over. Well, the Regency will be lovely. They'll find me very quiet."

We were across the bridge now, angling in along tree-lined streets on our way to Park Avenue. "There's my old church. I used to go there every Sunday when I lived at the New Weston. I hope when we reach the hotel my maid will be there. She's been taking care of me ever since I played Florence Nightingale on Broadway thirty years ago."

Her maid was waiting, and after several tearful hugs, Dame Edith was promptly shown to a luscious creamy-beige suite with great Victorian draperies overlooking Park Avenue. "Now," she said, whisking off her hat, "let's have a look at that schedule. I know you say *sked-yool* but we say *shed-yool*. Let me get me glasses. 'Eight A.M., the *Today* show.' Cripes! *Eight* A.M.! I never do anything that early! Will somebody be with me? Never leave me alone. You never know *what* I might say! Do I get paid? Good. I'm all for getting paid. Now I don't want to use me brain. I'll just relax and move about like a dummy and do as I'm told. Now, where's tea? It was ordered, but they're not exactly what you call rushing it up. What time is it? It must be—let's see—

135

eight o'clock at home." She goes to check the clock. "Twenty past nine. I think there should be some flowers here for me. I like flowers and attention. Check the desk and see."

Tea arrived. "Ava Gardner couldn't have it better than this," she said, stiffly gracious, pouring. "I shall require simple food, nothing rich for my stay. I'm on a bit of a slim. I don't drink or smoke. I only take one meal a day—meat and a vegetable, then fruit or pudding. The young people today do not live right. I grew up learning discipline. I was a milliner for ten years before I became an actress. Gracious. It was like going on the streets for a young girl to go on the stage. My family never adjusted. Father was a postmaster at the Wimpole Street Station and I grew up in a great Georgian house in London next door to Noel Coward." The great actress Ellen Terry took Dame Edith under her wing and taught her most of what she knows about acting. She became a legend, performing everything from Restoration comedy to war songs for the boys on the front lines in World War II. John Osborne wrote the part of the cockney woman into *Look Back in Anger* for her. Olivier calls her, simply, "the greatest." In 1946 she was knighted by the king, an honor reserved for very few women. According to her biography, she once even lived with George Bernard Shaw, although if you ask her, she merely narrows her great hooded eyelids and says crisply, in that powerful chamber-music voice: *"Who-o-o* told you that? Nothing that has ever been printed about me is ever true. There's nothing about me that is news. I'm a dreary person really. Except when I act. Did you see me as the Mother Superior in *The Nun's Story* or as Miss Western in *Tom Jones?* I felt alive then. I look only for the life in any part. Then I ask, 'Do I understand it?' Could I be that person? If I can, I do it. It was very daring for Bryan Forbes to send me a role of a derelict old lady rummaging about in garbage cans in a slum. But he knew I've always been daring. I'm the only one who ever played Rosalind in *As You Like It* and the nurse in *Romeo and Juliet* in the same season. Have another pastry?"

She took a large swat at something round and curly on the tablecloth which turned out to be a Napoleon. "I thought it was a bug. I can't see without my glasses." Had it ever affected her on stage? She ignored the question. "Look at the napkins. Aren't they lovely? I have lovely damask ones in England, but I rarely use them because it costs too much to have them laundered. We use excellent paper ones, very good quality."

She was right. There had been flowers at the desk. Lots of

136

hem. A bellhop bounced in with enough boxes of carnations, chrysanthemums, and long-stemmed red roses to fill a bus. Now we'll have to ask for jars to put them, won't we? I stayed at the Meurice once and they brought me the loveliest fruit and I thought the bowl was mine so I jolly well took it."

The subject switched to actors. "Wasn't it sad about Vivien Leigh? I saw her only a few nights before and she seemed quite gay. There are too many actors today and they don't peak up. They won't take advice, either. I can't stand old bores who go around saying 'When I was young' but I do know one thing. There is no discipline today. Kids are snapped up for the telly and films as soon as they learn to stand up straight. They have no training and many of them go to psychiatrists! I've never heard anything so ridiculous. I know of no actor of my acquaintance who goes to a psychiatrist. I certainly would never go to one. It's over here that you do that sort of thing, where you have so many Method actors. There are a frightful lot of chichi classes in the Method but it's such bunk. To me, there is only good acting and bad acting. The rhetoric no longer seems to come from the heart as it used to. But I'm no good at talking about the past. I live for now. I'm much better now than ever before and my best days are still to come. And now"—the great hooded-cobra eyes narrowed and took deadly aim—"you must GO!"

Dame Edith Evans stalked across the room, eyes blanching to the color of moonstones, pausing to delicately finger a red rose, then closed the door, well aware that no matter what people say about her she is one Dame they will never call Edie.

Melina Mercouri

APRIL, 1967.

YEARS FROM NOW, when we're all dead and gone, they'll still be talking about Melina Mercouri. They'll talk because, in an age full of plastic people, she was the real thing. She brought pride and distinction to her country at a time when

137

it had been forgotten, then reached out and broke the hea
of the rest of the world with the brooding brilliance of h
Technicolor smile. In Greece, when she appears in publi
they leave their olives and their goats and riot in the street
And on Broadway in *Illya Darling*, the $400,000 musica
version of her triumphant movie *Never on Sunday*, Ameri
cans are getting their first close-up of the woman called Me
couri and they like what they see. On opening night the
threw flowers on the stage and she threw them right back
They clapped to the rhythms of the bazouki, they stood o
the top of their seats and cheered until after the lights cam
on, and clamoring for more, they followed her to the Para
dise Greek restaurant (no Sardi's for this girl), where arme
policemen held them off with guns as they threw bottles a
the walls and danced on the broken glass until four in th
morning.

The critics said "No," but the critics do not buy tickets an
the paying customers are stepping on each other trying to ge
in. Melina, in her Pepsodent grin and charming disorga
nized English, beams at the lines in the street: "The mornin
after we have ze bad critics, ze people they come and stan
in line all the way to Lindy's. We make a hundred thousan
dollars ze first week and they send to me 300 telegrams
violently denouncing all critics. Is good, I think. Ze Ameri
cans, they love me, yes?"

They love her, yes. But why? She is not really beautiful the
way they make her look in a man's tuxedo in the pages o
Vogue. She is not really young (41). She has too many teeth
and if you look closely, there are tiny date-colored bruise
under her eyes. But none of that matters, for onstage or off
with or without Jean Rosenthal's lighting, Melina Mercour
has an undefinable quality that brings a thousand years o
Greek history bursting into glory when she opens her arms
and a mysterious charm that unlocks the secrets of women
through the ages when she opens her heart.

"Undefinable" is a good word for Melina, yet everybody
has a private idea of what she is *really* like. Behind that
ravaged, exclusive Tiffany lamp of a face, beneath those
glimmering eyes the color of the Gulf of Corinth, there are
many masks. She is called sexy, but the thought of it makes
her burst into a banshee wail. "Why the critics say for them I
am a 'splendid dish'? I am not Bardot. I do not sell *that*. It
takes great courage at my age to take my clothes off and
show my body onstage. I am scared to death when they
gasp." To others, she is a great character to read about in
magazines. She sits in Rudolf Bing's box at the Met, never

138

goes to parties, prefers eating Spanish paella in dives on Horatio Street to posh watering holes like "21," and once arrived twenty minutes late at a very exclusive private luncheon for the executive editors of *Life* (a big deal previously reserved only for honored guests like Elizabeth Taylor and President Johnson) in beret, mini-skirt, Betty Grable sweater, black boots, and a mink-lined Dior trench coat, announcing: "Ze Loren—she has for her eleven covers—me, only one. You owe me ten more." She is a spoiled brat who pouts when she must go to bed early, a vulnerable child who constantly touches the people she loves to be sure they do not go away, and a woman of ageless maturity who says, "My man can have as many affairs as he likes as long as he is a friend to me when I need him." She is all of these people, playing a thousand parts at once. Total woman.

But observe for yourself: The scene is her suite at the Dorset. It has been a bad week. "Catastrophe!" she yells. Her father is ill in London. Her husband, Jules Dassin, is leaving for a business trip to Europe. She has still not recovered from the bad reviews of *Illya Darling*. The news has just arrived of political upheaval in Greece. The Leftists, who she supports, have been overthrown and a military junta established by King Constantine, whom she does not admire. Melina lies on the sofa, her hair, the color of melting butterscotch, cascading over the pillow. Several Greek women are feeding her consommé with a silver spoon. She refuses to eat. Hysteria. "No planes will fly from Athens. Machine guns in front of the Hilton Hotel. Troops at the border. No elections. If I am there, I would be in jail for my people. All day I telephone to the American Embassy for news from Athens and all they say is, 'Do not worry. When will the record of *Illya Darling* come out?' Po po po. How can they think of something so silly when the fate of my poor country is at stake?" She fingers her green Greek worry beads. Despo, her best friend since childhood and the Greek chorus to Melina's Electra, chants "Poor Greece" and fingers her *yellow* worry beads. Her brother Spiros Mercouris (Greek men add an S to their names) fingers *blue* worry beads. Occasionally doors open leading to other parts of the suite mysteriously revealing a whole entourage of Greeks, all fingering their *own* worry beads. The house sounds like a den of rattlesnakes. "With Melina," whispers Despo in a voice two octaves south of Melina's own Dietrich purr, "you never lie. She wants always to know everything bad. She is pessimistic. On opening night, she wants to know right away the review of Walter

139

Kerr. Not me. If the truth hurts, feel free to lie. You know something terrible? Do me a favor—don't tell me."

Melina talks about everything at once. "Why the Equity of Actors don't send a telegram on opening night, hey? Twenty Greeks are here first time in history of Broadway, yes? Is triumph for a small country. For me *Illya* is a Greek oper ation. I say to myself we will come twenty Greeks and show America what Greece is like. For six months we live a nightmare. So many people come in and express an opinion my head aches. Everything is changed. You re hearse all day until you are so tired you cannot judge any more. A musical, it costs so much it spoils the soul of an actor. Every day I tell them it will be a catastrophe! They expect very much from us, yes? Now the show is so changed is more like Broadway than Greece. Still, I sing a song in Greek and we do the Greek dances and in a small way we talk about Greece. It is not a loss."

Melina puts on her Cardin men's pants that zip up the front and throws Dassin's coat over her shoulders and we leave for lunch. A Greek woman races after us and shoves a roll of ten-dollar bills into Melina's pocket. "My friends are everything to me," says Melina. "She care not for money," says Despo, "because in Europe she knows it is one day worth much and the next day nothing."

On the street, orange sunbeams play with Melina's hair a she announces we will all go to Chinatown. "Too far," protests Spiros. Melina pouts. "Mexican food," she cries leading the procession past open manholes. Three stree workers stop their drilling and wave, "Hey, Melina!" W walk past ABC and three TV reporters rush up to her and beg her to "Come on up to the newsroom and meet the boys!" Melina kisses them and waves, strutting through the traffic like a Greek goddess transplanted to 1967.

We end up at Romeo Salta, where the waiters fly at us like gulls in a storm. Melina takes her shoes off and sips sambuca with coffeebeans in it. "Even in Greece they think I drink but I never had a drop of whiskey in my life. My grandfather was the mayor of Athens for thirty years and my father a member of Greek Parliament. They taught me to represent Greece like a diplomat. It was like a curse. My childhood was a parade through the streets of Athens. The people of Greece knew me before I ever became an actress. Every single day I saw 150 people. My house was always open. If we had money we fed 100 people for lunch, if not we served pea soup. My family never wanted me to be actress. My grandfather wanted me to be prime minister of Greece. He
140

wanted me to be a boy. All my life I wanted to be masculine. My favorite line in *Illya* is when I say 'I am man enough to cry for you.' But with the years, I change. I am a woman now."

When she was five, she ran away from home and her mother found her with the sailors in a bazouki club passing the hat. Her family knew from then on that Melina would be an actress. She appeared for the first time in 1945 in *Mourning Becomes Electra* and the critics told her to go home to her palace and stay there. "I wanted to make suicide. But they could do nothing to stop me. I became ze star." She also became a wife at seventeen. "He was very rich. He never worked a day in his life, but he gave me freedom, tenderness, power. I adore him. I love him very, very dearly now. When I am alone in Greece I go to his house to stay. My room is closed all year until I come there. Greek men are wonderful. They give you a child to raise, leave for another woman, and you stay friends. Our love affair was finished many years before Julie. Then I meet Julie in Cannes in 1956. I go there to win the award for *Stella*, my first film for Michael Cacoyannis, which I make at same time I play Lady Macbeth in Athens. I am there forty-eight hours, but I do not win. I meet Dassin. I didn't know nothing when I met him. He has teach me everything."

Dassin, who had been blacklisted by the Hollywood film industry during the McCarthy witch hunts, was in Cannes without a passport. Melina's father pulled strings, got him to Greece to film *He Who Must Die* starring Melina. "From there I am with him eleven years. Love affair, dahling, very beautiful. After that, the bad time comes. Julie had no divorce for five years. You know how it is to go with a man who has a wife and three children? The press hated me. We had no money. Living in hotels. Mama is crazy. My father is crazy. One Sunday in Paris, my best friend from Greece visits us. She says to Julie, 'Before you, we drink our coffee, we go to the bazouki, we loved everything. Melina was a happy girl. Now we can't even go to a film without worrying what it is about.' I realized I had changed very much as the mistress of Julie so he said 'Ah, so—' and he wrote the story of *Never on Sunday*. United Artists gave us $64,000 and we make the film in Piraeus. Is first comedy for me. The happiest time of my life. Our house was filled with—how you call it—*extras*. Everybody dancing. The Greeks refused to be paid they loved it so. That's why I will always have tenderness in my heart for this story. It was more than a film. It was my life with Julie, my return to Greece. Before this, nobody wanted me. Articles in Paris against me. People say terrible

141

things because we are not married. After this, I am offered
forty scripts. Great films. Hollywood. But *always* whores.
said NO. I will show you I can play drama, so I do
Phaedra. A great triumph. And always, even after Julie and
I are respectable and married, we dream of making *Illya* for
Broadway. Hélas, here I am. Po po po."

We are back on the street. She is Athena in the sunlight
talking about New York. "I will always remember the Amer
icans. Why they love me, eh? The matinees are the greatest
audiences anywhere in the world. And the people are very
good to me. Tony Perkins comes to my dressing room every
night to kiss me, like we were lovers. After the bad critics
come, I am very sad, so ze Edward Albee send for me to
come to him. We drive in ze Greenwich Village and suddenly
from the taxi I see a Greek flag waving from his window. I
am very happy again. Bravo, *bravo* for the Americans!"

We are back at the hotel. A crowd gathers, applauding
Melina in the street. She smiles and the air turns several
shades lighter in color. Then, as quickly as it is summoned,
the magic disappears in the revolving doors, lost in the sound
of Melina's worry beads.

Otto Preminger

AUGUST, 1966.

TO GET THERE, take Highway 61 north from Baton
Rouge, drive twenty-six miles until you come to a sagging old
building in the middle of the road called the Boll Weevil
Café, with its "Colored Only" sign blazing in the 101-degree
heat, round the bend and stop in front of a celery-gray
house, its paint stripped and peeling in the noonday sun.
Standing on the porch, waving his hand in greeting, wiping
the rolls of sweat that pour down his face like raindrops, is
Otto Preminger, the movies' own aging Peck's bad boy.
"Welcome to Louisiana—you can say anything you like
about me—*anything!* I am not Arthur Penn!" he roars in
greeting.

He means it. Now on location with *Hurry Sundown,* he's a
142

long way from "21" but he's still his own best press agent. Actors hate him. Critics say he hasn't made a decent film since *Laura*. But the Big O (as he is called on the set) doesn't care what anyone says as long as they don't leave him out of the conversation. And there's not much danger of that, since he makes more news on his locations than most of the stars. Still you have to search for it, because he surrounds himself with paid pros whose jobs are to keep the press from finding out anything not in the press releases. Scripts are not allowed out of the production office. The actors take oaths to say nothing. Five minutes after he gives you the run of the place, a press agent beckons and whispers, "Mr. P. says you are not to ask anything about local politics or the race situation."

You begin to find out why. The company has had nothing but trouble. Georgia (where the 1,064-page novel was set) called it a "rich man's *Tobacco Road*" and wouldn't even discuss the possibility of filming it there. Then Gene Callihan, two-time Oscar-winning art director and set designer who did *The Cardinal* for Preminger, talked him into going down to Louisiana. Baton Rouge was his hometown, he knew the area and all the right people. So Preminger surveyed locations, sent Callihan to plant cornfields, build dams, and construct sharecropper cabins on the state prison property at St. Gabriel.

On June 1, the company arrived in Baton Rouge. Rooms and offices for more than a hundred people were taken at the Bellemont, a colonial-style motel with a Confederate flag blowing above the entrance and a reputation for hospitality to movie people. (Less than a year before the *Nevada Smith* company had stayed there without incident.) But this was the first film ever made in its entirety in the South using Negro actors in leading roles. Somehow, word got out that Preminger was there to make a film about "niggers gettin' the best of the whites" and trouble started. Preminger appeared in person to thank the people of Louisiana for their broadmindedness in allowing such a controversial film to be made there, only to be followed on the program by Governor Wallace of Alabama. A bad beginning, to be sure. Then tires were slashed on the company cars. Several cast members received telephone threats. Everyone was housed in a section of the motel, like an army encampment, that is guarded twenty-four hours a day by armed state troopers. The actors, without exception, feel like the poor relations of an aristocratic family, hidden away from the plantation in seclusion and embarrassment. Diahann Carroll, who rarely journeys out after dark, says: "You can cut the hostility here with a knife. I'm not a fighter. I usually smile and then go into my room and cry my eyes out. But down here the terror has killed my taste for going anywhere. Everything was supposed to be checked out before we got here. That was the company's responsibility. You just have to say what the hell, you took the job, so shut up and do the best you can."

The next mistake was to choose St. Francisville as the "typical Southern town" for the film. Located in Feliciana Parish, with a population of 936 (you won't find it in any almanac) it is the kind of place where ladies wear gardenia corsages to the drugstore, where men in ice-cream suits still sip bourbon toddies on their porches at sundown, and where you are nobody unless your family has lived there at least 100 years. A fading remnant of old-world decadence, it is white Protestant, old-guard, and crumbling. It is also the center of Ku Klux Klan activity in Louisiana. To this area Preminger has brought an integrated cast to film a story of post-World War II white trash being outsmarted by poor-but-honest Southern Negroes. It is subject matter to which the townspeople are anything but sympathetic. As one local man says: "It's like going to the Vatican to make a movie about Martin Luther, or going to a synagogue to make a film putting down the Jews."

Attitudes have ranged from unfriendly (several Negro members of the cast have been refused service in local restaurants) to condescending (Rex Ingram was introduced locally as Uncle Remus). On most locations policemen are needed to hold back onlookers. Not here. "You never see anybody, man," said Robert Hooks, a fine Negro actor from Broadway who is keeping a diary of the experience. "You can feel the eyes watching you behind lace curtains, though. Like they could cut your heart out." One prop man went to a laundromat to dye some towels for Diahann Carroll's bathtub scene and was chased out by a man waving a shotgun screaming, "Get outta heah with those nigger towels!" (He swears the Negro washing machines were the only ones with clean water.) The mayor has tried everything to get the company out of town without bloodshed. There was talk of moving to Plaquemine, another nearby town, but after one day there the heat from the overhead arc lights burst the sprinkler system and flooded the local hospital, causing $1200 in damages. So Preminger plunges on, trying hard to wrap it all up by mid-August.

The scene at the old house continues, with Madeleine Sherwood and Michael Caine. Caine learned his Southern accent on a tape recorder while making a British film in Berlin. Miss Sherwood, who has played a variety of Tennessee Williams roles, has no trouble with hers. She sits on an ancient divan, munching a Hershey bar and reading a 1946 *Screen Stories* with June Haver on the cover. Donna Danton, a young actress from New Orleans who plays the sluttish daughter of Miss Sherwood and Burgess Meredith, flies onto the screened-in porch, brushing away the flies from her pretty face. "Do you want this chair in the shot?" she asks, motioning to a rocker.

"My dear young woman, ve do not pay you to be an interior decorator. Ve pay you to *act!* Just say your lines, please!" Preminger is so angry, the saliva runs down his chin in the heat.

Outside, the owner of the house surveys her newly planted Hollywood rose garden full of hidden microphones. "We haven't had this much excitement since the neighbor's boy fell out of the fig tree. This house was built in 1825. Least they could do is give me a new paint job."

Lunch at a local Catholic mission. Preminger is all smiles as ceiling fans blow hot air on the cast, eating cold sandwich meat and watermelon. "I love locations. Some directors hate the expense. To me, expense is no problem. Here, ve get extras who are real people. The scene ve shot in an Episcopal church last week could never be duplicated in Hollywood. The people sang their own hymns, said their own prayers. Local extras move different, talk different. They are not disillusioned actors who never made it, or whose Daddys bought their SAG cards. Two years ago a box arrived with hundreds of pages of a new book called *Hurry Sundown*. I was interested because it perfectly re-created the conditions in a small Southern town in 1946. It's not about racial problems. The white hero succeeds only after he teams up with a Negro. It was the starting point of the basic human story going on in the South now. It also has romance. Jane Fonda and Michael Caine are like Rhett Butler and that girl—what's her name—"

"Scarlett O'Hara?"

"That's it, Scarlett O'Hara." Word came that the mayor refused to close the streets to traffic. "Call the governor!" bellowed Otto. Then the smile again. "There are problems on every picture. Sometimes you win, sometimes you lose. Cardinal Spellman thought *The Cardinal* was about him so he wrote letters to everyone to refuse us cooperation. But he had no influence." He brushed away the flies on his iced-tea glass. "Mayor Lindsay asked me to do part of this film in New

145

York and I refused. If they want to make more movie there, they should control the unions more. In New York an eight-hour day begins at 8 A.M. Down here, the eight hour begin whenever I call the crew, which is good for the nigh scenes. Also in New York you must hire a New York assistant for every Hollywood person you hire. Here, I can control everything, hire anyone I want."

And fire them, too. He has already fired the scriptwriter, a head cameraman, a few crew members, a secretary who was the daughter of the mayor of Baton Rouge (and who annoyed the cast by sunbathing on a Confederate flag), *and* Art Director Callihan, who negotiated all the construction contracts without even the aid of a scenic designer. "I was notified by an assistant while I was in the hospital recovering from an operation," says Callihan. "That's the way Otto does business. I still don't know why."

Burgess Meredith, who plays a cantankerous judge, says: "Otto's bark is worse than his bite. He's developed that monster image because the only way he can control people he doesn't trust is to bully them. I've done four films with him. *Cardinal* is the best. Otto's victim in that one was a little girl who had to wash my feet in the death scene. She was so terrified of him she spilled water all over the bed. Otto just yelled, 'RELAX!' at the top of his lungs. He thinks he's handling people but he only terrorizes them."

Michael Caine says: "The old bird's great if you don't let him hang you up. I come from a whole line of summer-stock companies in England, where the first words of every sentence begin with 'You can't,' so I'm used to it. He loves to embarrass actors in front of other people to tear down their egos. He's only happy when everybody else is miserable. Still, if you can keep his paranoia from beating you down, you can learn a lot from this guy."

A few nights later, the group was back in town to do a scene with Jane Fonda, Diahann Carroll, and Madeleine Sherwood which takes place in a white ladies' room. Miss Carroll, in a lemony summer dress, enters unlawfully and is slapped across the face by Miss Fonda.

"Miss-uh—" (Preminger often forgets the names of his actors.)

"Diahann Carroll," someone reminds him.

"It's too melodramatic, dalink." People stand on toilet seats, peer over the tops of the rest-room stalls at the black oscillating fan, white naphtha soap, and toilet paper stacked on the floor. He insists on absolute realism. Outside, giant wind machines blew clouds of bug spray into the black sky.

Preminger needed a sign saying "Whites Only." Shooting stopped while a prop man searched the vicinity. The gas stations yielded only "Colored Only" signs, but the right sign was finally located on the segregated toilet door of a state ferry boat. A group of menacing toughs had threatened to pitch the prop man overboard into the Mississippi River if he didn't throw away his screwdriver and return to land. "What's wrong, can't you svim?" yelled Otto.

By 11 P.M., a sign had been painted and Miss Carroll had been slapped so many times the tears were running down her face. A note arrived from the Ku Klux Klan, demanding that the company be out of town by midnight and never return. The Big O threw up his hands and hustled the actors into station wagons. Two cars of armed men had pulled up off the curb. The streets were deserted. Everyone drove back to Baton Rouge in silence and fear in a motorcade guarded by armed state police. "Because I played a few Nazis I'm ripe for criticism. I am not a tyrant. Sometimes I am impatient, but I'm not a tyrant," said the Big O, breaking the gloomy silence around him. "The legend is paling now," he added, as a state trooper pulled alongside the car to check the number of occupants inside. Everyone nodded, but nobody believed him for a single minute.

Michael Crawford

APRIL, 1967.

EVERY SATURDAY NIGHT, when most Broadway stars celebrate the birth of their weekend by heading for the nearest cocktail party, Michael Crawford races down the stairs backstage at *Black Comedy*, grabs a taxi, and heads home to play Monopoly. Waiting at the door of his pad on Central Park West are his wife, Gabrielle, his daughter, Emma (age one), and anybody else foolish enough to oppose him. Everybody sits around on the floor eating lamb and Yorkshire pudding off the coffee table, drinking orange squash out of Woolworth glasses (one of the American guests invariably has to go out for ice, because the British always

147

forget it), and playing Monopoly like it was going out of style. It *has,* but not the way Michael plays. He uses both the London and the Atlantic City boards ("That way you can pass Go twice!"), and guards the money like it was the Bank of England. Oh yes. He *always* wins.

Two rolls of the dice and he already owns Trafalgar Square and Mayfair. Bob Dylan wails on the phonograph. "He's the answer to everything that is crap!" swoons Michael. "I hate everything phony. Before *Black Comedy* was a hit, we never got asked out. Now it's a smash, so we get two invitations a day. We don't go out much."

Doesn't sound much like two swinging Mods from swinging England. But, in spite of Gabrielle's mini-skirts and Michael's Carnaby Street ties, that is the last thing in the world they want to be. "We had that lot," says Michael, blinking two robin's-egg-blue eyes from the boyish milk-and-Wheaties face that has made him a box-office blockbuster in England. Four of his films—*The Knack, A Funny Thing Happened on the Way to the Forum, The Jokers,* about two zany brothers who steal the crown jewels from the Tower of London, and Richard Lester's *How I Won the War*, costarring John Lennon—have had equal success in America. In all of them the fresh enthusiasm in Michael's Punchinello face stands out like Raggedy Andy with freckles. It's a face which—unlike his British contemporaries David Hemmings and Terence Stamp—seems destined to be laughed at. He doesn't mind. He is not even remotely interested in dramatic parts. "All I want to hear is people laughing. In *White Lies,* the curtain raiser of our show on Broadway, I'm a sad little fellow and it depresses me. Three of my films have been for Dick Lester, who is my best friend. I haven't made the big money yet, but I've done them all for fun. That's a lot more important than money." The radio played "Strawberry Fields" by the Beatles. "John Lennon wrote that while we were in Spain with Lester's last film. Now Murray the K is calling it a trip. John had no such thing in mind. He's great. He'd come in and sit crosslegged on the bed with his guitar or we'd take his Rolls to the beach. You should see his Rolls— even the hubcaps are black. Geraldine Page plays the Beatles every night before she goes onstage!"

For Michael, a fascinating revelation, because life itself is fascinating and there is still hope for a world in which an actress like Geraldine Page can play the Beatles before going onstage to glory. Everything involves him because involvement keeps him jumping and energy prevents boredom and boring is something he has never been. He can sit up all night

148

n P. J. Clarke's shouting "I'm sorry, you're wrong!" to
Harold Pinter, then turn around and spend an hour de-
cribing how he watched a man killed in the New York
raffic. And through it all, an innate sense of comedy. When
Gabrielle brings in the food, he chides, "She burns every-
hing, that girl. Ever had a burned hard-boiled egg?"

"You lying ham," says Gabrielle, who looks like all the
paintings of English maidens on old-fashioned taffy boxes and
seems pretty enough to be a movie star herself.

"Crafty as a wagonload of motors," says Michael, diving
nto the mint sauce.

His real name is Michael Dumbell Smith. John Lennon
thinks it's the funniest name he's ever heard and is writing a
song about it for the Beatles. His father, a pilot, was killed six
months before Michael was born. His mother remarried a
grocer and Michael was sent to convents where "the nuns hit
me a lot." Then he was sent to a choir school, where "the
principal got ten years soon after for having it off with the
music mistress." He left school at fifteen. "I don't regret
anything that ever happened to me in my life except school,"
he says. "I hated it and I didn't learn a thing." After that, his
mother died (he still can't go near a hospital) and he was
raised by Kay Kendall's sixty-year-old Dad. He wrote 100
letters to the BBC and got his start playing young parts on
radio broadcasts for children. Two years ago he met Gabrielle, who was a disc jockey at the Pickwick Club, a smart
discotheque owed by Tony Newley and Harry Secombe.
They were married in Paris by the British Consul, who had
to perform the ceremony all over again because the first time
they took their oaths on his diary instead of his Bible.

Sending such innocents to Broadway was like sending Han-
sel and Gretel to the witch's oven. She stayed on her father's
farm in Kent with Emma while Michael moved into the
Algonquin. He went to two parties and nobody spoke to him.
He didn't like the food. The TV didn't work. All alone on
Christmas, his holiday dinner consisted of "a turkey sandwich, cold tea, and tears." He spent "thousands of dollars" in
trans-Atlantic phone calls. His best friend in New York was
the operator.

Gabrielle and Emma arrived in time for the Boston opening. The reviews were great. "A rumor started that I should
be watched because I was so good I might become difficult.
That made me laugh. I lost so much weight I was down to
135 pounds. I came back from Boston and we had no place
to live, so we went to the Plaza, still green and airsick from
the shuttle flight—I think those guys are taxi drivers on their

day off—and filled in enough forms for me headstone an
then this guy about sixteen years old says, 'It'll be thirt
dollars, can you afford that?' It made me so mad I asked fo
all my forms back and they wouldn't give them to me. So
says, 'One Michael Crawford autograph is no good—yo
need five to get a Jimmy Cagney' and we left." They foun
an apartment (John Gielgud's), he got a dressing room at th
theater ("the size of an ant's navel—I put a bed in and now
have to stand on the bed to stay in the room"), had hi
opening canceled because of a blizzard and by the time th
critics saw him he was down to 125 pounds. "Everybody yo
read about came. President Kennedy's sister. Tab Hunter
Everybody. People come up on the street now and tell m
how much they like me. In England, only the cockneys woul
do that in pubs."

With success, of course, came Sardi's. Michael on tha
subject is like an Elaine May skit. "The show was a hit, see, s
I get my first invitation. It's like an institution. We're in
formed by our host we're at a *hot* table. Why that area nea
the door is *hot* I dunno, because in March the cold air blow
right in on you there. Anyway, we're a hit so the service i
great. We even got seven shrimp in our cocktail." ("
counted," said Gabrielle.) "So next time," he goes on, "
decided to be host. We took some guests and got a *hot* tabl
again. Everything was hot, including the waiter, who told m
my ten-dollar tip did not include the captain, who had jus
kicked him in the shins. I was so embarrassed I gave him
another five dollars. It cost me seventy bucks and we only
got six shrimps in the cocktail." ("I counted," said Ga
brielle.) "On my third and definitely last trip, I booked mysel
on the phone. 'Yes, Mr. Crawford,' they said. I made it
Sardi's knew my name. I was really excited. We were ushered
past the *first* hot table, then the *second* hot table, and ended
up in the garage—that's the spot near the kitchen where al
the waiters kick each other in the shins. It took twenty
minutes to get a drink, for which the bill was put right on the
table under my nose, and the service was definitely not up to
the hot tables." ("I only got *five* shrimps in the cocktail," said
Gabrielle.) "We mentioned the fact to the waiter and he
said, 'If you don't like it, you can sit upstairs next time.' I
guess *that*, in New York, is the supreme punishment—to be
put up with tourists. We go to Downey's now, where *every
thing* is hot except the beer."

Michael hates phoniness. Period. "It's the same in London.
Everybody trying to be first—find the right club, go to the
right places. Here it's Sardi's, there it's the Ad Lib or Sabil

la's. When *The Knack* opened in London, we found ourselves accidentally very 'in crowd.' It meant absolutely nothing. London has become unbearably pretentious now, full of little girls walking around in skirts the size of a man's handkerchief."

Michael begins taking photos of everyone with his new Polaroid camera while Gabrielle sits on top of the sofa barefoot reading Russian proverbs aloud: "The church is near, but the road is all ice; the tavern is far, but I'll walk very carefully." Everyone laughs. Emma is brought in to say hello by her nanny, a sexy blonde named Pam. "She's going to stop traffic when she grows up," someone tells Michael. "You mean she'll be a lady cop?" he roars. Emma messes her diapers and does a quick vaudeville exit.

The game continues. Michael is building hotels on everything but Victoria Station. John Normington, an actor in *The Homecoming*, mentions the American actors picketing shows with British cast members. "I don't blame them for being angry," says Michael. "I sympathize. American actors in England should be given the same rights we're given here. You can't do all plays there with strictly British actors. We can't say 'Hiya, baby!' any more than Americans can say 'By Jove!' But how many of those blokes carrying signs outside *Black Comedy* can take the falls I do eight times a week? After each show I want to come outside and hit those guys in the nose. I wanna say, 'Why don't you cut out the crap and try to get some work for yourselves instead of running us down?' The problem should be resolved by British and American unions over conference tables and not by actors carrying placards on street corners. I'm paying seventy-five dollars a week to American Actors' Equity just for the privilege of acting onstage here. What Americans pay in England is nothing compared to that. Then I perform extra Actors' Fund benefits without pay to benefit who? American actors, that's who. I'm black and blue from head to toe, I've got eight pulled ligaments in my leg and bruises all over, and when I limp out of the theater at night, these bloody bastards are walking up and down with signs saying 'English actors will be working next year—will you?' It's depressing to feel you're not wanted here. They give us the feeling 'You're no damn good—we can do better.' Well, *do* it."

Not, he hastens to admit, that *Black Comedy* is the greatest thing since canned soup. "It's a crude ballet, like a clock, with a cast of eight cogs that need precision movement. Now, nearly three months since we opened, the timing is off. It's time for the watchmaker to come back and take a look.

151

Five weeks after we opened, Peter Schaeffer tried to redirect the curtain raiser, *White Lies*, because so many people were walking out, but he's no director. And in *Black Comedy*, for instance, I have to move furniture to lines—if a sigh is four beats too late I'm on the other side of the stage four beats too early and the laugh is dead and I've lost one of the best moments in the show. Still, we've had only one rehearsal since we opened. This is Broadway, but it's not professional. I mean, how can an actress like Connie Stevens miss shows because her plane has a flat tire? In England, you can't even get permission to fly to Scotland for the night.

"I dunno. I'm a very young man, but I want things to be right, you know? Everybody seems to think it's better to put up with things that aren't right than get involved. But it's the public that suffers every time. We need someone now to say, 'O.K. you lot, let's clean it up and give the people their money's worth.' "

"Michael is very conscientious," says Gabrielle. "When I had Emma he had the morning sickness *and* the labor pains."

"I don't work hard at being anything," said Michael. "But if I ever get rich and famous I'll probably change. I'll probably"—he strives hard for the worst thing he can think of—"I'll probably buy Sardi's and sell it to Jim Downey cheap."

It was five A.M. The glasses were empty, the food was eaten, Michael owned everything on the board, and the bank was bankrupt. A pink wet dawn was shining through the terrace from the gritty sky. "He cheats," said Gabrielle on her way to bed. And outside, waiting for the rickety elevator, we could still hear Michael, counting his money.

Hayley Mills

UP IN HER PENTHOUSE TOWER on the 37th floor of the Sherry-Netherlands Hotel, the girl in the mini-dress balanced a glass of liquor (something red and daring swimming in a room-service glass) in one hand and a cigarette curling purple smoke into the air-conditioned air in the other. It was Hayley Mills, but you had to look twice to believe it. There was a time (it really wasn't that long ago) when you could get a green sour-apple grimace out of even your very best friend by simply mentioning the name. A teen-age Melanie Wilkes. Sweet. Too sweet. More peppermint-candy sweetness than anyone over the age of fourteen could stand without the aid of an Excedrin.

Well, there's a new Hayley Mills now. Freckles and choco-late-ice-cream smudges have long since been replaced by mascara and hot-pink lipstick. Hayley is a woman now. Just a tiny slip of a thing, really, but a full-fledged woman all the same. Twenty-one years old and ready to meet the world on her own terms. The last time she hit New York she came to plug a gushy little Walt Disney family film under the dictatorial aegis of a very stern father (John Mills) and a watchful mother (writer Mary Hayley Bell), who screened everyone before they entered the room and quickly showed them the door when the questions got too close for comfort. "Do you smoke?" or "Do you wear a bra?" Like that.

This time Hayley was back, more Sandra Dee than Shirley Temple, and ready with the answers. Snugly nestled in a suite with very grown-up gold-and-white-stripe wallpaper to plug a new film, *The Family Way*, in which she plays a married woman desperately trying to aid her impotent husband in the clumsy newness of sexual intercourse. She smokes. She drinks. She wears nightgowns. She even has a nude scene standing in a bathtub, and the censors are not happy. (In England, the film has become the Number One box-office smash in spite of an "Adults Only" rating and in America, where censorship is almost as silly, it has met head on with similar seal-of-approval problems, only recently winning a "Morally Unfit for Children" rating.) To top that off, Hayley was not living in the Sherry-Netherlands with her family, but with her new boyfriend, Roy Boulting, a much-married, 54-year-old British producer who, with his twin brother, John, directed her in *Family Way*. No bleached-blond beach boys with ho-daddy haircuts for this girl. "Goodness, some people are so old-fashioned, aren't they?" she says if you ask her about it.

Hayley answered the door and led the way up an ornate brass staircase past walls of framed playing cards, like the set of a Peter Sellers movie ("Very flush, isn't it?" she giggled gaily), to one of the two bedrooms, apologizing because she and Boulting were "a little mixed up with the appointment

153

schedule" and would I mind waiting a few minutes until they could get rid of "these boring people" in the living room. Through the bedroom her transistor radio tinkled merrily above a floppy pink hat and a pair of high heels she had kicked on the floor. The wait was brief. From downstairs, a whistle from Roy. The visitors had gone and the coast was clear. Settling down on the sofa next to him, Hayley started right in about the nude scene. "Do you honestly think people will come just to see Hayley Mills in the raw? How awful. Quite honestly that scene does not warrant all the publicity. It is a very integral part of the film and there is nothing dirty-minded people can get a kick from. I didn't relish the idea at first—the bathtub was only the size of this coffee table—and it was also very cold. We filmed in the winter. Every day I dreaded the moment when I would have to take off my dressing gown for that scene. The thing that unnerved me most was this man on top of the set who just sat there directly above me the entire time working a crossword puzzle. Anyway, after the initial wetting I didn't mind. The whole thing was handled with great taste by my director here."

She punched Roy on the arm with her fist. "Ha ha," said Boulting, a virile guy with a beanbag face and a Mod haircut who doesn't look anything like fifty-four years old and who bounces about with more vigor than most of the syrup-lidded Muscle Beach movie idols Hayley's own age.

"Do you know what he made me do?" asked Hayley, tickling Roy in the ribs under his starched white Carnaby Street shirt. "He made me rehearse in the tub without *any* water."

"Ha ha," said Roy, grinning fiendishly.

"Anyway," continued Hayley, "I treated it like I was doing a love scene. The only difference between a love scene and a nude scene is that in a love scene you have to worry where the noses go and in a nude scene you worry about where the fanny goes."

They blew smoke rings, grabbed each other like bear cubs, lost in the hilarity of Hayley's pun, and when the smoke cleared, she said, "It's not a sex film. Besides, kids today know more about sex at the age of eight than their parents do. Especially now, with sex education taught in school, kids should be told the facts of life in a straightforward, truthful way. Sex isn't a dirty subject, is it, Roy?"

"Ha ha," said Roy.

"This," pointed Hayley, "is the first time I've ever played a married woman. *Any* woman, for that matter. I signed with
154

Walt Disney when I was thirteen to do five pictures. I enjoyed working for him but those films were very restricting. Conveyor-belt jobs. So goody-good, you know? And there was this image I created which was hideous. I wasn't supposed to be seen drinking or buying cigarettes or smoking in public. The reasoning was that the audiences for the Disney films were very young, and if they saw me smoking eight cigars a day, why shouldn't they? So I'd spend three months in Hollywood, then go back to England and do a quality film like *Chalk Garden* or *Whistle Down the Wind* so people wouldn't say 'Oh, Hayley Mills, *Christ!' Family Way* isn't the first good film I've done. Trouble is, all the good ones I've made are the ones nobody ever heard of. All this talk about me growing up is a surprise to everyone but me. I've had my own apartment in London for a year now. Oh sure, I led a pretty sheltered life as a child, but it was for my own sake. There was always a member of the family along on trips if I needed help. But in the long run, I feel it was bad for me. I had to break away, make my own mistakes, learn to have confidence in myself."

Hayley's older sister, actress Juliet Mills, was the first to urge her out of the nest. "Stand on your own two feet," she said. When her Disney contract expired, Hayley took a flat with her eighteen-year-old brother Jonathan, who works in a London film studio. The family was outraged. Then Hayley's first film under her new flag of independence turned out to be *Family Way* and unknown to them both, her costar turned out to be her own father, who stood by on the set watching austerely while his director fell in love with his daughter. "I know he knew instinctively what was going on, because he was always making funny remarks which made me angry," says Hayley.

"All directed at me," added Roy. "Don't ask me why I fell in love with a little girl the same age as my own children. Ask her how she could fall in love with a miserable, ugly mugger like *me*. I'm fifty-four years old with a wife who still has not divorced me and a large number of children." How many? "Too many. When we met, Hayley was not even twenty-one yet. Our relationship was very formal during the film. Wasn't it, darling?"

Hayley threw her blonde curls back and giggled. "To all intents and purposes."

"I always said I would never become emotionally involved with an actress, but the theory proved impossible in actual practice. Now people want to know if we'll marry. Of course we will, but in England if you make a statement like that to

the press they will hold up your divorce forever. Mine is a
ugly business that has been going on for several years. It wa
supposed to be final May 23, now they've lifted it again fo
'further evidence.' So I don't know when we'll be free t
marry."

Annoyed by the subject, Hayley stuck out her tongue, mad
a green face and darted up the stairs looking a bit like Lad
Jane Grey in a mini-skirt on her final lap to the Tower o
London. When she was gone, Boulting added: "When thi
thing began to get serious, I asked her, 'Hayley, are yo
looking for a father image?' She said, 'Hell no, I have a
father with a strong enough image as it is, and I don't nee
another.' I don't want her to leave the guidance of he
parents to be guided by someone else. That would be exchang
ing one childhood for another, wouldn't it? Anyway, isn'
that a middle-class myth about marrying when you are bot
young so you can discover beautiful things together as beauti
ful youths? I've been married three times. The first time m
wife and I were twenty-two, completely ignorant, incompe
tent, and incapable of conducting a thoughtful relationship
It's a hoax perpetrated against the youth of today, like th
one about beautiful families—peel away the layers of mos
big families and you'll find they all hate each other."

Hayley popped back into the room. "I heard that. My
family is very happy."

"Nonsense. It's a professional family with an image that i
only just now beginning to lose its force. It's been a long time
a-dying."

"Darr-lingg," hissed Hayley, eyes narrowing beneath black
eyeliner. "Our work was our lives."

"See what I mean?" said Roy. "I think the Redgraves are
much healthier. All individuals. They never were concerned
with presenting an image."

"Well, I grew up that way. What happened to us jus
happened. I can't remember ever living like a child. We had
tea with Dad in his caravan on the set of *Great Expectations*
and followed him around on tour. He'd be onstage doing
Shakespeare and Mother would be off somewhere writing a
book and the three of us kids would sleep in the matinee
boxes on Nanny's day off. I was no more than six. I never
had friends my own age, only my parents' friends. I never
really liked boys my own age because they bored me. Still
do. Oh, there was one character, but that was more of a
brother-sister relationship. When I met Roy, I never considered age. I tried to force myself away from the idea of love,
but that was idiotic. I tried hard. Went to Africa. No good.
156

Came back to London, saw him again. Went to France. It was something I could not deny and after a while I said, 'Why should I?' Since I met Mr. B here, I've—"

"—stopped biting your nails," finished Roy.

"Right. A nasty sight that was. Now I want to go under hypnosis to stop smoking, but I'm afraid the neurosis would manifest itself in some other way worse than the smoking. I believe in hypnosis and also astrology. It's a very legitimate science. I don't follow rigidly what it says in the paper every day, but I've learned a lot about the character of people born under certain signs. I'm Aries, Roy's Scorpio. The news is very bad there. Still, my father is Pisces and Mother is Aquarius and they're not supposed to get on either."

"They don't," said Roy.

"Shut up."

It was almost time for them to dress for the swank cocktail party Warner Brothers had arranged to introduce them to the press. "Christ, what a bore," said Hayley. "You never get used to it. I just finished a new film in Singapore— a Noel Coward play called *Pretty Polly* about a mousy girl who has a torrid affair in the Orient. No nude scenes, but it's pretty sexy. Now I think I must turn to the stage and get away from movies for a while. I'm the only member of my family who has no stage experience. I played an angel on top of the Christmas tree once and also a bee. But I want to play an evil bitch in something. Can you see me as an evil bitch, Roy?"

"Ha ha," said Boulting, patting the remarkable child-woman on the fanny as they headed up the stairs to take their baths and meet the public.

Lynn Redgrave

IF YOU SAW HER WAITING FOR A BUS, you'd never believe it. Treetop tall (5'10") and all kneecaps, with hair that never seems to have met a sylist, a little round mouth invented for devouring hot-fudge sundaes, and a chubby

figure that changes weight according to her mood, she ce
tainly doesn't look like a star. In the words of her ow
father, she is "like an enormous lorry driver."

Yet baby sister Lynn is the newest star in the famou
Redgrave acting family: Her father is, of course, Sir M
chael; her mother, Rachel Kempson; her brother, Corin, an
her sister, Vanessa, who made *Morgan!* glow. In *Georgy Gir*
Lynn captivated a discerning audience at the recent Berli
Film Festival and helped the movie win a grand priz
Watching Lynn, some moviegoers may find comparison
sailing through their memories like comets: funny as Jud
Holliday in *Born Yesterday*, touching as Julie Harris i
Member of the Wedding, haunting as Giulietta Massina in *L
Strada*. In *Georgy*, Lynn is a combination of all three, wit
fish and chips on the side; one of the sad, overlooked misfit
who live other people's lives, glow in other people's spot
lights, hold other women's babies, and watch other peopl
fall in love. (When her roommate has a baby, Georgy ha
the labor pains.)

On a recent first trip to New York, she brought some o
the magic with her. She seems, at first, like the kind of gi
who drops by for tea and stays to spill cream on your carpe
and play hopscotch on your heart. Something of Georg
remains. But, like some pudgy Cinderella who suddenly find
her big square foot fitting firmly in the glass slipper, Lyn
Redgrave wears it with style. Snuggled warmly into her suit
at the Sherry-Netherlands, she greeted her guests as the
sailed in, one by one, reinforced by a press agent who herde
them in and out of a rainy afternoon.

Georgy, or Lynn—it is difficult to tell where one begin
and the other leaves off—plopped on a peppermint sofa
sipping her new fame like syrup through a straw. "The firs
thing I did was head for Reuben's and gorge myself. Then
saw Angela Lansbury in *Mame* and went to a real New Yor
eat-out. It was a simply smashing house with a garden in th
back and we ate a whole side of charcoal beef and it wa
simply super! I also did the *Today* show before the sun cam
up and walked back to the hotel along Central Park at eigh
A.M." The glow faded as she glanced shyly at the press agent
"The rest of the time it's mostly been the insides of elevators
and taxicabs."

How did all the fame come about? "Well, it's a long story
and beginnings are best. I never wanted to act, though all
my life the rest of the family was always getting dressed to
go off to the theater. I was always practically speechless with
shyness, so I'd kind of mumble and run off into the garden

when people called me a Redgrave. I went to an ordinary day school run by a terrible drunken lady who hated us all. Vanessa had gone there before me and her behavior paved the way. I was a shepherd once in a Nativity play and said, 'There's a star.' The first part of my life was spent in that awful school and going to the seashore for holidays and Stratford in the summer when my father played there. My sister and I have a nostalgia for our childhood. It wasn't long ago—I'm only twenty-three—but kids today grow up too fast. My sister's baby has already been to America three times.

"I didn't think much about my father being a star. I mean, if he had come into prominence suddenly when I was older, it would have been different, but he had always been famous and he never brought it home. Unlike a lot of famous actors, my folks love acting, so there was nothing dreadful about it, nothing to hide from the children. I went to the theater more than most children, but very little of it rubbed off. I remember seeing Joan Greenwood in *Peter Pan*. I cried because I couldn't fly. I also fell madly in love with Alan Ladd, but I didn't even bother to see my father play Hamlet because it interfered with the last installment of my favorite kiddie show on the radio. I was very normal. I was never allowed to smoke cigars or go to nightclubs as a child. I mean, I wasn't Portland Mason."

She clapped her hands and kicked the heels together on her Mary Jane shoes and told about her father being knighted by the Queen. "We all got dressed up in our best hats and went to the palace, and there was this terrible orchestra in curly Whig wigs playing *Salad Days* and *Oklahoma!* while Daddy was being invested. You get there ages ahead, and when royalty enters, everybody curtsies. Just as the Queen Mother arrived, all the little children had one mad rush to the loo accompanied by a befuddled wigged footman. I was dying to get inside the ladies' room at Buckingham Palace just to see what it was like, but never made it."

In the spring of 1959, following a terrible fracas with the drunken headmistress, she left school a term before graduation. "Father was never very good at facing our teachers but he wrote marvelous scalding letters. One of his letters got me expelled. I didn't know what to do, so I took a short housewives' course." (Pause.) "That's a course for ... short ... housewives." (A guffaw, followed by a feverish ladylike blush.) "Actually, it was a cooking course. I wanted more than anything to cook for rich people to pay for riding lessons. Nothing worked out. So I asked my sister Vanessa

159

about acting, and she *didn't* say forget it. Daddy paid for
year of drama school, but I found the school was a trap.
was attending and working in scenes to please the other
students, not to learn. I had to throw most of what I learned
away."

Still, she was lucky. She floated out into the London street
looking "absolutely wrong for everything" and landed a tiny
part in a Royal Court production of *A Midsummer Night's
Dream*, directed by Tony Richardson, who at the time had
not yet met and married Lynn's sister Vanessa. ("Few people
realize I met him first.") The production, in her words, was
"disastrous." But in the cast were a few other unknown
fledglings named Rita Tushingham, Samantha Eggar, and Ni-
col Williamson. Like the measles, they all spread to other
things. For Lynn, it was a small part in Richardson's movie
Tom Jones. "We took over an old mansion in Somerset, and
there were so many horses in the stables that when I wasn't
working I could ride. One night Albert Finney and some of
us raided the crypts and tombs underneath the vicarage
where the family's ancestors were buried. It caused a stink
and they almost canceled the film and we had to have the
grounds reconsecrated by the bishop. Behind the scenes it
was as bawdy as the film. Super fun!"

Sir Laurence Olivier noticed Lynn in *Tom Jones* and called
her in for an audition with the National Theatre at the Old
Vic. "I got the job for a year, so I got my own flat in an old
Victorian house near Hyde Park, and everything started
happening!" One year turned into three, and she became *the*
young actress in London to watch. As the fat, stupid flapper
in *Hay Fever,* she stole whole scenes from Edith Evans, and
as the mute daughter in *Mother Courage*, she brought the
Old Vic to its feet with tearful cheers. There was time out
between stage ovations to impress moviegoers as Rita Tushingham's roommate in *Girl With Green Eyes* but it is as
Georgy Girl that Lynn finally turns from a toadstool into a
truffle.

Tea arrived and, to the press agent's delight, the conversation switched to the film itself. "Well," Lynn began, adding a
dash of sugar to her visitor's teacup, "they didn't want me.
They tried to get every girl in London, and I was about the
hundredth choice for Georgy. Only Silvio Narizzano, the
director, wanted me immediately, but I was still nobody and
meant nothing at the box office, and they wanted a name to
play opposite James Mason and Alan Bates. Then after
everybody else fell through, he still wanted me."

"She's overly modest," said the press agent urgently.

160

"No, I have no shame about being second choice. During that shooting I met an actress friend in an office who asked me what I was doing. I said *Georgy Girl*. She said, 'Oh they wanted me for that part, but I didn't take it.' I wasn't mad. I mean, if you're the one who ends up doing it, then *you* are the lucky one. At the Old Vic when I auditioned, they wanted another famous actress, but I ended up playing her roles. I got the applause, not her. It all cancels out in the end."

Is she like Georgy? "Well, I looked the part. I gained fourteen pounds for it. I'm a terrible compulsive eater and now I'm always on a diet. I live on steaks and salads. Everyone thinks I'm the horsey one in the family, but we're all plump. Vanessa is not a natural-born willow."

The future seems "simply super" to her, but there is still that element of self-doubt which makes most great actresses greater. "I have a lot to learn yet. I still find it terribly difficult to cry, especially at eight-thirty in the morning. I'm not the slightest bit methody, although when I did the mute girl in *Mother Courage*, I went to a school for autistic children and studied their obsessions. One child had a shoe fixation, couldn't go to bed without them on. I used it in the play. An awful lot of my acting is still hit or miss. Never quite sure whether to trust my intuition or not. Up to now I never had a lead. I didn't know if I could do it. I mean, when you're bad in a walk-on nobody notices, but if you have to carry the whole bloody film, that's torment. So far my way's been right, but I know the day is coming when I won't have a great director and a great script, and it'll be a disaster. I have to be ready for that."

In the meantime, there are other things, like Russia: "After *Georgy Girl,* I toured there with the National Theatre. I got lost on the streets of Moscow, and people got off buses to take me home. They came to the stage door clutching great bunches of flowers that had withered during the performance, and gave them to all of us with love. Saying good-bye was an emotional crisis, and I must go back."

And there's her own life to live, away from the glamour of being a kooky-girl success: "I love to be alone in my flat. I'm terribly tall, so I need long, tall rooms. I love enormous movie epics I can laugh at and lose myself in and not worry about how it all was made. I love Carson McCullers novels and things I can't eat because they're too fattening. I love to cook and I make a wonderful dish called lemon syllabub for my friends. I'm not a member of a swinging set. I hate Gilbert and Sullivan and boys with long hair and discotheques. I never say 'What really with-it swinging thing can I do now?' I just sort of swing on my own."

The press agent was swinging her toward the door. It was time for another interview. She pulled on her raincoat over her black-velvet see-through Mod dress with the white Peter Pan collar. "The whole family lives within twenty minutes of each other. We all like each other's work and each other as people. Vanessa takes the spotlight one week, I get it the next." The door was closing, and she was still talking. "My father said he'll retire and we can all send him the ten percent!" Then she was off to see more of what success is all about. Today the insides of elevators and taxicabs. Tomorrow the world.

Beryl Reid

OCTOBER, 30, 1966.

TEA AND SYMPATHY WITH SISTER GEORGE began shortly past four. *Without* the tea. "I'm probably the first British actress you've ever met who loathes the stuff," she said, disguised for the day as Beryl Reid and looking twenty years younger than she does onstage at the Belasco. She peeled off the top of a brand-new bottle of unopened Scotch, mixed it with ginger ale in an oversize wine glass (veddy British), and gleefully grumbled when her guest sent her back for ice. "You Americans can't do without your ice. In England we never use it. But then our liquor is not 100 proof there, either. In America, one Bloody Mary with lunch and you can't speak to anyone for the rest of the day."

Settling down with the ice cubes still rattling nervously in her glass, she looked like the last person in the world anybody would ask to play a butch, cigar-smoking lesbian in *The Killing of Sister George* or anything else: offstage, to the surprise of everyone who meets her, Beryl Reid has a bubbly laugh, chicly coiffed hair (strawberry blonde, not battleship gray), girlish dresses, and skin that looks like an ad for Johnson's baby powder. "Everyone expects me to meet them at the door in pants, brandishing a hockey stick. I'm

162

only five-foot-three. When the stage manager met me at the airport with my tiny little feet and my silly little hat he didn't even recognize me from the photographs taken onstage. Something very physical happens to me on the stage. I feel a whole different shape. When I appear in revues in England, I usually play sixteen to eighteen different characters in one night and I never look the same."

It has been an unnerving morning. The night before she had been exposed for the first time to the American theater's diseased and yawning dog—the theater party—and the experience had left her visibly shaken. "It was the worst audiance we've ever faced. They sat on their hands and didn't laugh at anything, not even the sight gags. And—the height of rudeness—you couldn't see a thing during the curtain calls for all the people running up the aisles. Never seen anythin' like it in me life." She had also just been shown one critic's pan of the show in which he compared it to *Life With Father,* with *her* as the father. She read aloud: "Beryl Reid struts around, cigar in hand, a top-notch impersonation of pugnacious John Bull in drag." Then she collapsed with a roar of hearty laughter. "I must say that's hardly my own conception of myself. What bad luck that he didn't have a better evening." Then, "I shall have a brandy rather quickly on that one," with a leap to the kitchenette.

"Mostly they've been wonderful to us, though. Bette Davis came to last Sunday's matinee and told me I should play Sister George in the movie instead of *her!* Imagine! 'I feel strung-out—destroyed,' she told me. I've also been taken to some frightfully expensive restaurants. I saw David Merrick in Sardi's, but I just did a silent curtsy as I passed his table. We won every conceivable award in London, you know, and it was wonderful to have that year of success, but to bring it here was terrifying. Everybody made guesses for me. Some said, 'They'll go raving mad about the play.' Others said, 'They'll love you but hate George.' Harry Secombe, who had a nasty experience here in *Pickwick,* said, 'They won't even come.' But they did. Of course, some people never get a clue to what's going on. Me Dad, who's eighty-four, came to see it in London with a lady friend, and after the third act, turned to her and asked, 'Now, were they just sisters?' 'No,' she said, 'just good friends.' " More throaty laughter. "Eight out of ten nights the American audiences have screamed bravo at the end. The rest of the time, I play for the minority. You just have to say, 'Thirty percent of them out there like us' and play for *them.*"

Still, enough hippies have jumped on the play's bandwagon

163

thus far to make it the play of the season to argue about on the jet-set cocktail circuit, to ensure a steady flow of business at the box office and to prompt Miss Reid to move out of her suite at the Algonquin for a longer stay in a sunny apartment on West 72nd Street. "This is a challenging city, but I'm not accustomed to cities. In England, I live in a thatched-roof cottage near Windsor. Why, you don't even have any nightingales here. And the noise—my head is full of cotton rags. But I took this little flat because it's close to Central Park, and it has an oven and I've bought a liver grinder and a few things to make me feel at home." She produced her latest acquisition, a dime-store garlic crusher, to prove her point. Eileen Atkins, who plays her tormented girlfriend in the play, also lives in the same building. "That makes it nice. People are always warning us to be careful or we'll get raped in New York, so this way we can share cabs home together at night after the show."

If it comes as a shock to find someone so womanly playing a bloke like Sister George, nobody is more surprised than Miss Reid. In England, where she is a famous comic on the order of Lucille Ball, her background illustrates the history of a British tradition Americans know little about—the music hall revue. She was born in Hereford, England, of Scottish parents. Her father was a real-estate agent-auctioneer and her brother (the only other child in the family) is a scientist who used to invent cake mixes for Betty Crocker. Her mother died two years before she won the role of Sister George. She says her family is totally unimpressed with "all that show-biz twaddle," but she is happy about that because it has given her "a fine sense of balance. Once a man sculpted my head in Stefano marble and put it in the Royal Academy and nobody in the family said 'How marvelous,' just 'Oh good' and 'That's nice.' "

At the age of three, the family moved to Manchester, the second largest city in England, where she began doing imitations of stars on the radio and won a talent contest at the age of seventeen. By 1937 she was making two pounds a week (about $10) in a little summer show in North Yorkshire ("near Charlotte Brontë's moors") doing impersonations of Gracie Fields. What followed, she insists, was a "long and uneventful career in which everything happened slowly." She played vaudeville houses and music halls throughout England and hit London in 1949 in a revue called *After the Show*. Radio and telly picked her up and she became one of the stars of a fabulously successful show called *Educating Archie* with such stalwarts as Harry Secombe and Max Bygraves.

he developed a character called Monica, "sort of a frightful-top-drawer girl," she said, spitting through her teeth like Gloria Upson in *Auntie Mame,* "who falls in love with a ventriloquist's dummy." Very silly but the British loved it and when she invented a second character called Marlene of the Midlands, Beryl turned into a star overnight. "That Marlene was even sillier than the Monica character. She was a foul, beatnik type who wore telephones that lit up for earrings. She kept me eating for ten years, plus a year at the Palladium. Things don't happen like that in America. I still take the Marlene character on tour and do routines. Like Bob Hope. I stand up and say, 'Good evening each,' and I'm on."

She also starred in some hit revues, like *One to Another,* in which she and Sheila Hancock did a sketch written for them by Harold Pinter (everybody loves comics in England) and a film with Peter Sellers called *Dock Brief.* ("You wouldn't remember it, luv. I got murdered in that one.") When *The Killing of Sister George* came along she was still doing the Marlene character on Sundays at dour places like the Royal Festival Hall. Even after she was an established star in *Sister George* the taxi drivers would stop in front of the stage door and yell, "Hi, Marlene, luv!" through the windows.

One night when she was playing Marlene, producer Michael Codron, who had seen her in a music hall revue, sent her the script of the play. She couldn't believe it. "I went to two friends—a writer and a sculptor—and asked their advice. The writer said, 'Don't go near it with a barge pole.' The sculptor said, 'It could be the turning point in your whole life.' I decided the only way to step forward in my career was to take the bull by the horns." Word got out that London was in for something smashing and on opening night everybody turned up. Gielgud came. Edith Evans came, declaring, "I don't know what everyone is so shocked about. I was raised on Shakespeare, where they say every four-letter word in the book and call it art." Noel Coward and Margaret Rutherford and—wow!—Brian Epstein, the manager of the Beatles, came. The audience cheered and stomped on the seats and tore up the programs and threw them in the air. After the show, Beryl Reid was the toast of London. "It's a vaudeville tradition in England to say good night to the night watchman. Everyone calls them 'firemen.' So I was leaving with Noel Coward on my arm and I stopped and said, 'Good night, fireman,' and Noel turned to everyone and said, 'Isn't she mah-velous? She knows everybody's name!' "

But what about playing a rough old lesbian, night after night, who makes her poor roommate drink a cup of her own

165

bath water? Bit of a sticky wicket, wot? "Well, I didn't know what to do with the role at first, but I didn't want to be a total monster, so I started with the shoes. Everybody knows George is a dike but she's got to wear shoes she can walk to the BBC in and not give herself away on the street. I think the wardrobe mistress was sorry she ever met me. She kept presenting me with new shoes and I kept saying, 'No, no, I've got to walk to the BBC' and nobody knew what I was talking about. I found the ones I wear onstage—olive-green suedes with little stacked heels—after trailing up and down the streets of Bristol before we opened in London. They're perfect, because they show George's human side, her bid for femininity. Frank Marcus wrote this role for a clown. 'When George is at her funniest, she's at her saddest' I said, and played her that way. You begin by thinking 'Christ, she's bloody awful,' but in the final analysis she's the only really honest character in the play. Everyone else cheats *her*. Val May, the director, gave me some words to lean on when I got confused and the best one was *indefatigable*. In the end, when the girlfriend leaves her all alone and she's faced with the hideous future playing a cow on a kiddie show, I think of that word and I know I could be a good Clarabelle Cow if I put my mind to it and I'll find a helluvanother girlfriend, too."

The buzzer rang and in from the sunny day to say hello popped Eileen Atkins, looking pink and girlish and at least *ten* years younger than *she* does onstage. (There must be something wrong with those lights at the Belasco.) There was only one more question. "Are we lesbians?" Miss Atkins blurted. They both fell on the sofa in a chorus of giggles. It was the wrong one, but they seemed amused by the subject.

"Good heavens, luv, I hope nobody thinks *that*," laughed Miss Reid. "Even though we have received some un*believ*able mail."

"Should we tell about that?" asked Miss Atkins.

"Well, I guess not. It wouldn't be fair," said Miss Reid. "A lot of these poor girls seem to confide in us."

"Very sad," said Miss Atkins, shaking her Raggedy Ann bangs.

"I get all the daft ones—all the nuts—because they think I smile at them from the stage," said Miss Reid. "One dotty old man about eighty even found his way into my dressing room one night and tried to shake hands with the mirror." Summoning all her music hall training, she acted out the cene in her living room and had everyone doubled over with laughter.

"One man," said Miss Atkins, trying to get a word in edgewise, "wrote requesting photos of my legs in various shades of colors."

"In New York," said Miss Reid, "we've been warned not to go into Central Park after dark. But I speak to everyone in the street—bums and all."

"It's the taxi drivers I worry about," said Miss Atkins.

"Did you notice the one last night?" asked Miss Reid. "He moved the mirror three times to have a look at me legs."

"Anyway, we're not lesbians," said Miss Atkins emphatically. "Actually, I've been married nine years but I haven't had the energy to go and get the divorce. I can't even keep a rubber plant."

Miss Reid added: "And I just got *my* divorce. I've been married twice. Twelve years this last time. We get too set in our ways. When men get married they stop being lovers and start being husbands."

"How boring," said Miss Atkins. Then, suddenly, it was dark outside, and time to go back to the Belasco for another cup of bath water.

Jean Paul Belmondo

SUMMER, 1965.

VENICE, Italy.

Edith Piaf was just beginning the last agonizing chorus of "M'lord" on the jukebox when the wooden doors of Harry's Bar swung open and Jean Paul Belmondo sauntered in wearing a Robin Hood hat, a green turtleneck sweater, white chino pants, and cowboy boots. It seemed a dramatic enough entrance for France's most popular film star who had shown up unannounced at a rain-soaked Venice Film Festival so lacking in real celebrities the journalists had begun to interview each other.

He was accompanied by a French press agent who was to act as an interpreter ("The poor bastard can't speak a word

167

of English," I had been told on the telephone earlier), and after he finished doing the autograph bit for two college girls from the University of Michigan, he settled down in a captain's chair, ordered a straight pernod, pushed his hat around backward, stretched his lanky legs under the table, and lit a cigar, the way Gary Cooper used to do in the old days when he talked to Hedda Hopper in the Warner Brothers commissary.

"He's ready now," the press agent nodded.

"It is always good to meet the Americans," he said through the press agent. "They love me in America, you know. All my bad films. Take *Backfire*. It played a week in Paris, but in America they stand in line to see me. I do not blame them. I am worth standing in line to see. I have no phony modesty. I am the man of the hour. I enjoy it. Why shouldn't I? Tomorrow I could be selling tickets to revivals of my own films."

Three weeks in the lemony sunshine of an island south of St. Tropez, where he had filmed Jean Luc Godard's latest eccentricity, *Pierrot le Fou,* had left his face with a burnished orange glow. He had attended the gala unveiling of the film the night before at the festival and seemed quite happy about it, in spite of the mixed response of catcalls, whistles, and bravos it had received from a standing-room audience of critics and movie buffs.

"I think it is a good film. But one can never be sure with Godard. Being in a Godard film is great fun. I never can enjoy all the funny things we did because I am so afraid suddenly that I missed the point of why we did them. I get the feeling that Godard is telling me something I do not understand. He leaves everything up to his audience."

Pierrot le Fou is no exception. It is filled with the usual Godard cynicisms about self-defeat and the destruction of the innocent in modern society, the Godard trickeries (while a TV set blares news of Vietnam, there is a close-up of the red "SS" portion of an American ESSO sign), and the Godard private jokes (Belmondo insults an American film director, who turns out to be Samuel Fuller). It is possible, as with all Godard pictures, to argue just whose films have been borrowed to make up the whole. But one thing is certain—it would not be the *same* film without Belmondo. It is *his* sandbox and Godard has allowed him to wallow audaciously in it in fruity, sun-ripened Technicolor: Belmondo takes a bath *au naturel.* Belmondo does a Gene Kelly musical number on a deserted beach. Belmondo smashes a cake in a girl's face. Belmondo smokes a sad cigarette in bed, his head sting on a Picasso clown. Belmondo drives a Ford Galaxie onvertible into the ocean. Belmondo faces center screen and ads Robert Browning to the audience with a parrot on his oulder. Belmondo pours a drink on a naked woman at a aked cocktail party. Belmondo impersonates Michel Simon. elmondo asks a garage attendant to "put a tiger in my nk." Belmondo spends the night with a girl only to wake up e next morning with a corpse in the next room. His dience cheers. He is once again the Belmondo his fans ave come to expect—the innocent, tough little grease mon- y in the wrinkled seersucker suit, the twentieth-century arlequin saving the bad, rouge-cheeked Columbine from the angsters with the walkie-talkies and driving the getaway ar while the soundtrack grinds out music from old Republic oston Blackie serials.

"They compare me to Humphrey Bogart and John arfield. Nonsense. I am *me!* But like those other ugly men, have come along at a time when the public is ready for a hange. Am I a good actor? I don't know. But my training in he fight ring taught me how to do all my own stunts. I have een nearly killed twice, once in *That Man from Rio,* and nce in *Pierrot.* I never read the critics. Let them call me hat they like. One thing they can never say about Belmondo s that he was just another pretty face.

"I always pick my directors first, then the film. If I like a irector I'll even walk through a shot without any pay just to ork with him, like in *Band of Outsiders.* I always trust Godard. I do not trust myself. I have no self-confidence. I ead about all the ways to act from the Americans and Jeanne Moreau has tried to teach me how to get inside a character, ut I am too simple and unsophisticated to learn. Sometimes try to become the character, like the fellow in *Breathless.* But it does not work with Godard. He knows too well what e wants out of me. I myself am often lost, and I rely trongly on my director to think for me. But I do not like to e intellectual about films. I hate actors who are always nalyzing themselves and their films. I am like the gunman in Godard's *Alphaville* who says, 'I am too old to discuss. So I hoot.' I am too simpleminded to talk about acting. So I just rush my teeth and be there."

What does he think of American films? "For me they are wonderful. But I think you take yourselves too seriously. For years before I became an actor I would sit for hours in the John Wayne movies and the Jerry Lewis films. But the Americans think they are corny. Nobody can make Westerns like the American, but you think they are in bad taste. And certainly no director in Europe has ever been able to make a musical like Vincente Minnelli. In Paris we have festivals of old MGM musicals, and after all these years you still have to stand in long lines to see *An American in Paris*. Yet Hollywood has given up on musicals. It is very sad."

He has always been popular with his leading ladies. "I have worked with the best ones in Europe. Moreau. A very wise woman, knows all the answers before you ask the questions. We are very good friends, but I think she has no real fun in life. Anna Karina. Such intelligence behind that little-girl face. She can do everything—sing, dance, make biscuits. Geraldine Chaplin? I think she is too young, not ready for this business, but I liked her. Out of them all my favorite is still Jean Seberg. She is just what all Frenchmen want the American girls to be like—beautiful, happy, friendly, with both feet on the ground. And one of the greatest actresses in Europe. Yet she was laughed at in America. I sometimes think the Americans are very stupid people indeed."

A crowd had gathered in the bar and someone had unplugged the jukebox to catch every word he uttered. "Pay no attention, they follow me everywhere. I almost never go out in public. I am married to a very nice girl who also hates to be stared at. Mostly we just put on old clothes and go to the beach or to a cinema. I do not believe wives should mix in their husbands' business, especially if it is show business. I never allow my wife on the set. It does not pay. When I was making *Pierrot le Fou,* Godard and Anna Karina were like a cobra and a mongoose, always glaring at each other. It is not healthy."

What about other women? "Listen, I am only thirty-two years old. I'm not dead. And please remember, I am French. I am happily married this year, but next year? Who knows? I never plan ahead. For me, life is an improvisation." [Shortly after the interview he left his wife to have a well-publicized affair with glamour girl Ursula Andress.]

In Europe he is known as a fast-take man, and one of the reasons most European directors beg for his services (aside from getting the biggest yield possible out of his capital at the box office) is that he does his job, causes no trouble, and gets his picture in on time. In *Pierrot*, however, he has one line in English—a simple "Sure, New York, yeah, Hollywood" and it took Godard thirty takes before he could pronounce the words in English. "So you see, I will never make a film in America. Why complicate my life? I am too stupid to learn the language and it would only be a disaster. I would love to make a cowboy film, but can you see me sitting on a horse with Mickey Rooney's voice dubbed in on the soundtrack? It would be silly if I could not communicate, n'est-ce pas?"

Belmondo skimmed off his pernod, ignoring the water chaser the waiter had set beside him. Then he cocked his Robin Hood hat at a forty-five-degree angle and winked at the college girls in their Michigan T-shirts. Everybody laughed as they went into a mock fainting gesture, and in that fleeting moment I suddenly knew Belmondo had answered his own question. He can communicate, all right. He sure can communicate.

George Peppard

THE NERVOUS PRESS AGENT shifted his feet outside the honey-beige suite up on the thirty-ninth floor of the Hotel Pierre. From inside, the sound of a toilet flushing. Then a doorknob turning. "You're on your own now," he said, dashing into an elevator down to the daylight safety of the Fifth Avenue traffic.

Behind the door, faintly visible through a hazy cocktail of blue cigarette smoke, pacing the room like a prize jaguar in a velvet cage, was Hollywood superstar George Peppard. Polite, suspicious, careful. He looks like an all-American basketball player who has suddenly inherited his father's business. The grin is boyish, like maybe he'd like to choke down a handful of ginger snaps with a glass of cold milk. But the blond hair on the strong, sturdy head is flecked with gray and instead of milk the unsteady hand in the button-down Madison Avenue broadcloth shirt sleeve pours straight Jack Daniel's on room-service ice. An expensive substitute, perhaps, but that's what happens when nice guys turn into movie stars.

Surprisingly, the movie star talks sense. Sure, he's in town on a publicity jaunt to plug *The Blue Max*, a reserved-seat, wide-screen epic about the German Air Force in World War I. Why else would he be wasting such a sunny summer afternoon? Sure, he also knows what it feels like to be

171

treated like a garbage collector by some of the highbrow critics. He knows, too, there are those who feel he started out to be a good actor but gave it up along the way. He laughs about it with feet on the ground. "Hell, I'm not much of a fan of my own work. I look at myself on the screen and I say, 'O.K., stupid, do something!' But stupid never does. Sometimes, though, I fool myself, like in *Home from the Hill*. When I saw that one, I said, 'Atta boy! Stupid strike again!' I think *Blue Max* is the best film I've ever done, and also my best performance. But it still doesn't excite me. All too often I try for things that never come off."

Why? The boy works hard enough. For *Blue Max* he even became a pilot. "I read a book on Von Richthofen's flying forces in Germany with accurate flight photos and decided there was no way to fake a man in an airplane on film. When you draw back from a close-up and show the whole plane, it looks phony if the same actor isn't still behind the stick. So I took flying lessons and made my first solo flight with Frank Tallman, who flew the plane in *The Carpetbaggers*. He was a partner of Amelia Earhart's copilot and mechanic, Paul Mantz. Anyone can learn how to fly, but the main drawback is the expense. You only need forty hours to qualify for private piloting, but by the time the picture started I already had a multi-engine rating and two hundred hours of flying time. Now I have my instrument rating and I just passed the test for a commercial license. After all the preparation, I got to the location in Ireland and learned that Fox didn't want to insure me. The film was already budgeted at six million dollars." He took another sip of bourbon. "I used a strong arm. They insured me."

A plane flew over the treetops in Central Park. He rushed to the window, ice cubes rattling in his glass, and checked it out, measuring the distance with a cocktail napkin held at arm's length. "I learned not to drink and fly. So you know I worked hard, because I *love* to drink!"

Now that *Max* has been launched, Peppard can relax. The reviews are pretty good, but it wouldn't have mattered. The things he has to say about critics are largely unprintable. They are based on personal experiences born of a career which has, from the beginning, been turbulent. First, there was the New York period: "It was right out of Tennessee Williams. Four P.M. till midnight working as a bank clerk on Wall Street. That's the loneliest place in the world, eating in the Automat at ten P.M. looking out of all those dirty glass windows at a deserted section of the city, making sixty dollars a week before taxes, dreaming all the time of getting somewhere. I lived in a cold-water flat on Bleecker Street, then on Seventy-sixth Street, then Ninety-sixth Street. I worked as a cleanup man in a motorcycle shop, then spent a year trying to get a hack license to drive a cab. When I got it, I drove one night and the next day I got a 'Lamp Unto My Feet' and never drove the cab again."

Then, the New York-to-Hollywood period, fresh from his success in the play *End as a Man* and its movie version, *The Strange One,* when he was being written up in the columns as the hottest new Actor's Studio discovery since Paul Newman. The minute you hit Hollywood from the New York school you're a man without a country. Everybody in New York accuses you of 'going Hollywood.' Everybody in Hollywood calls you a 'New York actor.' When I got there, the casting agents said, 'You're a New York actor, aren't you?' I would say, 'No, just an actor,' secretly nurturing in my heart a superior feeling because I really thought of myself as a New York actor. Well, I didn't know how hard it was to make films. It seemed to me all those bad actors in films were just lazy. Every week I'd gloat through the smugness of *The New Yorker* movie reviews, putting Hollywood down. Even laughed through the reviews in that rag, *Time*. They held the same premise I did, that Hollywood was filled with overpaid, underworked people, all turning out garbage. You can always say, if you wanna play Beethoven take more music lessons.

"Then along came *Home from the Hill*. There was nobody in the cast who was my concept of a great actor. But we spent four months of hard work and physical unpleasantry in the swamps of Louisiana and Texas, fighting off mosquitoes and water moccasins and chiggers. We worked our asses off. Vincente Minnelli had done a good job. Eleanor Parker and Bob Mitchum had done a good job. I thought George Hamilton and I had done a good job. Then the reviews came out. They were *dismissive*." He said the word like he had bitten down by accident on some strange spider. "The same people saying 'George's gone Hollywood.' Well, the truth was I had gone to Texas, Mississippi, Louisiana, every place *but* Hollywood. Nobody cared anything about the goddam agony of trying to arrive at an emotional level through personal analysis in the middle of the swamp. I felt like a man coming out of the ocean with water in his ears. I said, 'Fellas, ya lost me!' and right then, I changed my mind about critics, about movie stars, about 'going Hollywood.' "

The rest you know. The lawsuits, the divorce, the eight-room house in Beverly Hills, the well-publicized marriage to

173

Elizabeth Ashley, the terrible tinseled potboilers for lots of money. George is honest about it all. "I went into *The Subterraneans,* which I also really believed in. After that, couldn't get arrested. When I saw what a trap I was in under my MGM contract, I asked for better pictures. Instead, I got crap like *Operation Crossbow*. After *Carpetbaggers* I suddenly became a valuable property and I got lots of offers. Suddenly I was being offered $250,000 plus ten percent of the gross for outside producers. I begged to get out of my contract. They wouldn't let me. MGM treated me like a piece of real estate, so I sued them. I will *not* be told what to do. When I bailed out of *Sands of Kalihari* later, I was afraid Paramount would sue me for a million dollars, which is exactly what they did. Don't think I haven't fought for better parts. I have." This fall he'll be in New York for three months, playing a sort of Sixties beatnik in a picture called *What's So Bad About Feeling Good?* "It's a farce about this disease which hits New York and makes everybody happy," he said, trying to work up some enthusiasm. "For those of us who have been in analysis, it'll be fun."

The phone rang. "Hello? No, Elizabeth and I do *not* work together except for charity. We tried it once. It was called *The Third Day*. We don't do it anymore. . . ."

A lot of time and several drinks later, he was loosening his tie, straddling a chair backward, and pointing a finger. "I've had just enough bourbon to tell you what I think of people who sneer at what I do. It's a big mistake to think I'm making a lot of money and turning out a lot of crap. It's not always my fault. I'm the first one around who knows crap when I see it. When *The Third Day* came along, I wasn't just broke, I was up to my ears in debt. An actor's responsibility is to keep his career going, not how much art he can turn out. I've got an agent, a lawyer, a public-relations firm, a business manager, an ex-wife, two kids, and Elizabeth Ashley. Responsibilities. I also love fresh broiled Maine lobster, but I sometimes have to do without it. I've got to do what comes my way. Bear in mind, I didn't produce those pictures, I only acted in them. I'm in my middle thirties now. I'm not bitching, because I've made a lot of money. But I can do more than I've had the opportunity of doing. I can't control the opportunities.

"People say, 'Come back to Broadway where you belong.' Hell, nobody's going to offer me *Man of La Mancha* or the king in *A Lion in Winter*. I'd love to do a play if there was a playwright who wanted to write a play for me. But what's so great about Broadway? It's as hardhearted as Hollywood.

You get treated in both places according to your saleability. Most plays spend three hours on the problem of whether somebody is going to get laid or not, and you know as well as I do it's not that big a problem."

A red balloon was floating up above the trees in Central Park. Peppard looked like the basketball player again. There was a noise in the next room. "Come in here a minute, babe!" he yelled.

Elizabeth Ashley peeped around the door facing, back from an afternoon shopping trip. She looked healthy and spruce, hair in a Lana Turner head wrap. "George gets so violent," she grinned.

"There's nothing super about being an actor," he continued angrily from the liquor cabinet. "Maybe you think it's hard to have the face I have and be a serious actor. Hell, it's hard to drink as much bourbon as I do and be an actor. Because we're fantasy people as figures on the screen doesn't mean we're fantasy people. Some are undersexed, some oversexed, some lucky, some not. Laurence Olivier is in my opinion the greatest actor in the world, but he isn't always lucky. Look at what *he* turns out for money. An actor should only be judged according to what he does with the material he has. Lots of movie stars fight and scratch to get a role. I've never had the need to exercise my problems by saying, 'I'd be a better Hamlet than so-and-so.' If I played Hamlet, he'd be just like Jonas Cord in *The Carpetbaggers*—A man in a quiet little agony. I could never play Hamlet, so I don't eat my heart out worrying about it. I could have gone to Sweden and made Ingmar Bergman films. I don't worry about that either. At its least, acting is a craft, at its best it's an art. It's just a moment out of time. It's not the most important thing in my life, but it's how I make my living. So don't anybody criticize me because I was in a lot of crap! Sometimes you're lucky to even get crap!"

Peppard stormed out of the room as Miss Ashley led the way to the door. "Come in here, babe!" roared the voice from the bedroom. She smiled softly. The door closed onto the grim brick silence of the hotel-lobby corridor. As the cigar-smoking stage manager used to say to the girls in the line at Minsky's, the interview was over.

Franco Corelli

SEPTEMBER 17, 1967.

SPAGHETTI SIMMERED ON THE STOVE. But Franco Corelli, age thirty-eight, exhausted from rehearsing twelve hours a day for his appearance as Romeo, age eighteen, in Gounod's *Romeo and Juliet* at the Metropolitan Opera, was not thinking about food. Sipping his favorite drink (creme de menthe and milk) from a crystal goblet, he slumped in his easy chair, played with his tie, occasionally burst into a rapturous arpeggio, then brooded like Heathcliff. Offstage the opera tights of ancient Verona replaced by a powder-blue tailored suit, he looks like an Italian Rock Hudson. His fans call him the greatest tenor since Caruso. The bravo-shouters follow him around like the coming of a new Messiah. Impresarios pay him as much as $10,000 a performance to grace their stages, making him the highest paid tenor in the world. Women throw roses onstage when he appears. To them all he says "Pooh."

It is what Corelli thinks that matters. When he hits those high C's, he carries them all to the top of the ceiling. He knows that. He is called the king, but underneath there is the throbbing urgency of a little boy wondering, after every triumph, if he can do it again. He is torturedly self-critical. "I have many *demeriti*," he says. "I have nightmares of music. I sleep music. I see notes in my dreams. I never rest, because I am always trying to improve myself. If I have three months of absolute freedom I use them to project my technical instrument. Without that, I am nothing. Now I worry about Romeo. I have too big a stomach. Today I had a little coffee and no lunch. I spent eight hours standing. I am very tired. Even when I take an hour to rest, I study the score. French is not my language. I must also look right for Romeo. I refused to wear a blond wig. Where does it say Romeo must be blond?"

"Franco, I like you as a blond," says his wife, Loretta, the

176

ower behind the throne, the one who can handle him when nobody else can.

"No, *non molto buono*. Leslie Howard was a blond in the movie. No good." He has seen the movie five times and even invited Norma Shearer to his opening. "Also, they tell me I'm too old. Youth has nothing to do with it. Now Zefferelli makes a film with teen-agers playing Romeo and Juliet. That too young. This is a story for all ages. It's also a true story. For the feeling of it I went to Verona to visit the Capulet house. I took many photos. The house is all covered with vines and there is an enormous amount of tourists. You have to stand in line to see Juliet's tomb and then the tomb is empty. But I'm glad I went. Now I will play Romeo my way. Everybody sees him differently. Perhaps you think Romeo looks like Lex Barker. Gounod saw him noble and romantic. My Romeo will be hopelessly romantic because the music is sweet, like sugar, and also because I too am hopelessly romantic."

True? "Oh yes," says Loretta, smoking a pipe with imported Dutch tobacco, "*very* romantic."

"Romeo explodes one moment, cries the next," says Corelli, "just like me. When I told people in Italy I was coming here to do Romeo, they gasped. They see me as interpreter of more violent roles because they think of me in real life as violent."

Small wonder. In the short fifteen years he has been singing, he has developed the reputation of a monster. He once leaped off a stage in Naples and raced to a loge box to beat the hell out of someone who booed him. Annoyed onstage in Rome, he burst into a rage and drew a sword on fellow singer Boris Christoff, and not long ago, during a Met tour of *Turandot*, he bit Birgit Nilsson in the neck because she held a high note longer than he did. Nilsson wired Rudolph Bing the next day: "Cannot sing in Detroit. Have hydrophobia."

Similar stories flourish wherever he plays, yet mention the word "temperament" and the massive Corelli hands jut out like a director, framing a scene. "I give so much time to my career, to give the ticket payers their money's worth, that if someone is rude to me I am rude back. Then I get the bad reputation. Why is this? I don't smoke, or drink, or go to nightclubs. I sacrifice everything. Some singers grow up with a fantastic voice. Not me. I had never thought of singing until I was twenty-three. Singing was a hobby. My father was a shipbuilder for the Italian Navy and in Italy it is a custom that the son does the same work as the father, so I was studying

177

to be an engineer. There were four children. Nobody in m
family was musical. I sometimes heard Caruso on the radio
but I wasn't crazy about opera. Then one day I went in th
car to Florence with a friend who was to audition in a
amateur contest. As a joke, he entered my name too, an
when they heard me sing for fun they offered me thirt
dollars a month to stay and see what I could accomplish.
didn't learn anything but I went to Spoleto and sang 'Celest
Aïda' and won the biggest competition in Italy. Even the
my family don't want. 'Many beautiful voices in the worl
singing for pennies,' said my father. The technical require
ments for *Aïda* were beyond me, but I still won over all th
other tenors in Italy. So I knew it was my destiny."

Three months later, he was starring at the Rome Oper
and the following year he was appearing opposite Mari
Callas at La Scala. Today he is on top and the friend wh
entered his name in the amateur contest is a governmen
employee in Italy. And he has done it all without a lesson. "
avoided voice coaches, because everybody told me the
would ruin my voice. So I learned to sing with friends an
listening to records. I have people to teach me the scores, bu
everything else I teach myself. I did not choose or look fo
this life. It was fate. I have the eternal feeling that I am
never prepared because I was not prepared in the beginnin
and I have no training. It is a great responsibility I have. M
own specialty is that I can hold high notes a long time. They
come to see me perform and I can see them in the audienc
timing the notes with their watches. They want the maximum
from me. They come to my dressing room and say 'You hel
the last note ten seconds shorter tonight than usual, what'
wrong?' Forty-eight hours before a performance I am com
pletely alone. I speak to nobody. I watch TV. I live in hel
because I am so aware of the need to live up to what the
require of me. And still I get the bad reputation.

"Critics? Ridiculous. When I began, I had many faults, bu
they loved me. Now that I am much better they criticize every
move I make. They even write that my fan clubs disrupt my
performances. I have no fan club. I have never tried to
romance the public. I have never paid a claque to applaud
Caruso spent two hundred dollars a night for paid applause
The greats do not pay. But when the claque of one of my
divas boos me because she has paid them, I get very mad
Then I lose my temper. In Italy it's even worse."

Singers are crucified there. If a diva cracks on a high note
in Italy she has to apologize publicly in the papers for creating
un scandalo! Corelli grew up in those opera houses and he is

fraid. "The tragedy of opera is that every singer thinks he is the best singer in the world. This makes socializing difficult and jealousy is everywhere. After a glorious career of forty-two years, one of the great tenors, Giacomo Lauri-Volpi, told me, 'There is no glory in singing.' He spoke of many singers, old and new, none of them were friends. You can't have a big Otello and a little Otello who are friends, because nobody wants to be the little Otello. Many say the voice is a gift of God. But too many opera singers think they *are* God. There is the problem. When another famous singer gives me a compliment, I clap my hand over his mouth because I know the praise is insincere. I do not go to see other tenors."

But other tenors see Corelli. He has opened more seasons and played more roles in more opera houses than any other tenor. At La Scala in 1962 there was an eighteen-minute standing ovation after his duet with Joan Sutherland in *Les Huguenots,* something which had not occurred there in thirty-five years and has never happened at the Met. Next season he will open La Scala with Verdi's *Ernani* and the Met with *Adriana Lecouvreur*—making him the only tenor in the world honored by opening the same season of both houses twice in one career. And still he needs to be constantly reassured, even during intermission. Nobody is better equipped for this job than Loretta. "Don't interview me, I must cook and make his bed," she protests. But she is always by his side, taping his voice for errors, photographing him for his album covers, holding a mug of water in the wings. "I know one tenor's wife," she says, "who turns on all the water faucets backstage to drown out the sounds of her husband's voice. Santa Maria! I would rather suffer in the theater than suffer at home."

When he isn't working or studying, Corelli goes to the movies. He loves Bette Davis, is dying to meet Melina Mercouri. Joan Fontaine is one of his biggest fans. ("I told her she could have him for one week," winks Loretta, "and I guaranteed she would send him home in two days.") He likes some American pop music, "but not rock-and-roll. My records could never outsell Nancy Sinatra." He has never sung an opera in English, but once recorded "O Holy Night" for the Firestone gas stations across the country and sold a million copies. "I will never perform in a contemporary opera. About as modern as I get is Prokofiev's *War and Peace* and that was derived from the eighteenth century, so it isn't modern. But that does not mean grand opera can't be modern. A big two-hundred-pound woman standing in the center of the stage singing *Traviata* is to me ridiculous.

179

Opera is changing because we have the movies. We are going soon to the moon. Why should opera be the only thing old?"

He would like to make movies (he starred in the screen version of *Tosca* and after his Met debut was offered a Hollywood contract), but it "depends on how well I learn English and none of my friends will help me." As for the future, "I ask nothing. There is no need for illusions. Some live for the applause. Not me. If the day comes when the public does not respond with applause I will not feel any different. I don't want it if I'm good or not, only if I'm good. There is no glory in singing. When the strain gets bad over the years, a singer's career stops. Even now I go onstage and my hands turn to ice, I tremble and my knees give way. A man can get eight or ten more years out of a career than a woman. Some tenors sing up into their sixties, but sopranos never. Caruso and Gigli both died with their voices still strong. I know now when I am good and I know when I am bad. I also hope I will know when to retire."

Dinner was served, but Corelli's mood was somber. "I stay out of drafts, I don't go with women. That was the ruin for many singers, not me. For five years I've been very good and still I get the bad reputation. I think now I will start being bad and see what happens." Bristling uncomfortably at the horror of such a thought, everybody ate in silence. Then, as quickly as it had been summoned, the storm cloud passed over his face and the Phantom of the Opera seemed, once again, just like any other happy Italian—passionately attacking his bowl of spaghetti.

Gwen Verdon

FEBRUARY 6, 1966.

THERE ARE SOME PERFORMERS, rare as blue butterflies, who carry around their own lightning. It has nothing to do with the color of their skin, or how many octaves they can sing, or how many times they've played *Hamlet*. When the footlights hit them, *sock*. It comes across. It's a special ift, intangible, which bridges the gap between adequacy and greatness. To define it borders on betrayal, but Jolson had it, and Fanny Brice, Chaplin and Garland. And this tall, freckled girl with "big bones and long muscles" and a head of hair that looks like a tomato surprise that just exploded, named Gwyneth Evelyn Verdon.

Enchantment. That's what she's selling in *Sweet Charity* over at the Palace these nights. And everybody's buying, from the ghosts of Nora Bayes and Houdini up in the flyloft to the critics out front. Well, maybe a few critic-type people were less than jubilant about the show itself (if only musicals didn't have to have books), but they all bought Verdon. There was even a lawsuit over opening-night tickets, one man wanted in so bad. I don't blame him. When she waddles out on the stage as Charity Hope Valentine, the Ginger Rogers of the Fan Dango Ballroom, her little chin stepped on by the world but still held high, her heart a hotel men walk through as regularly as the eleven-o'clock news, with a little red heart tattooed on one arm and a shoulder-strap Lois Lane purse hanging on the other, she melts hearts. After a five-year absence from the Broadway stage, the kicks may not be quite as high as Lola's (she is forty years old now, and a grandmother) but the Verdon brand of dazzle still casts a lovely light.

If there is still any doubt about her durability as a star, ask the chorus. That is, if you can get their attention. There is such a close family feeling in *Charity* that cast members are "insiders," all others are "outsiders," and rarely do the twain meet. Dropping by the theater one afternoon, I found the chorus glued in the wings, watching the star rehearse like proud parents at a PTA meeting. Out on the stage, Gwen hopscotched through her paces, flinging her legs about in leotards and paratrooper boots like a Raggedy Ann doll coming apart at the seams. Her father, who flew in from California for the opening, was serving coffee from a Broadway delicatessen. The camaraderie seemed unreal: no temperaments, no fiery glances, no inflated egos. (As Gwen's standby, Helen Gallagher, jokes: "The company that drinks together, stays together.") The star finished her number, bowed to the applauding electricians, stopped to exchange a few dirty jokes with the dancers, then led the way down a narrow flight of stairs to her dressing room, which she designed herself in shades of "Army khaki green."

She wrapped a mink coat around her rehearsal pants ("I'm sick so much of the time, I don't want to catch cold"), ran fingers through her hoydenish hair ("Please don't write about my 'flame-colored tresses' ") lit up a cigarette (she chain-smokes), and sprawled on her chaise longue, while her husband and the show's director, Bob Fosse, sat in a little Victorian chair reading *Variety*.

"Everybody wants to know what I've been up to since *Redhead*. Well, let's see. I got married and did some TV and took dance lessons from Cyd Charisse's sister-in-law and had a baby, named Nicole Providence, who'll be three in March. I had all this stomach trouble, and two of the biggest specialists in New York treated me for ulcers and hepatitis and all the time I was only pregnant. Gee, it makes you wonder about doctors, right? Then one night we had nothing to do so we went to see that Fellini film, *Nights of Cabiria*. Well, I just hated it—so depressing—but Bob, he's the movie buff in the family—remember him in the old MGM musicals?—he just loved it. He couldn't sleep. So he woke me up at six A.M. with a nine-page Americanization of it and he got me all stirred up. We changed her from a prostitute to a dance-hall hostess, because in New York the whores are either elegant with posh lives, then nobody would have any sympathy, or they're bums, then nobody would care. I guess people will compare me with Giulietta Massina, or be disappointed because the show has an unhappy ending. American audiences always want you to get the fella and eight kids in Scarsdale, but how many people actually end up that way?

"We went to a dance hall to observe the girls. They still wear the old Lana Turner hairdos and wedgie shoes. Forty-five-year-old gals dressing like it was 1942. Boy, are they tough. One saw me eyeing her and she said, 'What are you starin' at, sister?' Bob used what he saw. He's a Method choreographer. He works the dances out of the characters. You know, he went to school with Brando and Jimmy Dean on the GI Bill. We've been working sixteen hours a day on the show, but now we're not going to do anything for a while except stay home with the baby. She's already a show-business veteran, travels back and forth with us to the Coast, and loves to stay at the Beverly Hills Hotel. The first word she ever said was 'bellboy.' "

Gwen throws herself into her work so completely that she usually collapses at least once during each run. At her age, the pace isn't easy. Between acts, she adds energy by drinking beef bouillion with soda crackers and two tablespoons of cottage cheese ("Lots of potassium, you know"), and takes a special-formula vitamin pill that Cornell University made up for pilots on bombing missions during the war "to keep the fat built up on the nerve ends." She loves working for her husband because "he doesn't boss me around. Of course it's bad, too, because when we go home at night we take the show with us. We usually rehearse in Dinty Moore's kitchen while they fold up the tables and do the dirty dishes after closing. They know us so well there, they even keep food in the refrigerator for us. Some of my best numbers through the years have been choreographed in there in the wee hours of the night."

Though she has been dancing since the age of two, she has never been stagestruck. "I had a crush on Fred Astaire, but I only met him once, and I never got to dance with him. Of course the reason MGM hired Bob was because he looked like Astaire, so in a way I got him after all. Did you know he was the first Dobie Gillis?" Fosse peered over the top of his *Variety* and frowned. "Then there was Chaplin. I still dream about him sometimes. I dreamed the other night he brought me a daisy." She grinned shyly and her face lit up bright red as she hugged her knees.

Gwen Verdon does not sound like a star. But she never lived like one, either. Her background might stagger the imagination of a writer of class B movie melodramas. Born in a twelve-dollar-a-month bungalow in Culver City, near the MGM studios. Her father was an ex-gardener from England who worked as a studio electrician. Her mother was a combination bank clerk-ballerina who named Gwen after a London woman who outraged her family by marrying a Chinese opium smuggler, then committed suicide by leaping into the Thames. Gwen had rickets as a child, plus a series of other diseases following a hernia operation at the age of two which left her, she says, "gimped." She was so knock-kneed and pigeon-toed she wore ugly, corrective-therapy boots and the other kids called her "Boots Verdon."

Her mother died in 1955, but Gwen still remembers the day she tore up the doctor's letter that said both of Gwen's legs would have to be broken and reset to straighten them. "She wanted me to be a great dancer more than anything. She would say, 'That child is like a wild sunset. She *will* dance!' I danced." Gwen enrolled in a class taught by Marge Champion's father, learned the buck-and-wing and the waltz clog, and at the age of three, entertained at the big MGM Christmas party thrown by Marion Davies. At six, she was billed as the "fastest little tapper in the world" at the Shrine Auditorium. At thirteen, her measurements were already 36-24-36. At fifteen, clad in a thin rubber bra, panties, and a mixture of gold powder and glycerine applied nightly by her mother, she danced at a place called the Florentine Gardens

183

with two other unknowns named Lili St. Cyr and Yvonne De Carlo. At sixteen, she married Jim Henaghan, a minor gossip columnist and a member of Louella Parson's staff. There was one son, Jimmy, twenty-two, a Hollywood TV actor and father of Gwen's grandchild. Her marriage lasted five years, during which she gave up dancing (to her mother's horror), scrubbed floors, and followed her husband around, often writing his column for him and spending lots of lonely evenings sitting in cheap burlesque houses watching the baggy-pants clowns, from whom much of her present dancing style originates.

Then there was her unhappy movie period, when she assisted choreographer Jack Cole in teaching the screen's glamorous but awkwardly earthbound first ladies to appear to be talented. She was Monroe's torso, Hayworth's feet, and Grable's rear view. Then she would stand aside and watch them get the gravy in the close-ups. In *David and Bathsheba* she was cut in the South because she was an Egyptian Negress dancing for a white man ("It was the Bible, what could I do?"). In *Gentlemen Marry Brunettes* she was in competition with Jane Russell and the Eiffel Tower. ("Guess who lost?") Sandwiched between were chores staging at the Lido in Paris ("Easy job; when in doubt, just bring on the nudes") and bits in two Broadway shows—*Bonanza Bound*, the only Comden-Green musical to post its closing notice between the first and second acts in Philadelphia; and *Alive and Kicking*, in which she danced with her boss, Jack Cole. The critics were hardly aware of her big Broadway debut, but Brooks Atkinson did note the next morning that the easiest way to remain invisible was to dance with Cole on the same stage. Fighting tears, she headed back to Hollywood to teach Monroe how to bump and grind.

It was the last time she was invisible. Her next show, in 1953, was *Can-Can*. More problems. Lilo had Gwen's numbers cut from seven to four, arranged to have her offstage at the end of three of them so there would be no applause, and managed the curtain calls so that she was upstage behind a bench. "I was so unhappy I wanted out. By the time we opened all I remember saying was 'Oh Boris!' eight times and 'What's on the menu?' I don't really blame Lilo. She was the star and I was stealing the show. In the theater, that's like another woman in a marriage triangle." But on opening night, the audience stopped the show cold, screaming for Verdon. Michael Kidd ran around the side of the building and through the stage door to get to Gwen's dressing room, pulled her onstage in a towel, and as one *Can-Can* dancer calls, "The only sound louder than the audience stomping feet was Lilo gnashing her teeth in the wings."

Gwen laughs about it all now, but she doubts if she will er make another Hollywood movie. "Their idea of a movie ar is a gal with big bosoms who can do a couple of chorus cks. Besides, I'm not box office. Who'd pay to see me in a ovie?" Since she has passed up most of the stars she once orked for (more awards than you can count, and one of e few dancers to ever appear on the cover of *Time*) a few ave come backstage. Marilyn Monroe used to hide from the ess in her dressing room, or drop by on her way to the ctor's Studio. She is very fond of Grable, says she "is the ily one who never let them cut my numbers. I taught her w to dance in a potato sack with pie plates on her feet. ie always said 'Don't give Gwen the leak light,' meaning the ght from the star's spot that might spill over on the next rl. She always made sure I was lit properly."

Gwen does not think she is sexy. "I kid sex. Why, the Lola imber in *Damn Yankees* was staged right down to the inute I touched my hair. The really sexy girls have got it d they don't have to put up billboards to let you know iey've got it. I used to tell Mitzi Gaynor and Marilyn to get it there as though they were saying, 'Stand back, boys, ou're looking at a woman.'

"I have never tried to analyze my popularity. I don't even ke to read about it. Carol Haney once told me, 'Gwen, the ublic has given me a reputation for being gamin and ador- ble and now when I try to be gamin and adorable what used be little gestures onstage are as big as elephants.' I've ever wanted to be anything special. As a child, my pop ould come home and tell me all about the big stars he had t that day at MGM, but all I ever wanted to hear about ere the monkeys in the Tarzan movies. It's the same now. : takes me a long time, but once I decide to do something I y so hard to be perfect that I am never satisfied. It's not mbition, because I do carpentry and I approach it the same ay. It's a character flaw."

She did her bantam-rooster walk across the room and niled her incendiary grin as she pointed to the gold lettering n her dressing-room door. "They even took down the piece f paper stuck up with Scotch tape and put my name in gold tters. I guess they think I'm going to be around awhile."

The mob scene clamoring for tickets in front of the alace gives evidence that nobody ever doubted it. There iould be a better way to welcome Gwen Verdon back to roadway, where enchantment belongs, but as the man in the

box office counting the money says: "There ain't enou[gh]
confetti in the city of New York to do the job up prope[rly].
Amen.

Geraldine Chaplin

DECEMBER, 1965.

THE PAST YEAR has seen the world saturated with t[he]
starry-eyed doings of a willowy wisp of a girl named Geral[d]-
ine Chaplin. Her photo stares out at you from practical[ly]
every coffee table in America. From the *Dr. Zhivago* set [in]
Madrid hard-nosed reporters have swarmed like swamp l[o]-
custs around her dressing room waiting for her just to s[ay]
good morning. Newspapers and magazines record her eve[ry]
sigh. Geraldine Chaplin gypsy dancing at the Feria de Sevill[e].
Geraldine Chaplin presented to society in a white Castill[ian]
gown by the Aga Khan. Geraldine Chaplin parachut[e]
jumping. Geraldine Chaplin having a bull dedicated by [El]
Cordobés in the bullring. Geraldine Chaplin in Lebano[n]
gowned by Ricci, getting more attention in the slick maga[-]
zines than Jean Shrimpton. It's Geraldine Chaplin all th[e]
way: swimming at Monte Carlo, frugging at the Piper Clu[b]
in Rome, living it up as the darling of the jet set. And wh[y]
not? When you're the daughter of Charlie Chaplin and th[e]
granddaughter of Eugene O'Neill, a girl has to do som[e]
thing!
More incredible than the vast amount of publicity she ha[s]
received, however, is the fact that she has yet to be seen o[n]
the screen earning it (what if the girl can't act, Virginia?),
fact which has Geraldine herself a little more than worrie[d].
In New York a few days ago to publicize the opening [of]
Zhivago, the Chaplin girl took time off from the wearyin[g]
routine of blowing a trumpet for a ten-million-dollar movi[e]
to let her hair down and speak of more serious matters. Lik[e]
her life, and what will become of her if her acting fails t[o]
impress the world, to which she has already been overex[-]
posed.
Orange sunbeams darted off the gilt-edge mirrors on th[e]
186

rupy beige walls of her suite on the thirty-eighth floor of
e Waldorf Towers ("All this space just for me, and a
tchen, too"). Three dozen scarlet roses popped and bulged
om vases ("They were so lovely, but they keep it so hot in
re they just burst open from exhaustion," she informs her
est). Nowhere to be seen is the publicity man's make-
lieve about-to-be movie starlet. Instead, the real girl paces
rvously on the beige carpet, occasionally jumping in the air
th glee, giggling girlishly, racing to the window to exclaim
ver a helicopter that cruises the Manhattan skyline, gurgling
it something that sounds suspiciously like "Gollygumgee,"
d finally flopping in the corner of the room, her arms
rapped around the back of her head and her coltish legs
anging over the edge of a lemony Waldorf sofa in their
hite vinyl pop-art boots.

In person, she is not really pretty; her face is too round,
er forehead is too wide, her hair is too long and tied with a
ondescript rubber band, her lips are too pale (she wears no
akeup except eyeliner), and two unusual black moles ap-
ear prominently under her eyes. Watching her brings visions
f bubble gum (which she chews constantly) and lemon
rops, of little girls in dotted Swiss dresses ordering Shirley
emple sodas in Sardi's.

When she talks, it is another matter. She is frank, open
nd bright and, like an overindulged child who has just helped
erself to an extra piece of forbidden fudge, a wee bit pre-
ocious. "I know I've gotten everything because I'm Charlie
haplin's daughter, but I'm not ashamed. Why shouldn't I
ake advantage of it? When I first left home to become a
allerina, I was terrible, but I ended up on the front pages.
nly one of twenty little dancers in the chorus of *Cinderella*,
ut you'd have thought I was Pavlova. Sure, they were
xploiting me. My father was furious! Now that I have
ecided to be an actress, I get more offers than I can
anage. If my name was Annie Smith, I would have noth-
g. But nobody ever said this was an honest business. Be-
ause of my name, the right doors opened. Now it is up to
e to make it pay off."

Looking back, it seems to have paid off from the begin-
ing. She was born in Santa Monica, California, on July 31,
944. Although she insists she looks like her father, she more
losely resembles her mother, the former Oona O'Neill,
whose marriage to Chaplin was strongly protested by her
wn father because she was only eighteen and the famous
ilm star was fifty-five. Geraldine ("Friends call me Deanie,
which all started because my little sister Josie couldn't

187

pronounce Geraldine") spent the first eight years of her life i
a rambling mansion in Beverly Hills. She remembers almo
nothing except a wishing tree in the back yard. When she wa
seven and her brother Michael was five, both children wei
extras in Chaplin's film *Limelight*.

"I suppose that was really my professional debut, but
only had one line. In the scene I see my father coming dow
the street drunk, see, and I say, 'Mrs. Allsop is out.' My litt
sister Josie was only two and she kept following me aroun
the movie set and every time I would say my line she woul
say it too. We did the scene about fifty times and finally,
just screamed, 'Daddy, Mrs. Allsop is *out,* for Pete's sake
He never used me after that."

By the time she was eight, a combination of income-ta
problems and unpopular political sentiments had cause
Chaplin and America to fall out of love with each other, s
the family moved to a big country house in Vevey, Switze
land, where they have lived ever since. America would lov
to have them back now, but Chaplin has refused to retur
"He is not bitter about being called a Communist, or abou
the way America treated him, so why should I be? I woul
be silly to say I hate America because of what happened t
him," says Geraldine.

For an eight-year-old American child, it was quite
change to be carted off to Europe. "Michael and I went t
the village school where nobody—even the teachers—spok
English, and we couldn't even say 'Bonjour' in French. It wa
awful, but we learned the language in five months. We ha
to. I can now speak five languages. But at home everythin
remained American. We were brought up on chewing gun
and hamburgers and regular hours—lunch at noon, dinner a
six. At Halloween we dressed up like witches and on Chris
mas we hung up our stockings. It was a strange life, and th
Europeans thought we were all crazy. The crazy Chaplins i
the big house on the hill, they called us. We had no friends
only our animals—two wolves, badgers, mice, a crow, ai
eagle, a fox, two crocodiles, and a pet rat named Rodney. H
was a big ugly sewer rat who lived in a drawer and ate raw
eggs and salad. If the doorbell rang, he'd be the first one a
the door. I loved him the best."

When Geraldine was ten, her father sent her away to a
convent. ("Daddy is a fanatic for discipline.") For the nex
seven years, she spent very little time at home. "When I wa
seventeen, I left for good. I've been making my own mone
ever since. I get nothing from home. What I do is m
business. Of course my father always complains. He gave m
188

lecture when I went away to study dancing in London, he
lectured when I got my apartment in Paris, I suppose he'll
have another lecture prepared when I get home after the
opening of *Zhivago* in New York. He never *ever* writes
letters or telephones me, but I hear it all through
Mummy."

Geraldine studied ballet for two years in London, lived
with a Polish family until her money ran out, moved to Paris,
where her brother Sydney's wife, Noelle Adam, introduced
her to a movie agent who got her a small part in a Jean Paul
Belmondo movie called *A Beautiful Summer Morning*. It has
never been released in America and she calls it "one of the
worst movies ever made. If David Lean had seen it, I would
never have gotten a part in *Zhivago* or anything else."

During the Paris period, she lived in a dark basement
pied-a-terre with a six-foot python named Emma, which she
finally gave to a zoo. ("She wouldn't eat anything but live
mice, which I had to feed to her by hand, so I finally had to
give her up.") She still keeps the room ("I only sleep there")
but either travels home to Switzerland or stays with her
brother Sydney in Paris when she is not working. "I go home
more than I used to. There are eight of us kids, so far. I say
so far because with my parents there could be another one
any time. When I go home, all the kids get out of school and
the whole family comes down to the station to meet me. I
spend most of my time changing diapers and drinking Cokes
and talking to Mummy about my life. And I get a lot of
sleep. Daddy makes everyone go to bed by nine."

Geraldine has a dual citizenship, American and British, but
cannot vote in a foreign election. She has very few friends in
films, one reason being "I fall in love with all the actors I
meet. First, it was Marlon Brando. I still have a crush on
him. Then Belmondo. Now it's Omar Sharif. When he walked
on the *Zhivago* set in Spain, I took one look and said, 'I can't
act with that man. He's too gorgeous!'" Another reason is
that she is too serious to take actors seriously. She has, for
instance, more than three hundred records, and only one is
by the Beatles. Her tastes run more to Sibelius and Bach, and
she'd rather read Katherine Mansfield than Ian Fleming. "I'm
really not the interesting person all the columnists say I
am."

For someone who claims to be dull, she does some fascinat-
ingly offbeat things. Like parachute-jumping. "That's my
favorite sport. I learned in Oxford. Not the tacky Army
parachutes that look like camouflage. A girl could break her
neck that way. I mean the lovely feminine chutes that whiz

189

down. Your mind goes, your body goes, life and death do
matter. I gave it up finally, after landing in the middle of
highway with cars going by in both directions."

Recently a surgeon friend had her disinfected and dress
in a very unglamorous sterile mask while she watched h
first lung operation. "Men faint, girls don't. I just stood the
holding someone's hand for support; it turned out to be t
patient's. It was so beautiful. I could see his heart beati
and once the blood spurted right up toward the ceiling. (
course I couldn't eat meat for a month. They removed a lu
and a rib, just lying right out on the floor, and then t
patient woke up squeezing my hand and I could hardly s
him for the tears. I cried my eyes out. It was more thrillin
and moving than any play acting on the screen."

Whether these interests are phases or part of the real gi
nobody knows. But Geraldine is adamant on the thing th
interests her most—her career. "Listen," she says, her Si
mese-cat eyes narrowing pointedly, "for 20 years I was noth
ing except 'Charlie Chaplin's little girl.' Now I live m
own life and I have my own chance. It is the be all an
end all for me right now. When you are a child in th
Chaplin house everything is easy. But when you make you
own decisions it's different. When my brother Michael mar
ried a woman eight years older than himself with two chi
dren, Daddy went into hysterics. When I went off to Londo
to live on my own instead of going to college, Daddy ha
hysterics. He'll probably have hysterics again when my littl
sister leaves home. But he has Mummy, and they are ver
much in love. And please remember, he is seventy-seve
years old. We live on two completely different planets. S
you see, I have to make good. I never think is this the righ
thing or isn't it. When you start that nonsense you never hav
any peace. I just follow my instincts. Daddy has never see
anything I've done, but he is the best critic I have. He ha
taught me how to tear down a character. 'Slug your guts ou
is his philosophy of acting. Never mind the talent, just wor
hard. As long as he's around to teach me, I'll never stud
acting. Who could ask for a better teacher than Charli
Chaplin?"

As for *Zhivago,* she insists that Julie Christie steals th
film. "She's today, so modern. Of course everyone in the film
helped me. They knew I was unsure, nervous. David Lear
would whisper in my ear, 'Of course I'm probably wrong, bu
try it this way,' and when it's right he makes you think you
had all the ideas yourself. I called everyone 'Sir,' even the
script girl. Alec Guinness would take me aside and say,

Relax, old girl.' I was prepared for horror after growing up hearing my father talk about film people. But there was no tension, no bitchiness."

Even before the film had been released, before she had even proved herself as an actress, the solid-gold Hollywood forefinger was beckoning. Geraldine looked down at her knobby knees peeking inquisitively out from under her Baby Doll dress. "What if I'm bad, I mean not just adequate, but really *bad*? What if Charlie Chaplin's daughter cannot act and cannot communicate?" Then she smiled a smile so rapturous that the roses nodded in their vases and the room appeared to turn two shades lighter in color. In that instant, it just didn't seem to matter.

Leslie Uggams

MAY, 1967.

BEFORE *HALLELUJAH BABY!* OPENED on Broadway, one of Leslie Uggams' friends remarked: "How can she possibly play a Negro; she's never *been* one." At a time when it is considered an insult to show-biz liberalism to make even the most obvious references to race (they'll be telling us next that Anna May Wong wasn't really Chinese—she was just a strange lady with slanted eyes who liked to hide behind spiderwebs), it still sounded like a bitchy thing to say. But it is partially true.

Onstage, she stops the show by flashing her Lena Horne teeth, shaking her Vidal Sassoon haircut like a dustmop, and tugging out brassy songs disguised as all the poor little Negro girls in history—here a kitchen maid doing white folks' ironing, there a Congo cutie in a Harlem chorus line, everywhere clawing her way out of the hole. But in Leslie's real life there was never any hole to claw her way out of. She never climbed up out of the slums like Ethel Waters did; she grew up in a nice middle-class family on a nice block on a nice street in Washington Heights. She was not an unhappy child, laden with racial guilts; by the time she was eighteen, she had bought her own car, opened her own checking accounts, and owned her own credit cards. She never had to sing in Harlem dives like Billy Holiday did, she became an instant star on Mitch Miller's TV show and never left the top. When she married a white man nobody yelled "Scandal!" the way they did at Lena Horne and Pearl Bailey. In *Hallelujah Baby!* a white actor (Allen Case) tells her he loves her, yet nobody has threatened her, sent her hate mail, or jeered her in the street, the way they treated Diahann Carroll when Richard Kiley kissed her in *No Strings*.

Times have changed and several times a day Leslie Uggams looks into the mirror and tells herself, "You're lucky." She said it again the day after she read her own personal review for *Hallelujah Baby!* She said it pacing up and down in her elegant, high-ceilinged, eight-room apartment on Central Park West which she found without any of the problems Harry Belafonte had finding his. She lives there with her husband, Grahame Pratt, a Wall Street broker, a seventeenth-century harpsichord, some tomato-soup-colored carpets, and practically no furniture. She sat at the end of a long, empty room, leafing through a cookbook for a salad recipe for dinner, with the wind blowing around the eaves of the building. The windows rattled and her bodyguard, Thor, a Great Dane the size of a small automobile, occasionally took large bites of our knees and shoes as we talked. "I grew up in four rooms all my life. Now eight are not enough. We want to buy a brownstone. I guess people never stop wanting more, do they? My own life has been an easy one, though. We weren't millionaires, but the ends always met. My father was an elevator operator and professional floor-waxer. He still is. He runs an elevator on Park Avenue and refuses to give it up. He's very independent, but he's very proud of me. He's quite a celebrity in his building. He sang with the Hall Johnson Choir once, but he quit just before they became famous. My mother was a waitress and she took care of white people's children, then later she became a dancer at the Cotton Club in Harlem when Lena Horne was in the line. So *Hallelujah Baby!* does not really reflect my own life much, but my parents told me a lot of things when I was young, so it was easy for me to understand Georgina, the character I play. The Negro woman has been the Rock of Gibraltar a long time, while the Negro men were often stripped of their pride. My parents have been married almost thirty years and they are very happy, but my boyfriend in the play is still a lot like my own father. He was a porter on a train for years and fought to get a union going. You should hear his tales! Luckily I was saved from all that."

192

She thought a moment. If there was ever a time when she experienced bigotry firsthand, she couldn't remember it. In 1962, when the House Labor Committee held hearings on racial discrimination, she said, "I've really found very little resistance." It's true. When she was six, she was already stealing scenes from Ethel Waters on *Beulah*. From the start, she was treated well. "They wanted me to wear my hair in those terrible little pickaninny braids all over my head and Ethel Waters said absolutely not and she combed my hair long with two tiny bows."

She was one of the kids on Milton Berle's show and sang with the Billy Williams Quartet on the Sid Caesar-Imogene Coca hour. At twelve, she became "gawky and skinny," her voice changed and she retired. "It looked like the end." At school, she was editor of the year book and president of the student body in the same class with Brandon DeWilde, Olympic ice skater Carol Heiss, Herman Shumlin's daughter, Mary Martin's daughter. Most of them got married and had babies. Leslie plunged on. At fourteen, she sent in a list of songs to *Name That Tune*. One night at dinner the man on TV announced to a contestant: "Next week you will appear with your partner, Leslie Uggams." She grabbed her coat, got her hat, directed her feet to the sunny side of the street, and won $25,000. "It was like a scene from a bad movie with all the neighbors opening their windows and shouting 'We saw you on TV.' It made me happy because I knew I could go to college now and study psychology, but by the time I was old enough I was already a regular on Mitch Miller and I could afford it anyway."

Miller saw her on TV and got her a record contract. Then she became a star on his schmaltzy sing-along series as a kind of Sepia-tone Shirley Temple. The image bugged her. 'I was dying to bust out and do something wild and sexy. Even after I was twenty-one, people would still come up to me and say, Aren't you just a child, dear? Shouldn't you wear high necks with Peter Pan collars?' " She finally did break the mold, almost before she was old enough to be fingerprinted by the New York police, at the Copacabana, where she sang "all the sexy songs Mitch Miller wouldn't let me do" while a huge animated portrait of Mitch blushed bright red in the background.

She went to Australia two years ago, still breaking in the new sexy-broad nightclub image, and one night a young man came backstage and asked her and her parents to have a drink with him. "No," said Leslie, while her parents nodded "Yes, we'd love to" in the background. The young man drove

too fast, made a U-turn in the middle of the street, scare
Leslie to death. "Well, I'm glad we'll never see that m
again," she said in the safety of their hotel. The next after
noon he staged his own one-man sit-in and they were marrie
the following October. There had been several boyfriends an
the papers had already rumored she would marry Billy Eck
stine's son. When she announced her engagement, her fathe
didn't yell, "But he's a *white* man!" He said, "Oh no, no
again." Even the Negro press was kind. The headlines i
America read: "Leslie Uggams marries Australian Man."

About this time Arthur Laurents was writing *Halleluja
Baby!* for Lena Horne. Betty Comden and Adolph Gree
wrote songs for Lena Horne. The costumes were designed fo
Lena Horne. Everybody was ready to go but Lena, wh
walked out on the whole project. Enter Leslie Uggams. "
had no experience, except in *I Spy* with Bill Cosby and
little stock. They were considering Dionne Warwick.
couldn't believe it when I got the part." The ghost of Len
still overshadows every moment of the show, but Lesli
refuses to let it worry her. "I never thought of Lena at all.
mean, this was a very big thing and I had enough to worr
about without worrying how Lena Horne would do it. I ha
met her, of course. There is no Negro woman in the worl
not aware of her, but I'm not like her. She smolders and set
you on fire, I use more comedy and the voice is not th
same. We are sorority sisters—when I joined the Negr
sorority, Delta Sigma Theta, she pinned me. She's great, bu
I don't want to be another anybody.

"If you are a Negro, they love to label you. Diahan
Carroll was called another Lena too, at first. In this busines
you're automatically either another Dorothy Dandridge o
another Lena. But times are changing for us all. When
grew up there was only one Negro ballplayer, one Negro
superstar, one Negro this, one Negro that. The stage is gettin
more aggressive, but not movies. I was in one once, *Tw
Weeks in Another Town*. Of course you don't remember me
I was the chick in the feathers who sang while Kirk Dougla
talked to Cyd Charisse. I'll never do that again. I want to
play the South too, but I won't. When Diahann Carroll and
Bobby Hooks came back from filming *Hurry Sundown* in
Louisiana, they told me about it. Nobody is going to tell me
where I can go and can't go. I'd get lynched for sure
because I'm so hotheaded."

Suddenly she remembered. There *had* been a time when
somebody treated her badly. "I haven't thought of this in a
long time. I was on a kiddie talent show, one of those things
194

with the audience-applause meter, and if you won five times in a row, you won a car. A little Negro boy won the week before, so when I went on they weren't about to give it to two Negroes in a row. I sang and they cheered so loud that the applause meter would have broken, but my mother stood backstage and watched them tie the clock back. All my relatives were watching and I had to explain why I didn't win when I really *did* win. I cried and cried. My mother looked me in the eye and said, 'We *never* cry.'"

She walked to the door in her floor-length, pop-art, red-fuchsia-purple-yellow-orange-chiffon gown, a full-fledged Broadway star who looked like she had never heard of a Peter Pan collar. She opened the door while Thor threatened to tear the visitor into shreds at the slightest wrong move. "I've always been a very determined girl. I'm not a good loser and I do not accept defeat. Tying that clock didn't stop what I was going to do with my life one bit. I never cried again."

Bill Cosby

IT'S SUNDAY AT MIDNIGHT, when most people in the world are asleep. But at the Flamingo Hotel in Las Vegas, Bill Cosby is getting ready to go to work. Out in the lobby a secretary from Des Moines, Iowa, tells her friend: "I don't care if he *is* a Negro; he's the sexiest man on TV." It's a reputation Cosby has built quietly and unobtrusively, from his days as an Ivy League ballplayer at Philadelphia's Temple University to his Emmy-award-winning role in *I Spy* as the first Negro man to ever star in an acting role on his own series. Cosby doesn't mind a bit. "Hell, they gotta look at something."

For this night on the Vegas Strip, it seems like they've all come to town just to look at *him*. Twelve million people a year crowd into Vegas to gamble and take in the shows (so many that the casino operators joke, "If you don't gamble, you're ahead of even us") and it seems like half of this year's quota is standing in the Flamingo lobby, waiting for reserva-

tions to Cosby's show. The ones who get in are never disap
pointed. A lifetime of taking the white man's knocks has lef
most Negro performers with chips on their shoulders. No
Cosby. His act, which nets him an additional $25,000 a week
to add to the six-figure salary he gets for filming *I Spy,* is wr
and funny and nonracial. "People," he says, "accept m
because I'm not controversial. Most of them don't even think
of me as a Negro. When I first began telling racial jokes, the
Negroes looked at the whites, the whites looked at the
Negroes, and nobody laughed, so I had to tell all the joke:
over again. I was beginning to sound like a P.R. man for Dick
Gregory." So he dropped the salt-and-pepper gags and made
his own world come alive onstage, telling stories about the
poor little outcast saber-toothed tiger who lisps because he
only has one saber. Or the Wolf Man who tells his barber
"Just a light trim around the legs." Or Noah, hearing the
voice of God telling him to build the Ark: "C'mon, man, who
is this *really?* Am I on *Candid Camera?*" Even when bigotry
occasionally creeps in, it's funny. Talking about a whit
childhood bully, he tells the audience: "I went to grea
lengths to make friends—even let him drink out of my
orange-soda bottle without wiping it off."

The audience laps it up. They file out into the casino, stil
laughing, past the keno players, roulette wheels, and one-
armed bandits. Chandeliers bounce white heat off ebony wall:
while jazz combos play show tunes and everywhere there is
the deafening sound of silver dollars crashing into piles from
chrome-plated slot machines. Backstage, the women gather
in their minks and sequins—pregnant wives whose husbands
wait for them sheepishly near the blackjack tables, airline
stewardesses waiting to catch the late night flight back to Los
Angeles, shy secretaries on vacation from their routine office
jobs, soaking up a little wickedness and giggling to each other
about it. All waiting for Cosby, who is inside his dressing
room soaking wet from the stage lights and the hot Nevada
night. Sitting with him are Mel Tormé's wife, Jan, who has
dropped over during Mel's show at the Hacienda to say
hello; a music publisher from Los Angeles named Joe
Shribman, who is also Rosemary Clooney's manager; and a
Vegas character named "Big John" Hopkins, a Herculean
ex-fighter who acts as Sammy Davis' road manager. Sammy
is taking the night off from his own show at the Sands and
Big John is playing Cosby's "bodyguard" for the evening.
Pandemonium reigns. Engaging Cosby in conversation is a
decidedly cluttered affair. He bolts. He leaps. He talks about
three topics at once. "My wife isn't here tonight . . . must
196

l her . . . How is Mel's show doing? . . . Do you think
yone was offended by that joke where I teach the praying
antis to become an agnostic? . . . Let's" catch the Ritz
others at 2:30. . . . Is the car out front? . . ."

I hadn't noticed one Negro girl in the mob outside, so I
ked him if it bothered him, having so many white girls
aiting for him each night? "Hell no, it should've happened a
ng time ago. Not just to me, but to the whole race setup. I'm
t the physically attractive kind of guy movie stars should
, you know?—although Belmondo isn't either and he's sexy
hell—but I mean it should've happened back with
elafonte and Sidney Poitier. It's funny, but psychologically
just didn't happen. Those guys still play Negroes when they
t, but I refuse to do that. In order for a man to become a
x symbol, a woman must like him, dig? On *I Spy* I'm a
nnis bum who is really an undercover spy. I don't sing, tap
ance, juggle, or say 'Sir.' I'm not a Rochester. This guy
play likes women—redheads, blondes, all kinds—he's a
hole human being. For the first time, a black man sees a
oman and wants to make love, to treat her beautifully the
ay a woman should be treated by any man. And it's not
one like a black man loving a white woman. Just a man,
eriod. Now how can black people watch only white people
ake love? That's an illusion wrongly created by Hollywood
p to now and I hope to change it."

He's done a pretty good job so far. He broke ground
here not even Lena Horne, Nat King Cole, or Sammy
Davis could tread, and *Variety* named him TV's Jackie
Robinson. At first, he was slated to play the familiar role of
olored second banana to the show's white star, Robert Culp,
ut the two men developed such a fondness for each other
hat Culp demanded Cosby's role be upgraded. The drive for
ivil rights gave extra acceleration to the need for a new
Negro "image" and Cosby's own warmth and lack of antag-
nism toward what Negroes often nastily call the "Mister
harlies" of the world made him a natural candidate. The
how has clicked to the tune of top ratings, Cosby is making
lmost enough money a year to repay the National Debt, his
ecord sales have tripled, his nightclub appearances are now
old out weeks in advance, he is more in demand for guest
ppearances on TV variety shows than ever before, and
Hollywood is writing scripts geared especially for him. No
ause-thumping. No flag-waving. Nothing but gravy.

*:30 A.M. Cosby and Big John elbow their way through the
mob to the parking lot. One woman runs along behind. "My

husband and I came all the way from San Francisco to se
you," she tells Cosby. "Then you better go back inside an
find him before he loses all his money—husbands are hard t
find, lady." Big John starts up the motor and heads his sport
car into the Strip, a blazing ribbon of purple light that cut
through the heart of the casinos with enough electricity to ru
Hoover Dam and so much glare you can read a newspaper a
midnight. At the Hacienda, we drop Mel Tormé's wife at hi
dressing room, where Cosby plays the ukelele and Mel sing
and everybody makes plans to meet for breakfast. Cosb
jokes. Everybody accepts him as though he has been in shov
business all his life. (Three years ago he was a college dropou
tending bar for sixty dollars a week and living in an upstair
room without plumbing over the Gaslight Club in Greenwic
Village.) Only occasionally does the race thing pop up. H
stops to buy a buck-fifty cigar and somebody asks him wha
kind he smokes. "They're flesh-colored, so I can have some
thing to identify with," he snaps, stabbing the air around hi
white friends with a brown cigar.

2 A.M. We hit Caesar's Palace, the new twenty-five-million
dollar resort hotel, where Big John buys us chocolate-ice
cream sodas. A sexy dancer from *Sweet Charity* named
Marguerite De Lane drops by the table. Shecky Green
drops by. Jerry Lester drops by. It's like a stand-up comi
convention. "Shecky," says Cosby, "they told me you were i
the audience tonight, so I said, 'Gee, I better do somethin
new.'" "You just do *anything* and it's *great,* man!" say
Greene. "Didja hear the one about the guy who drank outta
the wrong side of his mouth . . ." Bill tells the other comics a
joke, assuming the character of a drunk drinking out of the
wrong side of his mouth, and spills water all over his trou
sers.

After all the comics have done a routine, they leave and
Cosby is serious again. "I guess there are some bigots who
don't like me. There are still four NBC stations in the Deep
South who won't carry *I Spy*. A lot of so-called white liberals
still want Negroes to play only parts about 'the Negro
Problem.' They won't buy a Negro spy. But I never receive
hate mail. The worst letter I ever got was about a show we
filmed in Rome—some guy accused us of making the *Italians*
look like fools. I want people to identify with me regardless
of color. The minute you pull yourself away, you lose your
audience. The color white is different from the color black. So
what? We all have the same needs. I never sit down and say
198

What will white people laugh at?' Some of these shows cost 200,000 a show, so why take chances? Listen, before I'm rough, they'll make a movie in which I live next door to ack Lemmon. Why shouldn't I make all the old Cary Grant novies with Doris Day? If I can't find a producer to make nem, hell, I'll make them myself. That's my next move. here's no going back, only forward."

We talked about money. "I dig it, but Uncle Sam is looking ver my shoulder all the time. They oughta fix it so a guy an become a millionaire in peace. Everything is in the bank, aby. My kids are going to college. I tell college kids today, Don't be a dropout. The dropouts have all the jobs already nyway.' All my life I was a dropout. I dropped out of chool in the tenth grade in a Philadelphia slum, then got my igh-school diploma in the Navy. After the Navy, I went to 'emple on an athletic scholarship. I was twenty-three and I aid to myself, 'Finish school this time, baby, or it's Horn and Iardart's the rest of your life.' But I quit again. I only need ne more year to graduate. If I make enough money on *I py* I want to give up show business and become a physical-ducation teacher. I don't want to spend the rest of my life n a stage."

Cosby hasn't spent his money foolishly. He still sends hecks home to his mother in Philadelphia and his only two uxuries are a fancy car and a rustic, ranch-style house in a piffy white section of Beverly Hills. When Nat King Cole did he same thing a few years ago, hoodlums dumped garbage n his front lawn. Nothing like that has happened yet to Cosby. "I have two little girls, Erika and Erin, and if anyone ver threatens them, look out. I'm very short-tempered with gnorant people, and if any guy tried to dump garbage on my awn, he'd get filled with buckshot—colored man *or* white."

We talked about his wife and his eyes brightened like candles in a cathedral. He met Camille Hanks, a pretty tudent at the University of Maryland, while he was playing a mall club in Washington. Camille's parents did not want her o marry an entertainer. To get her away from Cosby, they ent her to live with relatives in Virginia. But love won out. 'When I played the Gaslight, I'd get off work at four A.M., leep till nine, drive to Maryland, buy her a hamburger, go to a movie and hold hands, then drive back to New York. This went on every day." They were married Jan. 25, 1964, in Olney, Maryland. "In choosing a wife I waited until I could afford it. I was scared at first, but after I got into it I realized it was my whole life, it's for keeps. In a marriage you have

199

to take all your habits and blend them and then bend a lot to make a better life for yourself. Up until the age of twenty-six I was a bachelor. The adjustment—*wow!* My wife's idea of marriage is like handcuffs. I report in, punch the clock, give her the money. She watches me like an eagle. I'm only kidding, but she does phone me twice a day when I'm in Vegas."

I asked how they manage to keep their marriage from getting stale. "We play it by ear. I don't want to have to tell her every day I love her just to reassure her. She knows it. Physically she is beautiful, but inside she's got them all beat. I mean, *women* fall in love with Camille. She's the only woman I know who never lets the claws come out. We get angry, we have fights, but this is for keeps, man. She sure didn't marry me for my money."

A white waiter apologized to Cosby for spilling coffee on the table and somehow the conversation switched again to The Problem, which for all his efforts to deny it, is always lurking just around the next sentence in his thoughts. "I'm lucky, but I'm not so stupid as to think just because something good happens to me it's going to happen to the rest of my race. What's wrong is that the whole Negro race has to keep proving itself. Why is that? For instance, if I had a Bill Cosby Special on TV with Belafonte, Poitier, and Sammy Davis as guests, you know what people'd say? 'Bill Cosby had all colored people on.' But if I had Lucille Ball, Sinatra, and Dean Martin, how many people would say, 'He had all white people on'? White people are always judging, but Negroes are not supposed to. If a white man falls off a chair drunk, it's just a guy. If a Negro does it, it's the whole damn Negro race. I don't want to be a crusader or a leader—I just want to be treated like a human being."

Black power? "They have a point. I mean, if a lion stalks a zebra in the jungle the zebra has no chance unless all the other zebras form a circle and stomp the lion to death. It's the only way, man. But I don't think there is such a thing as actual black power. If the Negroes had any military power don't you think they'd have done something by now? You can burn stores and break windows, but that's fighting a losing battle. 'Black power' are two words invented by the hysteria of the white press. I respect a man like Stokely Carmichael, though. He's the only man who can get black people together and make them aware of who they are. I'm not saying all black people are beautiful and right, but a lot of them are still being kept down. Think of all the black ballplayers and black actors who can't get a job. America continually cheats itself of great talent and entertainment. But I don't have time to sit around and worry about whether all the black people of the world will make it because of me—I have my own gig to worry about."

3 A.M. "Bill, baby!" yells the blackjack dealer as Cosby leads his group across the Caesar's Palace casino to a lounge called Nero's Nook. "Hi, Bill!" winks a Negro waitress in a Grecian costume. Five waiters rush up to seat him at a ringside table. The Ritz Brothers stop their show onstage to introduce him. The Mel Tormés and Negro comic Godfrey Cambridge join us. Debbie Reynolds waves at Cosby from her own table. Juliet Prowse blows a kiss. Tormé orders tomato juice, everybody else orders drinks on Cosby. Under the hot stagelights The Checkmates, one of the wildest groups in Vegas, knock everybody out in blue zoot suits with purple guitars attached to white extension cords, wailing air-conditioned amplified rock-and-roll. They jump off the stage and pull Cosby out of his seat. Cosby climbs onstage, still smoking his buck-fifty cigar, singing, ad-libbing, telling jokes. Mel Tormé jumps up and joins them all on the drums. The audience, mainly show-biz entertainers who have dropped by after their own Sunday night shows, goes wild. Flippo. Cosby is no longer the white man's Negro. He is in his element. It's one of those rare nights. It's Cosby's scene, the one *I Spy* watchers seldom see in their living rooms.

5:15 A.M. Cosby's entire entourage arrives at the Sands, for a breakfast of Chinese food. The Chinese chef, who usually opens up at this hour only for Sinatra or Dean Martin or Joey Bishop, does a deep bow in front of Cosby, who orders for seven people. Everybody talks at once while Cosby leans over to me: "I'm fascinated by all this. Meeting all my idols. I tell them, 'I love your work,' but the beautiful thing is that they say it right back to *me*. It's a great feeling. I don't want to make a life out of it, though. I'm making big money now, but it won't last forever. I always wanted things I couldn't afford. Well, today I can and they don't mean as much. I bought a '37 Rolls Royce and now it costs me $3,400 to get a paint job. Otherwise, I haven't been changed much by success. I started out making six dollars a night in a burlesque house telling Ivy League jokes to six sailors and a junkie, doing a routine about how Shakespearean actors talk. They didn't want some college darkie talking about Hamlet between bumps and grinds, so I got fired. I went to a beatnik dive—you know the kind—full of ugly Negro girls and ugly white men—sort of a Lonelyhearts integration. But they laughed. I was getting closer. Finally some cat called and said, 'Aren't you the one who does the funny bit about the guy with St. Vitus's dance trying to light his own cigarette?' I said yes. He said 'I'll give you sixteen dollars a night.' Big Time. What he really wanted was for me to open the joint at 7:30 before the regular acts went on at 10. Boy, the things they do to you in this business when you are nobody."

"That's nothing, Bill," said Mel Tormé. "When I was getting started, my first big job had an announcer who stepped up to the mike and said, 'And now, ladies and gentlemen, Mel Tormé—the Velvet Fag!' "

Food arrives. Mel is telling everyone about the time he and Nat King Cole had to fight off a gang of Texas toughs with a ketchup bottle while Cosby consumes a breakfast of two orders of spare ribs, a pepper steak, pork and mushrooms, lobster in black-bean sauce, three egg rolls, shrimp fried rice, four cups of Chinese tea, and a Coke.

7 A.M. Everyone else has gone to bed. Cosby and Big John hit the Sands casino. "Let's win some of Sinatra's money back," says Cosby. There are seven sleepy-eyed people left at the blackjack table and one of the Righteous Brothers playing a nearby slot machine. Cosby sits down with his trench coat on and talks about women while Big John places his bet for him. "I'm a physical man. If I look at a woman and she hits me, it's always immediately or not at all."

"A smile?" I ask, yawning.

"Smiles don't make it with me. It can be just a walk. Then I have to check it out upstairs, because the face is no good, baby, if the brain is dead. I don't like mentally aggressive women that are always competing, especially if you're talking about love. It's all right in business, but love is no boxing match. Too many women wear the pants today, but I blame the men for that. My wife has seen me really angry only twice, but I never struck her. I told her with my eyes and she got the message. I hate a man who slaps a woman."

Cosby loses $900 in less than an hour. It's 8 A.M. The early-morning sun floods the casino with streaks of yellow light as a group of Nevada cowboys enter drinking bourbon and branch water. Cosby decides to quit before his wife finds out how much he's dropped at the blackjack table. "I'm gonna quit this crazy business too," he says, heading back along the deserted Strip toward the Flamingo. "They'll try to get me into a new version of *Porgy and Bess* or something and that's when I'll throw in the towel. Then when they forget all about Bill Cosby, the next generation of Negro swingers will come along and *they'll* do *Porgy and Bess*—1984 style."

A soft breeze was blowing in from the desert as we arrived back at the Flamingo, where Cosby was staying. A row of armed guards, handsome as movie stars, tipped their caps as Cosby entered the lushly carpeted lobby. "I'll sleep for ten hours now and then start all over again," he said. The day's fresh batch of gamblers were arriving from the airport as Bill Cosby waved good-bye, on his way to bed.

Peter Fonda

> *Here comes*
> *my past*
> *passing by*
> *my eye*
> *passing near*
> *my ear*
> *passing through my heart*
>
> *Oh the rain*
> *will never end until*
> *my past has*
> *passed*

—Peter Fonda

Peter Fonda was lying on his back, in a bathing suit of old cut-off chinos, out by his swimming pool up on Lime Orchard Road in Beverly Hills. He lives there, more or less a part of the society he's been rejecting since he was six years old, with his beard and his mustache and his wife, Susan, who was in bed with the flu the whole afternoon and his two great-looking kids, Bridget and Justin, and two cats named Bamboo and Hashish, surrounded by mountains and cut off from everything that even resembles the Establishment. He's so isolated you can't even find him on a map of Los Angeles. But

203

he's there, telling it like he sees it and trying to be his own man in a world that keeps telling him he doesn't see it straight.

Lying on his back, talking to a tape recorder, getting it down straight, the sun burning into his skin, with imported Helena Rubenstein's "Bikini" lotion turning his tan to butterscotch and a four-inch scar slashing across his stomach where he once shot himself with a gun when he was ten years old, drinking Carlsbad beer while fourteen Bozak-610 speakers played Vivaldi and Ravi Shankar and "Sergeant Pepper's Lonely Hearts Club Band," throwing it up to the hills above the tennis courts. "Peter Fonda. Even reading my name in print drives me around the hill, man. It's weird. I don't become Peter Fonda till I go down that road, then the public takes over. Here I'm just me. To anybody who comes up that hill, I'm just 'Hey man, what's happening?' But when I go down that hill, I'm the son of what's-his-name and the brother of what's-her-face. I want people to know I've got more going on. You're my proof!" He yelled to his daughter Bridget, age four, swinging naked on a swing up on the rise above the house.

"Huh?"

"I said you're my proof."

"Huh?"

"She's gonna drive some guy into the booby hatch."

Bridget is named after a girl who committed suicide. She was the daughter of theatrical producer Leland Hayward and the late Margaret Sullavan, who had been married to Peter's father before he was born. The Haywards' other daughter, Brooke, is married to Dennis Hopper, one of Peter's best friends and one of his costars in *The Trip*. The children of famous people. It's a subject Peter knows a lot about. "I loved Bridget. I was at a Broadway play, *Tenderloin* I think, and I went home and my father said sit down and have a drink. He never even *talked* to me, so I couldn't understand why he wanted me to have a drink, but I sat down and he kept saying, 'Poor Leland, poor Leland.' Bridget's dead from an overdose of pills and I was falling thirteen floors to the ground and all he's saying is 'Poor Leland.' Adults. All my life I've been supposed to respect them and there's nothing to respect, man. When I got busted for pot, my Aunt Harriet called me from Omaha and told me it was uncool so I told her it was uncool for her to tell me. She said it was wrong for me to do it to Susan and the kids. I looked around and saw my old lady sitting there and my kids playing and I didn't know what she meant. 'You won't be able to get Bridget in

204

a good school,' she said. The last thing I want is to send my kids to school. I want to keep them as far away as possible from organized politics, religion, and education. The only thing I owe my daughter is to tell her not to get pregnant."

Bridget joined us by the pool, still in the nude. She looks like a baby version of Peter's sister, Jane. Beautiful. Cheeks like ripe nectarines. "You wanna talk into this box, Bridget? When you get to be president of the world, you'll have to do things like this. You tell this little box here what you think about Daddy." Bridget wasn't having any. "What do you think about the CIA? What does Daddy always tell you about the CIA? Doesn't Daddy always say, when he picks up the phone, 'The CIA sucks'?"

The stillness of Peter's private world was shattered suddenly by the sound of a helicopter. High, high above the hill it came, hovering briefly over the pool and chopping up the Botticelli sky like a dragon breathing down on a meadow of butterflies. "That's one of the sheriff's spotters from the Los Angeles vice squad," he grinned. "They come over the house with telephoto lenses and take pictures to see if I'm smoking pot or taking LSD, anything to bust me on, and sometimes I take pictures of them taking pictures of me. *Hello, fellas, you dirty bastards!*"

He talks about LSD like it was a cache of diamonds he suddenly found hidden in a geranium pot. He's taken eleven trips on acid and he says they saved his life. "A year and a half ago, I had no self-confidence, no belief. All my life I was getting done in by the crewcut mentality of America that says if you have long hair you're either queer or a beatnik or on pot. I had a superego, an IQ of 160—all the ingredients. But they were so masked by my own viewpoint they couldn't come through. I was in terrible manic stages, found myself one day in the middle of Europe, man, out of my bird. I was oozing through the rocks. When I took my first acid it jolted me out of that. After LSD, I have seen the worst and I've seen the best and I know where I am on this planet."

His first trip was taken in September, 1965, in the middle of the desert with two other guys, a St. Bernard named Basil, and a medical supervisor. "We all piled into a stationwagon and I remember I had brought some dog food for the dog. I said something to him out loud like, 'Here, Basil, here's something to eat,' because he wasn't on a trip. He was straight, man, and I knew he was straight. I had been eating an oatmeal cookie that looked like it was alive with worms. You know how the top of oatmeal cookies look bumpy? Well, under hallucinatory conditions it looked like it was rippling

205

and worms were crawling in and out of it and I popped it in my mouth, man, and I could taste them. I was chewing these worms and swallowing them and—oh wow—what a feeling and I gave Basil this Gainesburger. Anyway, here was Basil and I said, 'Oh wow, hey man, you see I didn't forget about you, man.' I'm trying to remember what I said without paraphrasing it. Oh damn. Anyway, I said in essence that my ego wasn't so big I had forgotten about *him*. I had brought him food for his trip because he had come along on *our* trip. It was comforting for me to know, while I was eating this worm-filled cookie. Do you know what I mean? I'm not sure I've said what I meant. It was weird to me under acid to relate to this dog on a certain level. I didn't know what it meant not to have an ego, I just suddenly knew I didn't have one at that moment. I was really into the drug by then. Oh man, what a strange trip. The sky at one point looked like a Tiffany lamp shade but much prettier. Tiffany could never make one like this. And a plane came through, only I didn't know it was a plane. I was like watching something else, suddenly I saw the changes coming from above and behind me and I looked up and I saw them as waves coming through the air and hitting and bouncing off and I put my hands up like it was raining and saw these *things* bouncing off my *hands!* They were coming from the sky and finally I looked up and it wasn't the sun but it was sending all these waves at me. *I was seeing the sound!* And I focused in on it and it became a plane. Multicolored. *Flashing* in the sun and the sky in the middle of this Tiffany lampshade. Whew. That kind of deep visionary hallucinatory thing went on for about four or five hours. Heavy stuff. Then about three hours of milder stuff and then about four hours of longer periods of changes. Your first changes are multiple and rapid like movie editing—rattattattattt—then they get longer. Every trip is a different trip. Jesus, once the St. Bernard chased a frog or a big kind of horny toad under this bush and I went over to see what he was doing and the thing came out of the hole, only I saw it like a gigantic monster going ROARRR! and shooting flames out at me and it really blew my mind, man. We related to each other and were coherent most of the time when we weren't staring out into space seeing things. You're seeing different things but you're on the same trip, you know. I took other trips up in the mountains, once on a beach where I walked on the ocean, once here by my own pool, once with Bobby Walker, the son of Jennifer Jones. I think anybody who wants to take a trip should. Knowing there's a law against it. I don't mean to sound like I preach sedition or anarchy, but like there's also a law against oral copulation, man. So there's this law against LSD, but if you're serious about your head, man, and want to do some changes for it, there it is."

Outrageous? Maybe to a few apple-pie mothers baking brownies for the guys getting their arms shot off in the Mekong Delta. But not to the swingers, the generation Peter speaks to and for. They're tuning out the sound of Those Who Know because Those Who Know don't know anything about Moby Grape or the Mugwumps or Lothar and the Hand People or how to dry a crop of dreams in a Laundromat dryer set at "Cotton." They are fighting yesterday's problems. They hardly comprehend freak-out, much less the Hare Krishna Chant. So the kids in the acid generation learn their own way to live in a world inhabited by adults who screwed it up before they got here. And Peter Fonda's life is a perfect example of what they're fighting to avoid for their own children.

He was born in New York City February 23, 1940. His mother was a beautiful socialite heiress named Frances Seymour Brokaw, the second of Henry Fonda's five wives. It was the beginning of a childhood that makes *Elsie Dinsmore* look like *Jo's Boys*. He flew to California with his father when he was fourteen weeks old and always got shoved in the background hoopla of the horrible world of being a movie star's son. "Nobody ever told me anything, man. I remember the time Jane and I went to Jimmy Stewart's house and he and my father had heartburn and took Tums after dinner and I was so stupid I thought I'd be an adult the day I could take Tums." He was shuttled around to one school after another. At six he was sent away to a farm school in a canyon. "What kind of freaked-out parents would send a kid away at six to make his own bed?" When he was seven he moved back to New York, where his father starred in *Mr. Roberts* on Broadway. He went to boarding schools in New York, and to Fay School in Southboro, Massachusetts, where he so desperately wanted to belong to someone that he ended up writing love letters for the other boys. After two bad years of Gilbert and Sullivan, he wrote his own play, a take-off on *Stalag 17*. His mother committed suicide on April 14, 1950, and left him an estate of $60,000. A few months later Peter shot himself through the liver and kidneys with a .22-caliber pistol on the estate of S. H. Kress, the dime-store millionaire. He was rushed to a hospital in Ossining, New York, and given three blood transfusions. His father was off in the Virgin Islands somewhere getting married again, this time to his third wife,

Susan Blanchard. "Nobody told me the truth about my mother, man. I was ten years old and I didn't understand. I just knew she was dead and I was all alone. My father won't even talk to me about *today*, so he's not gonna talk about yesterday. There are too many yesterdays for him to get into, baby. I didn't find out how my mother died until I was 15. I was sitting in this barber's chair in Rome and I picked up a magazine and read about her doing herself in in an insane asylum. It blew my mind, man. And nobody to this day has ever told me anything. I just assumed their guilt."

Peter went back to prep school in Connecticut. He organized the Wampus Players and wrote and directed plays and drew cartoons of the faculty members. This caused resentment among the teachers and Peter's life was made miserable. "I finally left in my third year after I got in a fight with this alcoholic master. He said I was late for chapel and accused me of being an atheist. I said I was closer to whatever God was than he could ever hope to be. That upset him enough to call my old man a son of a bitch. 'Anybody who's been married all those times'—I didn't even know how many times it was at that point—'has gotta be a son of a bitch.' He had crossed me on a personal level, man, so I slugged him, knocked him out cold. I don't know if I did it in defense of my father, or because it was the first time *they* —the Establishment—had crossed over that personal line. But that was the end of the Establishment for me. I was sixteen when it happened. He was a man and I was a man and he was drunk and overstepped his bounds. He held no authority for me. That's the whole bag, man—who do you respect? The Congressmen and the Senators and the peace officers and the parents? What do they expect, man, once you catch them, once you know they're not telling the truth? 'Well, we'll let that one slide off and we'll see what else happens?' That's the way *they* live. That's not the way I live, or the teen-agers who are already finished with their rebellion. The Teen-Age Youth Revolution is a *fait accompli*. The manifesto was written a long time ago. I've been told all my life I must accept authority but all the authority I've ever seen has been rotten, man.

"After I cold-cocked this guy the other faculty members began doing things. Like my math teacher changed the answers on my exam. I began to really get spooked out about it. I told my father—he was off somewhere getting married again (this time to an Italian baroness, Afdera Fonda)—and I went home for the wedding and I told him things were getting rough and he was funny. He said, 'You want me to
208

you out of school?' And I said no, I'd work it out. I
ed taking phenobarbitol to calm down. You would've
ght I had malaria. I wasn't hip to getting high in those
, I was just getting doped up. Then I got in a fight on a
and they made me the scapegoat and I really flipped out
this guy told the headmaster I needed help. Anyway I said
nted to leave. I wasn't kicked out. I just quit. But I did
a certain amount of whatever dignity I had left at the
ent, which was very little. I called Jane at Vassar and
her I needed help and I must've been outta my mind
use the next day she drove up in a stationwagon and
d me hiding in the bushes talking to a bunch of dogs.
looked at me and said, 'Oh wow, I think you're Holden
field.' Every young cat who had gone through the same
ges, man, Holden Caulfield was their psychodrama.
nger was the Albee of that time. But it made me mad. I
flipping out of my skull and she thought it was great
use it was just like Holden Caulfield.
Anyway, my father was off in Europe so she put me on a
to my Aunt Harriet's in Omaha, Nebraska. What a
e! I landed in Omaha and immediately I was told that, of
rse, you'll have to go back to high school. And I said, 'I'm
going anyplace, man. You're crazy.' You gotta graduate.
gotta be a man. The whole thing about you gotta. They
't believe anything I told them so they just assumed I had
n kicked out of school. Nobody called the headmaster or
thing. I was lost. My mother had been in a mental
itution and my aunt was afraid I would end up in one too.
uld've become a professional killer or a robber or any-
g at that point. I was that close to flipping out to the
er side. But I was at least straight enough to know *she*
n't telling the truth. 'You gotta get an education.' But I
eed finally to go out to the University of Omaha to take
achievement test so at least they'd know where I *was*. I
k every kind of test and interview you can imagine. Some
them were so stupid and inane I started putting on the
ple who were giving them. I blew my cookie. The first
ng I was asked to define was the word *puddle*. Click went
stopwatch. I laughed and got up and walked out of the
m. The second thing they asked me to define was cat.
ck went the stopwatch. I said you're all insane, man, what
you mean define cat? So they gave me two boxes. One
d a pack of cards and the other had some categories.
rried . . . I don't know. Divorced . . . I don't know. I was
o dead on their test. There were three no's, six yesses and
rty-seven I don't knows. That's where I was. I was honest.

Then my father flew in from France and was sitting on
couch in my aunt's house and this guy told him I had
intelligence quotient of 160 and should be a sophomor
college and he yelled 'WHAT?' If he'd said I should be a
quarterback he probably would've been pleased. Now
finds out something cool is going on with his son—his kid
a brain. He couldn't just accept it, there had to be a pun
ment. I had to get my high-school diploma first, so since
only private school in Omaha was a girl's school I ended
attending college and graduating from an all-girl's
school at the same time."

College turned out to be just as sterile for Peter's kind
brain as all the other fiasco schools had been. "As a freshn
I took the same program of teaching that was given to
when I was twelve in grade school. I was bored out of
bloody mind sitting there. They were talking about *art* w
just the summer before I had met Picasso. I already kr
what Hemingway was all about, man, I had run into some
these cats. I had listened to Faulkner talk the way so
people listen to football games on the radio. They ca
Degas a *finger-painter*, man. Then this chick teacher ask
me to do a paper on Montaigne." He said the word like
had just found a tarantula in his algebra book. "He inver
the essay form. I had no use for him. The essay is n
creative. Everything I'd read of his up to that point had b
plagiarized, so I put him down in 500 words and I was gi
a grade of F. I read the paper over and discovered I had
misspelled word and one grammatical structural mistake
went to the head of the English department and raised h
'How can you mark me down just because you don't agre
This chick teacher thought he was a bloody genius and
didn't. I don't care if it's a bloody college or prison ward
the Superior Court of Los Angeles. I have to tell it like it
man. It's the only way to be. My way of telling it was to
my thing down on paper. I was bored by it, she was boring,
class bored me, I was only fulfilling my obligation. I fai
because she didn't like what I said—that was college. Th
sock it to you, baby."

But there he was, getting lectures about being an ad
from the adults, locked away in Omaha, living the kind
life his father wanted him to live because that's what h
been expected out of him by *his* father, and Peter was m
confused than ever. "I had been on a shrinker's couch whe
was eleven, man, and I'd been drinking five quarts of wine
day in Rome when I was fifteen and I'd been picked up
this twenty-eight-year-old woman who was married to an

210

ché in Rome and they had both picked me up in front of
Peter's Cathedral and taken me home and balled me and
lew my life out when I was fifteen and I was expected to
e home and date these nice girls in Omaha. And my
er's off in the woods someplace, and even when he's sitting
he same room with me, he doesn't know what to say and
hair's cut short the way he wants it and my aunt keeps
ng me I should take out this Zelda Farnsgrabber because
father is a member of the local Establishment and she's a
e girl, right? Well, the only chick I ever knocked up was
da Farnsgrabber and I got it on the first date and I stayed
until five in the morning and when I got home it was all
ht with my aunt because it had been this Zelda, and here
going to have to pay five hundred dollars to send her to
erto Rico and I haven't got the bread. So I sold a Christ-
s present, a shotgun or something I didn't want, and I sold
bought my freedom from Zelda.

He bought his own freedom too. He took $300 he had
ed and at the end of his third year he climbed into an old
rd and headed for a summer-stock company in Fishkill,
w York, where he would take his clothes to the laundro-
t and hide behind the drier naked and drink beer while
y washed. He also painted sets, ushered, did walk-ons, and
rked the lights. He was learning. He went to New York
d got a part in *Blood, Sweat and Stanley Poole,* a flop play
ich won him the Drama Critics Award as promising actor.
ree days later he married Susan Brewer, stepdaughter of
ward Hughes' former assistant, Noah Dietrich. The play
sed after two and a half months and Peter went back to
ollywood for the first time in years. On his own terms this
ne. He was tested for the part of President Kennedy in
-109, but his first film turned out to be *Tammy and the
octor,* which he now calls Tammy and the Schmuckface.
e got $15,000 for it. "I saw it and had to be hospitalized
r a week and a half. I'm just kidding. I only vomited." He
ught a car and went to London to do an antiwar film, *The
ctors,* which was a disaster. Then he did *Lilith* for Robert
ossen and although it was his best film, his part was heavily
t. He didn't get along with Warren Beatty and he received
actically no direction from Rossen. His fourth film, *The
oung Lovers,* was another flop. Peter went into a depression.
is mind was full of things he wanted to say and people were
ccepting him as an adult, but he still wasn't pleased with his
eative output. So he sank deeper within himself and with-
rew from the kind of society that approves of making
211

movies for money even if they don't say anything. His tr[oubles] began all over again.

On February 3, 1965, he was in Tucson when his b[est] friend, Eugene (Stormy) McDonald, heir to the $30-milli[on] Zenith electronics fortune, was found shot to death with [his] wrists slashed. A coroner's jury decided that since 32.4 gra[ms] of marijuana (enough for 125 cigarettes) were found in [the] dead man's apartment Peter should be given a lie-detect[or] test. Nothing ever came of it, but Peter got some pre[tty] messy headlines. The death of Stormy, who had been his b[est] friend since their college days in Omaha, left him visi[bly] shaken. "There's never a day that I don't think about my b[est] friend putting a bullet in his head. There's hardly a day [I] don't think about my mother cutting her throat. Ther[e's] hardly a day that I don't realize this girl whom I was in lo[ve] with who was almost like my sister, took pills and did hers[elf] in. And all the other people I knew who tried to do the[m]selves in. I have no sympathy anymore. Compassion. But [no] sympathy."

The most bizarre stage in the life-span of Peter the Reb[el] was just beginning. He became Peter the Kook. He wo[re] funky tinted shades and let his hair grow until it curl[ed] around his chin. He took to wearing cowboy boots and cra[sh] helmets and Navy Commander hats with tuxedos, and livi[ng] on raw eggs, bananas, milk, and Bosco chopped up in [a] Waring blender. His father gave statements to the press abo[ut] how he had given up on his children. Jane Fonda gave a[n] interview in which she said, "I don't know where he is, and [I] don't care." Like that. Peter was still fighting the world wi[th] proud tears in his eyes behind the motorcycle goggles.

The only company in Hollywood willing to take a chan[ce] on him at this point was American-International, an organ[i]zation which went into business fifteen years ago with som[e]thing called *The Beast With 1,000,000 Eyes* and had worke[d] all the way up to *How to Stuff a Wild Bikini*. *The Wild Ange[ls]* was made for peanuts. Peter got $10,000. The film to da[te] has grossed ten million in the United States and Cana[da] alone and has turned Hank's Bad Boy into an undergrou[nd] star with the No. 1 best-selling poster (showing him with [a] phallic motorcycle between his legs) in the arty paperbac[k] book galleries. Peter Fonda, according to the grass-roo[ts] underground, is the whole shirt. Zero cool.

All of which leads to Peter Fonda as the guy he is toda[y,] lying beside his pool, making a forty-five-rpm record [of] Donovan's "Catch the Wind" and accompanying himself on [a] twelve-string Guild acoustical guitar, watching a group [of] 's and their birds riding up the driveway on motorcycles. ey, I'm doing an interview, man, come back later." Talk- about everything. Like the time he was busted for smok- pot last winter. "I got a call in the middle of the night m this chick who said, 'Your friend's been busted.' So I ed a lawyer for my friend and about a day and a half r I got a call from my lawyer saying *You're* gonna be ted!' And what it amounted to was that his house had been led without a warrant and the cops said this guy was wing pot in his backyard. They found out I was part of it hat I was the guy's employer—he was like a secretary to at the time, he was my personal assistant on *Wild Angels* nd I had left a guitar case in his house with my name on About this time American-International was putting out all promotion material calling me a spokesman for the young- generation or something and the cops believed it. They ught I was the leader of a dope ring. So it was released to papers that they had busted *my* house, man, and it wasn't house. I wasn't even in town, man. I got hauled into erior Court in Los Angeles, no joke. I had to go in front a jury on a felony charge—possession of eight pounds of rijuana. If they had arrested me on the street with a key in pocket at least it would've been a legal bust. I got on the nd and I admitted I'd been to this guy's house, but not re than few hours. 'Well, Mr. Fonda, what was going on? aat did you see them do?' 'Well, I didn't pay any attention it was none of my business.' I took an oath that I'd tell the th and that was the truth. Fuck 'em. I'm working on a mula to blow up the district attorney's office."

He got off after Henry Fonda flew in from Arizona with a ard he grew for a movie Western and testified in Peter's fense. "I wore my hair long. I wore my double-breasted ts. I smiled at everybody. I wore my funky shades. Every- ng my lawyer told me not to do. I knew I wasn't guilty, t all of my principles were at stake. The jury was instruct- to find me guilty beyond a reasonable doubt and to a oral certainty. I think those words were repeated at least 5 times. 'Remember, ladies and gentlemen of the jury, it ast be beyond all reasonable doubt and to a moral certain- .' The DA said in his summation that the jury shouldn't be l astray by the appearance of the young defendant. 'You ust think about him just as though he was a Mexican.' This s downtown Los Angeles, which is made up of Mexicans. exican built. They were here before we got there and here s this guy telling them to treat me just like I was a exican. I nearly fell out of my chair. Two women on the

jury voted against me. I was not acquitted, because o
felony charge you have to have a complete, unanimous v
But ten to two to acquit is pretty heavy, so they dropped
charges. They figured they were doing me a favor, so I sp
right out and said, 'On the contrary. My sister's willing
back me for another trial. If you want to play, I can p
And this one I'll really win because I know what mistake
made last time.' I really dig my sister. Probably a great
more than she digs me and she *digs* me. I dig my father,
I have a great deal of compassion for him, too. I wish
could open his eyes and dig me and if he could dig me
wouldn't feel as much a failure."

He was arrested again on November 26, 1966, in front
the Fifth Estate coffeehouse on the Sunset Strip along w
sixty other hippies who were accused of disturbing the pea
Brandon DeWilde, who was with him, got away. He
jailed, but not booked, and at 3:45 A.M. he was released a
his press agent was able to prove he had been on the scene
shoot a documentary film on teen-agers. The film ne
appeared, but Peter did shock everybody by turning out *7*
Trip, a bizarre Technicolor curio directed by Roger Corman
big underground favorite with the *Positif* crowd in Pa
Corman had directed *Wild Angels* and Americ
International was hip to making some more of the kind
money that film grossed. So Corman's camera and Pete
knowledge of LSD was certain to be a yeasty combinati
They opened the movie and passed out kaleidoscopes to
square critics with a gimmicky come-on: "LISTEN TO T
SOUND OF LOVE . . . FEEL PURPLE . . . TASTE GREE
. . . TOUCH THE SCREAM THAT CRAWLS UP T
WALL. . . ." The critics weren't amused. Except for the f
out critics who always dig Jerry Lewis movies, the film
rotten notices. But Peter feels proud of it.

"I didn't do it for money, man. If I wanted to ma
money I'd discover a way to make food out of the ocean a
make a billion dollars because years from now the world
going to be starving and they'll turn to the ocean for s
tenance. The money I have doesn't come from movies, m
Movies didn't pay for all this. I got involved in the beginni
because the script I read was so beautiful, so incredi
honest—wow!—what an honest thing, that I decided to de
cate myself to making sure it was done right, that I we
against the advice of everybody else—my agents, my busin
managers, all the people I paid money to for advice—hea
of the industry and so on. Because I had been involved in t
drug scene, they thought coming out and doing a drug fi
214

s a very stupid move for me and I could see their point
all that. But I kept telling myself, Man, you gotta do this
vie! You just gotta do it! This'll be the first time you can
ke a movie and won't have to compromise once! It's got
D in it and that's all it needs. I kept telling Corman,
u're not gonna lose any money, man.' You can only make
ething good if you don't have to worry about making
ney. The ones who won't go see it because it's an AIP
e film will have to see it because it's a *great* movie. And
you make an exploitation film, you're still gonna make
ney. I said this to Corman in person, face to face, close
ugh in person meaning like personally, personably, in tune
h him. So I'm not copping out. He knew, or he pretended
know, he would never have to compromise. But he com-
mised. It isn't important how much because *The Trip* as it
nds is still an incredible American movie. Corman went
to Europe to make some racing-car movie with Fabian or
ankie Avalon or somebody before it was even finished
oting. The music wasn't even in yet. All the stuff we shot,
happened, everything went down as it did because Dennis
pper and I went out and shot it. All the stuff in the desert.
rman wouldn't spend the money. But he let me shoot it. I
d him I had the equipment, but I didn't, man. I had to go
t and rent it. If I had asked him for bread, we wouldn't
ve got it in the movie. Dennis directed and I ran."

"Not while on a trip, though."

"I took the trip straight. First of all, if I took acid for a
mera I'd look at the camera and the people around and I'd
y 'You dumb fuckers' and walk out the door or some-
ing. I'm not gonna play that game on acid, man. No, I did
straight because I wanted to see if I knew how to act. It
as a chance, man. The running sequences were shot by a guy
a wheelchair and another guy running behind with two sun
ns, man. It was underground-movie time, man. That's the
ay to make a film. I waited a long time before I even
gned the contracts to make sure I got everything I could
t. Like music. They had a contract to spend $3,000 for
usic. *Three thousand bucks!* I finally told them I would
ve them the music for that price and I would take care of
tting it done. So I ended up paying my own bread to get
e music produced, it cost me $7,500 which I didn't have.
ecause they didn't pay me that much to do the flick. But I
t a percentage. They made millions on *The Wild Angels*
d didn't give me a penny of it. And they worked me
vertime, too many days, and they didn't pay me for it. They
ve me about a thousand dollars worth of camera equip-

ment, though, enough to build my own darkroom with.
The Trip is gonna make so much bread, man—WOWWW
Can you imagine what's gonna happen like in Texas, m
when those kids in that drive-in get to that first nude l
scene, man? The naked scenes were my idea. Even my A
Harriet wants to see it. 'You've heard so much about it, n
SEE the pill going down!' See, there's this boat sixty-five f
long and it's gonna cost me a quarter of a million bucks a
in order to pay that I gotta make three million. Now I fig
five percent of *The Trip* means I get $50,000 for ev
million they make in profit. I think they are already makin,
profit. I'm not allowed to say how much it cost to make"—
yells into the mike—"but that's CENSORSHIP and not
lieving in CENSORSHIP, it only cost around $450,000
make.

"I like movies like that, without all the big-studio shit. *T
Wild Angels* was a wild film. I did all my own stunts, my o
motorcycle riding. We were illegal most of the time, eve
body did everything, we worked for nothing, we got it all do
in seventeen days. The Hell's Angels played the cops. They
as bourgeois as everybody else, they've got rules and regu
tions they live by. I walked in and they weren't sure if I w
gonna be right for the part, man, because I mean, look
me. I don't look like a Hell's Angel, man. But I knew wh
puts them up tight better than the Angels do and I had
good reason for being there because it was an an
Establishment film. It didn't prettify anything. It was new.
people say, 'Is that your criteria? Is that what makes it goo
because it's new?' First of all, people like that are bound
be reactionary anyway. There are always new Fords eve
year and I don't own any Fords. There are always new rifl
New plants. Not demolition plants, but growing green plan
Grass. Get it? *Grass?*" He makes smoking gestures. "No,
mean this kind of newness: films should be open to interpr
tation. I want to make the audience participate, not
vocally yelling yes and no, booing or hissing in a melodram
That's third-person participation. That's titillation. 'No, n
Doris, don't pick up the phone,' you say to Doris Day, who
about to pick up the phone to get a divorce from R
Taylor, 'Rod's changed his mind!' 'It's all over, don't do i
says you, sitting in your third-person seat. In *The Trip*, ma
you never have a chance to. First of all, the music doesn
give you a cue to what's coming on, nobody looks to th
door because it's suddenly opening, it's *zing!* You're goin
someplace else. You gotta watch everything. Even the corn
reprised so it makes cinematic sense, not just bucolic cra,
216

hat kind of participation, man, brings an audience in. They
g it."

Right now he's making his own movie about the Beverly
ills meter maids who ride along on their motorcycles mark-
g your tires with chalk so the cops can give out tickets. "It's
lled *Lovely Rita Meta Maid*. It's a song the Beatles wrote
d so I'm gonna do a movie with that as its theme and
ange pictures on the screen in a rhythmic pattern to that
usic and subliminally flashed in will be pictures of chicks
rewing cats with gun belts on and boots on and handcuffs
d night sticks, beating people while they're getting screwed
d stuff. Only *Rita* will never be shown to anybody, man,
less I show it on a pretty wild circuit, because nobody will
ant to see that. I mean they'll want to see it, but their cops
on't want to see it and the cops decide what everybody else
gonna see. Get that, Everybody Else? Does that make you
ad, Everybody Else? Does that make ya *sad*, Everybody
lse? Does that make ya *glad?*

"And then there's also the possibility of doing something
ith my sister. Listen, Jane and me in a film, right? Directed
y Vadim, right? Who's got one of the greatest love cameras
ve ever seen, a *phallus!* Jane and I as brother and sister who
ake nude pornographic movies directed by her husband, who
a porny moviemaker, and our old man is a has-been actor
ho's drunk all the time. Everybody would go see it."

The motorcycle gang was roaring up the hill again. "Hey
e interview's still on, man!" yelled Peter. They left, frown-
g. "They don't understand I'm gonna be president in five
ears," he said, grinning like a Mongol slave trader.

There was an enormous splash. We looked around and saw
small brown lump drifting toward the bottom of the twen-
y-foot end of the pool. "My God it's the baby!" Justin, who
n't even a year old yet, had fallen in. Peter leaped into the
ater and dragged the struggling baby up by its feet. He
ngled him up and down in a few spasmodic jerks and the
ater came pouring out of his lungs as he wailed his head
ff. "That'll teach him not to crawl around the pool," said
eter, putting the baby down on the hot concrete and drying
is tears with a warm towel. "I won't always be around. My
ather was never around when I needed *him*.

"I'm nude in front of my wife and kids all the time. We
wim out here in the raw. If you can become that intimate,
hat honest, without having moral hangups or copping out
nd going into a nudist colony, you're healthy. That's like
moking behind the barn or screwing in the back seat of a
ar. Here in California at a local museum, there was an art

217

exhibit showing a sculpture of two people screwing in th
back seat of a car. The parts of the car were assembled an
the door was open so you could see in it and it was a work
art for the comment it made on society. But the county supe
visor decided this shouldn't be viewed by people under eig
teen. I laughed because the only people I know who screw i
back seats of cars are under eighteen because their paren
won't let them inside the house. So they made a compromise—
the car door was left open at certain times and closed at othe
times—it shows how this man's mind must be. It shows tha
his kids, if they wanted to make it, would have to make it i
the back seat of a car someplace instead of being able t
groove with success on a bed. That's the American view
point. Now if you are able to groove where you want t
groove, you can take your clothes off and go swimming an
not get embarrassed about it in front of a whole mess c
people in check, because if society doesn't become too libera
it's easier to control.

"I'm called a very naïve person for thinking that way. I'r
called an idealist, a dreamer, a rationalist, every kind of fuck
ing name you can think of. I think I'm very non-naïve. I loo
at the people who believe in society and I consider *them* naïve
I could survive on this planet if it all went tomorrow. Most o
those people who want to put me down in the press, pass mora
judgments on me, put me in jail, they'd be jumping out o
windows because their gig got done in—either through
social revolution or a Chinese bomb. I'll be out there makin
fish hooks out of bones because I know how to, and I didn'
take an Eagle Scout test to do it. Or I can field-dress a deer
When I was five years old I had my first thoughts abou
death. There was a war on. I saw life as one whole war wit
everybody dead and I had nightmares. When I was nine and
ten, I was going through emotional changes that would send
me to the bathroom, racked with pain. They always wante
to take my temperature, and it was subnormal because m
blood pressure, my blood sugar, was way, way down. But o
course they never bothered to find out about that. I didn'
have any stomachaches or pains or sicknesses. But I couldn'
function because I was in such pain in my head. I was
manic-depressive then. At nine. And they'd say I was jus
trying to stay out of school. They did me in, man, and
couldn't tell them anything because I had no vocabulary. I
was just a nine-year-old freak. I always thought abou
suicide. I've popped pills, I've taken a quart of whiskey and
drunk it down like water, holding my nose. I drove a car into
a bridge at over a hundred miles an hour.
218

"Now I don't think I'll kill myself. Not since I took LSD. I found *me* on LSD and my eleven sessions achieved what it took Jane five days a week for five years on a shrinker's couch to accomplish. It was cheaper. I found out platinum spoons or plastic spoons—they're all spoons, man. They all feed you. And to think 'I'm better than you' is the biggest fallacy I know. Everybody else used to think that, so I did too. They were convinced that because I was Henry Fonda's son that something else was going on in my life and everybody had to either suck up to me or put me down because of it, one way or the other. It could never be anything else but that it blew my mind because being Henry Fonda's son— what did that mean? My father was never around, he never speaks any fucking words to me, he never said a bloody goddam thing. He's married to a chick now who was an airline stewardess, and she won't let my thirteen-year-old-half-sister Amy even see my films. But I talk to him now. I say 'I love you,' you know, like I could never love him before. But now I know that all in all he saved me. The fact that we had to spend a Christmas in Kansas and a Christmas in Detroit and a Christmas in a hotel room in Milwaukee, the fact that I was one summer here and one summer there and all over the bloody *world*—I discovered what Christmas was all about, what the word *family* meant.

"One of the first things I learned was that everybody has to find out what's going on *out there,* because they don't know what's going on *in here.* I point to myself when I say that. I'm not original, Christ said the same thing. People can't know what's in front of them, if they don't know where they've been. Christ said, 'If you see what's in front of you, all the rest will be revealed unto you.' "

"Do you consider yourself religious?" I asked.

"No, I consider myself part of the universe. The universe is a religion. Man is a religion. It's all heaven, it's all hell. Everything *is* everything. Death is just a change."

And that's where Peter Fonda is now. He's beaten the third-rate psychiatrists and the pea-brained cops and the hack writers and the Blue Book curiosity seekers at their own game. He's learned a man doesn't have to be queer to be sensitive or tough to be a man. He knows anyone who thinks he's totally secure is kidding himself. He's living it out a day at a time. "I have to be free in my head," he says, "I cannot be free in society."

There seemed only one thing left to ask: "Are you happy now?" But Peter had done a perfect swan dive back into the pool and he never heard the question.

Marlene Dietrich

DIETRICH?

This is what I know: First the rehearsal. It is three days before the opening. The Lunt-Fontanne Theatre is empty except for musicians and technicians. A lightman she had flown all the way from England is setting the spotlight for her entrance. It must be just right or she won't go on. Onstage, Burt Bacharach, an ingratiating, teddy-bear guy with windswept hair, is working out an E-flat-chord change for "Falling in Love Again" in chino pants and white tennis sneakers. Backstage, Dietrich is scrubbing down her dressing room. "Hello," she says, turning the room into instant Vista-Vision with the symphony of a smile, "you wrote that article where you said you didn't like Barbra Streisand . . . ah, yes, I remember." She knows everything everybody writes. Writers are her passion. Dietrich legs dazzle like white birches beneath a tight op-art dress. "I've been here scrubbing down this place with Ajax all week. I'm the queen of Ajax."

The room smells like Estee Lauder perfume. Dietrich steps over cases of champagne and boxes of roses, still clinging to their green-tissue wrappings. "Gifts from admirers. Why do they send me these things? It only means I have to send thank-you notes. They're probably from people I don't even know." She halfheartedly slashes a crate of champagne with a knife, then tosses the card on her dressing table unopened. "You are the first person who has been inside this room. Would you like to wash up or anything?" There was an enormous, tacky, lovable pickaninny doll propped gently on her makeup table, full of pins, looking like Br'er Rabbit's tar baby. "Don't you recognize it? It's the doll from *The Blue Angel*. And here's Papa's picture." Pointing to a framed portrait of Hemingway. "And this is my third most cherished possession, a pair of ballet slippers given to me by the Moscow Ballet. These are the only three things I carry around everywhere."

220

We went down to the stage, where a secretary stopped us
thank her for saving her life with one of her mamma-bear
 ndouts of vitamin-C tablets. (She is known to the people in
 r show as a walking medicine chest, always ready with a
 re for every ailment.) Bacharach sat at the piano, his eyes
 osed and his nose tilted toward the violins, and she sang a
 w antiwar song, "White Grass," which she brought back
 om Australia. "It's about a crippled soldier returning from
 e war, who finds his town gone, his wife gone, everything
 ne. And he sings 'I hear we won, hooray.' That ought to
 care the Bejeesus out of them on opening night. My daugh-
 r knows all the new songs because she listens to the radio
 ll day long. I don't have much time to listen. I'm always
 aveling. Aren't those musicians wonderful? I wrote it in my
 ontract that Burt could choose them. I couldn't make a
 ove without him. That's why I don't do more new songs,
 ecause he has no time to arrange and orchestrate them for
 e and I won't do anything without him. I also had my own
 uitarist and drummer and my own mikes flown in. You have
  put everything in your contract these days and then they
 ay you're difficult."

She rushed up onstage to inspect her pink scrim, which she
 lso had brought from Europe as a backdrop, and check out
  tempo change with the orchestra, then hopped down off the
 tage and joined me in the orchestra, sitting sideways in her
 eat like a young teeny-bopper. I offered her a cigarette. "I
 ave them up, darling, but you smoke. They aren't harmful.
 isten, they spend millions of dollars on cancer research, and
 hey come up with nothing, so they have to scare people
 omehow. Why don't they put on every bottle of Scotch
 Drink this and you will get cirrhosis of the liver'? Why don't
 hey write on every bottle of aspirin 'Take twenty of these
 nd they will kill you'? Smoke, darling." She sipped a glass of
 cotch and the talk was gay.

Suddenly a threat appeared menacingly in the aisle. A
 eporter with something slung over his shoulder. A tape
 ecorder? Or worse, a camera? No matter. Thunderclouds
 olled and the room turned dark. "Who are you?" she said
 n a loud Teutonic jolt. The violins frittered away and the
 rchestra came to a hush in a sigh of dissonance. "WHO
 ARE YOU?" The voice roared through the empty theater
 nd the laughing face turned into an Empress Catherine
 tare, cold as a glacier, as the man began to sweat, clinging
 o the wall for protection. "I . . . I'm waiting for some-
 ody."

"You aren't waiting for nobody. Come with me." She took

him by the arm and personally showed him the way ou
grim-jawed as the Prussian Army on the march.

Minutes later she was champagne-bubbly again, as thoug
the incident had never happened. The band wasn't seate
right, so she got up onstage and moved the furniture aroun
herself. The spotlight didn't land right. "They'll say 'Ladies an
gentlemen, Miss Marlene Dietrich,' and the light will sho
the big fat feet of the first violinist," she complained. Th
was no Circe, floating through the dreams of mortal men in
diaphanous gown. This was a woman working away th
afternoon, creating more problems than a dog has fleas an
solving them all in her own breathtaking way.

At six o'clock she told her chauffeur in a motherly way t
drive Bacharach to the airport to meet his wife (Ang
Dickinson) and we walked to Dinty Moore's for a steal
Stepping out of the stage door she was set upon by
toothless old hag with her head in a shredded scarf. One c
the autograph nuts who hangs around the door at Sardi's.
crowd gathered. "Oh darlin', I never thought I'd see youse i
person, I been waitin' all day, I got a present for ya," said th
crone, digging into a shopping bag full of old newspaper
"Don't worry, I'm not going anywhere," said Dietrich, show
ering this woman, who could have been her own age c
younger, with kindness. The cases of champagne and th
expensive gift-wrapped offerings from well-heeled Stage Doc
Johnnys waited upstairs, kicked into a corner, yet she waite
on the street with the patience of Job, the wind blowing he
lemony hair, for this autograph hound to come up with
penny from the bottom of an oily shopping bag. Lili Marlen
turning into a hausfrau.

We slid into a corner table and as she washed her stea
down with cold beer I discovered the best way to intervie
Dietrich is not to try. Given the time, she can summon th
inclination. The list of topics she will not discuss is as long a
your arm, but topping the list is her movie-star days wit
Von Sternberg. "I do not wish to be known as a movie sta
because, quite simply, I am *not* a movie star. I haven't mad
a film since *Judgment at Nuremberg* and that was a ver
special kind of thing. I may never make another one. I am a
international theater star now. It's so boring, all that tal
about the legendary Marlene and the legendary films of Vo
Sternberg. That's why I love Russia so. There was nobod
crying in their beer there about *The Blue Angel* because *Th
Blue Angel* never played there. They've never seen it. Thos
films are all right, but keep them in their place. Don't mak
them that important. I do not like to be interviewed anymor

y pansy film-fan writers, because all they want to know bout is *Blonde Venus* or *Shanghai Express*. There is a whole roup of people in America who do nothing but sit around in ark rooms in the Museum of Modern Art and watch old ovies. Don't they have anything more important to do with heir lives? I do with mine. Listen, I'm making fun of myself hen I walk onstage and say I came to America because I hought it was the most romantic nation in the world and en sing 'Blue Heaven.' I have a straight face and I say Here is a typical romantic song from one of my pictures' nd I do 'The Boys in the Backroom.' It's putting those ictures down, in a way. I kid myself *and* those films. I don't o the part of my show anymore where I came out like a an. I used to walk offstage one minute in the diamonds and urs, strip down stark naked, and come back on twenty-two econds later in tie and tails. But the girl who did that change ot married and I've never found anyone else who could do that fast, so I dropped it.

"I'm also tired of being called a sexy grandmother. It's nly in America that there is this obsession with sex. Artur Rubinstein is a great artist, but who gives a damn how many randchildren *he* has?" But she *is* sexy. And she does have our grandchildren, although she doesn't talk about them uch. Her family comes under the heading "private" and her rivacy is the thing she values most in life. "I can't stand any nvasion of my privacy unless I allow it. Even on opening ights nobody is allowed in my dressing room. I see everyone nstage. Invading my dressing room is like invading my edroom." But according to those who know her well enough o have met her family, she lives for her daughter, Maria, her on-in-law, William Riva, a toy and set designer, and their our boys. Two of them attend a terribly exclusive private chool in Switzerland (the one where the Shah of Persia's ids go) and people insist her money pays for their tuition. "I on't have a lot of money. I'm never solvent. I sold all my ewelry during the war. I don't live swathed in ermine and iamonds. I never owned anything. I rent an apartment n New York and one in Paris. I love America, because America took me in when I was in trouble and America has een good to me. We all thought Hitler would be out in two years, and when we saw he'd stay in, we never went back. Once you are derooted you stay that way. You can't grow roots again. With taxes the way they are here, though, you can't keep a cent. When I left Hollywood to join the army, it wasn't so bad. I wasn't taxed then. But while one department of the government was giving me medals, anoth-

er one was suing me for back taxes. I had to work off th
back taxes after the war, when I didn't have a cent."

The war in Vietnam is another of her favorite topics, and
although she is careful to veil her political views, they see
through in the songs she sings, like Pete Seeger's 'Wher
Have All the Flowers Gone," and sometimes even in he
talk. "What are we going to do," she says, leaning over he
plate, "kill Johnson?" She admits things have changed sinc
she fell in love with America. "I came here in 1930 an
became a citizen in 1934. It was absolutely wonderful then
Nobody was afraid of anything and you could say what you
liked. I am still a citizen. You don't change your citizenship
like you change your dress. But honey, it ain't the America
now it was then. I defend it in Europe, but I'm not proud
There's a fear now that wasn't here when I came. It's fear
that makes us weak."

Like the girl in Hugh Martin's song who lives at 5134
Kensington Avenue and can't get through to the boy who lives
at 5133, you can be in the same room with Dietrich and never
get close. It's just as well. Some of the friendships she has
formed over the years ended, dashed against the rocks, when
people got personal. And friendship is sacred. "All my friends
are dead," she says, and means it. She was never part of the
Hollywood scene and, except for possibly Billy Wilder, she
rarely visits anyone there. She always found a haven in New
York, where she blended in with the others who had escaped
the Nazis. People like Mady Christians and Eleanora Mendelssohn, from the Felix Mendelssohn family, who had
financed the career of Max Reinhardt and fled Berlin when
Hitler came to power. Women of beauty and wealth and
talent who would smuggle a pearl necklace or a Van Gogh
out of their left-behind homes and live on that. Then there
was the Paris crowd—Hemingway and Cocteau and Gerard
Philippe and Piaf—although she leans across the table and
intimates "Piaf needed me more than I needed her. She was
a Gemini." All of them gone now. "There is no one left I can
telephone at four in the morning if I need them. I always had
the public, of course, but that is never enough. It's the ones
you can call up at four A.M. who matter. But that's true with
everyone, isn't it? Nobody is really devoted to another person
or even to a project anymore. You can't shake people up
today. But friendship is still important and I'm very loyal.
Even if the few friends I have fail me, it doesn't matter. I
am always there when they need me. I won't let people know
I need them, because I don't want to burden them, but I
do *need*, just like everybody else."

224

She is hung up on horoscopes. "What sign are you?" she asks first thing.

"Libra."

"No wonder I like you. I'm Capricorn. That means a lifetime of trouble. Capricorns have to work for everything. But it's nice for others. We work for other people. Very conscientious, Capricorns." If she has a secret about how to stay young, she isn't telling. "I eat anything. If you don't like it, go jump in the lake." She loves German doughnuts filled with apricot jam and sardine-and-onion sandwiches on rye bread. She can stand at the sink, the steam in her hair, and rise up out of the soapsuds like the Phoenix from the ashes. She never wears red and spends half her life in aprons and blue jeans. Contrary to all the old wives' tales floating around about how her legs aren't her own, how her hair is a wig, how her face is held together by a tight mask—forget it. Everything is hers, and, as Lee Remick's husband said on opening night, "Even if they aren't, they sure belonged to somebody wonderful." Even with no makeup, sitting a finger-tip away, she looks like your kid sister, but mention beauty and she laughs. "I stay out of the sun, mainly because I don't have time. I don't bother much with myself. I wash and I go. I don't look at myself in mirrors. I sleep whenever I can get it. I wish I could sleep twelve hours a day, but my profession won't allow it. Last night I slept from two to six. Six hours. That's not bad."

"That's four hours, not six."

"I can't count. I never could count. There is one thing. My hands. I froze my hands once in the war and now when I sing I put them behind me because they turn blue when they get warm under the lights."

She hates almost everything written about her, especially reviews. ("Only fools keep press clippings.") Her most recent Gethsemane is a new book called *Dietrich* (what else?) by Leslie Frewin. "It's all lies, honey. People in my childhood made up, written from a clipping service. All lies. When people come up to me in the street with copies to autograph, I refuse." She hates television ("They've offered me the moon, but I'm still a virgin in that area. Who needs it?") and never goes to fashionable nightclubs. She'd rather give a small dinner party, like the one she threw for Sir John Gielgud when he came to America to do *Ages of Man*, for which she will spend the entire day cooking, then serve her guests like a maid and never sit down and eat. She will walk out of the room if anyone asks her about her legend, but she will spend hours talking about Las Vegas or babies or Bloomingdale's or the color yellow. "I have anxieties, like everyone else, but only about fate, growing old, things beyond my control. Not about me or my work. Right now the thing that worries me most is that if I do not get back to the theater there will be no opening night."

But there was. Sweatshirts were gone. Seats with their backs missing were gone. Maxwell House coffee cans full of cigarette butts were gone. And everybody came. Olivia De Havilland and Joan Fontaine came, and even smiled at each other. Merman came. Dietrich's husband, an unassuming California chicken farmer named Rudi Sieber, who has been married quietly to her for forty-four years, came. My God, even Tallulah Bankhead came, telling everyone it was the first time she had been to an opening night in twenty years. And when the lights dimmed and the pink light hit the star of the show in just the place she had rehearsed it, you couldn't hear the cymbals for the standing ovation.

There she was, looking peachy and creamy in waves of shimmering spangles, dodging the flowers they threw at her like rice. Mother Courage in sequins. And backstage, when it's all over, when she has finally pulled the curtains closed with her bare hands to stop the screams for more, she stands in the middle of the flowers sipping her Scotch and says, "There's a fly in here. It was flying around my head all night. I don't think I was very good. It's gone better." True there was no Hemingway to give her a glamorous introduction, no Cocteau to write poems to her in the press, no Piaf applauding in the wings. She's survived them all.

But the legend lives on. . . .

Governor Lester Maddox

OCTOBER, 1967.

> (*Governor Lester Maddox of Georgia is the only subject in this collection who is not a celebrity in the Klieg-light sense of the word. But because he is one of the most controversial, colorful, interesting, and infamous characters who ever rose to power in the American*

*political arena, he creates his own aura of ce-
lebrity that follows him around like a stray dog
after a hot biscuit. That's why he's included
here.)*

N MEMORIAL DAY, orange-hot sunbeams filtered down
through the magnolia blossoms and darted off the gold-leaf
dome of the state capitol building in Atlanta. The air smelled
like ripe bananas, ladybugs crawled lazily across the early-
morning grass, and yellow jackets sipped the dew dripping like
blackstrap molasses in the Southern heat. Traffic was slow
and it was easy to find a park. Everybody in town was at the
swimming pool, or going on a holiday picnic, or in their
air-conditioned houses watching ball games on TV. Everybody, that is, except Lester Maddox, the sixty-fifth governor
of Georgia.

Down at the state capitol, a limestone monolith which cost
$118.43 less than a million dollars of carpetbagger money to
build, ol'Lester was hard at work behind his desk. Lester
does not celebrate Memorial Day. He only recognizes
Confederate Memorial Day. And for the next four years, so
will the people who work for him.

It was early, not yet noon, but the TV reporters from the
local stations were already setting up cables in the marble
halls, hoping to catch ol'Lester's thoughts for the day. Not
that they expected to get much. One thing Lester Maddox
has learned since he's been in public office is that the press is
his natural enemy. They print cartoons of him, analyze his
vocabulary on their editorial pages, criticize his every legisla-
tive move, and make him the butt of more jokes than
Tallulah Bankhead. (Only that morning one reporter had told
me the latest Lester joke: Seems ol'Lester got constipated
on the plane to Washington to visit LBJ. When he arrived, he
dashed off the jet and raced to the men's room. A few
minutes of toil and trouble later, he couldn't find any toilet
paper in his cabin, so he banged on the wall of the compart-
ment next to him. "Y'awl got any toilet papuh in theah?"
"Not a bit," came the answer. Ol'Lester searched through
his pockets, came up with a crisp bill, and banged on the
wall again. "Y'awl got two fives fo' a ten, then?")

Wandering past polished glass cases filled with dirty, rot-
ing Confederate flags, I wondered what Lester Maddox was
really like. I had only seen him once, on television, waving a
pistol at a group of Negro youths who had tried to enter his
fried-chicken cafeteria called the Pickrick, drool running
down his chin, eyes bulging and crazed like a madman

227

undergoing withdrawal symptoms after twenty-five years (
heroin addiction. Now he is governor, a fact that ha
provided more conversational needlepoint for sophisticate
Atlanta than canned peaches or *Gone With the Wind*. "I'v
never interviewed a governor before. I don't know muc
about politics," I confessed nervously to one of the reporter:
a Dartmouth graduate from Ohio. "Don't worry," he reas
sured, "neither does ol'Lester."

Inside the glass doors marked "Office of the Governor" sa
a buxom brunette in slight makeup and a bright-orange dres
with two yellow porcelain pears on her left bosom. Her nam
is Mrs. Mary Beasley and she knows everything that goes o
in ol'Lester's office. When I telephoned the governor's publi
relations counsel, Bob Short, from New York, he put m
right through to Mrs. Beasley, who assured me, "Don't worr
'bout a thing, I'll see that you get a good story." She wave
me to a seat and continued with her telephone conversation
"I can't get a call in to the governor now 'cause Carolyn ha
so many calls waiting. You'll have to call back." A lot c
other people were waiting, too. There was a man in a whit
ice-cream plantation suit smoking a Havana cigar wh
looked like Raymond Massey as Abe Lincoln, forty-tw
Negro schoolchildren from Albany, Georgia, and a twenty
four-year-old war veteran from Jackson, Mississippi, wearin
a Purple Heart over a short-sleeve sports shirt who had com
to ask ol'Lester to march in a "Win the War in Vietnam
parade.

Suddenly, unspectacularly, ol'Lester himself was on th
scene, dodging the reporters, shaking hands like Will Rogers
chucking the Negro kids under the chin (carefully avoidin
touching their hair), and telling everybody "Howdy." Dresse
in a forty-dollar, olive-drab Robert Hall suit with a Masoni
pin in his lapel, he looks, at fifty-two, like a little fightin
cock. Hairy hands hang from their coatsleeves in animate
chunks. His round, balding head, too big for his stubby littl
body, rises above the rest of him, with a few tiny strands o
hair clinging for dear life to the crown, Dagwood Bumstea
style. Horn-rimmed glasses sag heavily against a network o
tiny varicose veins that threaten to fester and erupt on th
top of a nose supported by a red sunset of a face that continu
ally changes shades as his temper comes and goes. When h
speaks, he whimpers in a high-pitched, nasal voice, like Hen
ry Aldrich with hormones. "This the gentleman from N'Yok
C'mon and let's have us a li'l talk, son," he motioned, leadin
the way past the outstretched hands and ignoring Mrs
Beasley, who waved three telephones frantically at him.

228

In his chambers, blood-red carpets line the floors, black-
ther chairs rest comfortably against dark wood-paneled
lls, air-conditioning turned up to 65 degrees sends wet
ills through the bones, and in stark contrast, possibly as a
minder of its phantom past, an ante-bellum plantation sofa
th cream-and-rose-colored flowers nods graciously in the
rner. On his desk, a spray of disorganized bills to sign, state
cuments, assembly-meeting speeches, and a copy of
illiam Manchester's *The Death of a President* sprawl non-
alantly, almost covering ol'Lester's prize possession—a
gantic white-leather Holy Bible with his name engraved in
ld. Also in the clutter I noticed a statue of praying hands
inting up towards an enormous Confederate flag waving
st behind his leather chair, another paperweight of praying
nds holding down a copy of Robert Ardrey's *The Territori-
Imperative*, and, just beyond, a smaller, unobtrusive Amer-
n flag dangling precariously on a stick.

"I don't turn away anybody, no *suh*. You know they tell me
onald Reagan don't let *nobody* in to see him. Well, I don't
n my bizness thataway. I promised to be guv'nor of all the
ople, black *and* white, and I'm keepin' my word. Tell me,
hat do they say about me up yonder in N'Yok? They think
m some kinda nut? Well, I'm not. You ask me anything you
ant, heah?" (Out in the hallway, Carolyn was still getting
lls on the governor's phone. "Where IS Carolyn?" Mrs.
asley was asking anyone in the room willing to answer.)

I asked him about his campaign. "Well, suh, I knew I
dn't have any money. I couldn't put ads in the paper 'cause
body liked me and I already closed down my restaurant
ause the Communists in Washington had turned the state of
eorgia into a police state. So in October of '65 I went to
ork preparin' a platform which I published 50,000 copies of
d delivered by hand in my '64 white Ponyac stationwagon.
had no public-relations firm and nobody to write a speech
ven. I answered all the mail myself—traveled a hunnert
ousand miles and fifty thousand of that was in one car.
obody ran my campaign but me. I always been my own
oss and that's the way it's gonna stay. Cost me forty
ousand just to get in the primary and the run-off against
wo million that had been spent against me by my opponents.
never did even have a billboard. I been studyin' on politics
or thirty years and I ran fer lots of things, but I never did
in. This time I didn't see no way in the God's world I
ould lose. People were fed up with the Communist dictators
nd rabble-rousin' bolsheviki 'roun' here and I knew they'd
upport an ol' country boy like me. I tied me a four-foot
229

ladder on the top of my Ponyac and drove down the highway and evertime I saw one of them big two-thousand-dollar billboards put up by one of my opponents I'd just pull off the road, get my ladder out and nail up ten little signs all over their big'uns and ruin 'em all and it wouldn't cost me but a quarter."

He roared a high tenor laugh, rubbing his nose with his two forefingers. I asked him how much he got paid. He didn't flinch. "The salary was twelve thousand a year when I was elected—about eighteen thousand includin' commissions. They increased it to forty-two thousand five hundred a year for me. Hell, a mule couldn' live on what they used to pay. There was more money in sellin' fried chicken. I got a furniture bizness on the side now which the wife runs and I plan to go back into that when this is all over. You know I wuz a happy sonbitch in that restaurant. I still don't like to drive by there. It hurts my heart. I got into it with fo' dollars in my pocket and through the great American free-enterprise system enlarged it nine times in ten years till I was makin' half a million dollars a year before the Communist take-over under Lyndon Johnson. You know, the moral decadence in this country is frightnin'. Chillrun see their parents and executives in political life drinkin' and carryin' on, abusin theirselves on the taxpayer's money, and they think they can do it too. I know I cain't wipe this condition out, but I know if I c'n git others to follow my example we'll raise a state full of Christians down heah in Georgia. I wouldn' have opened my restaurant if I had to sell cocktails. It was a place you could bring the wife and chillrun on a Sunday night without fightin' off the drunks. Many of my friends do take a social drink, mind ya, but not me. I don't smoke either. You won find an ashtray in heah. Drinkin' and smokin' leads to more degeneracy. Just like some people want to integrate. That' their bizness. When the gov'ment tried to force my customer to sit next to Nigras I got mad. We don' cotton to that stu down heah. I'm a peaceful man and I always treated m colored hep fair with due respect and a decent wage. But I'm not gonna live next door, no *suh*. I've never been one to go mad and fuss. Those kind lose. But don' step on me."

I asked him if he ever had any regrets about the pisto waving incident that sent his image flying through the T cables of the world as a radical monster of the militar Southern-bigot variety. "Naw *suh!*" Did he think he had don the wrong thing, displaying his passionate hatred of Negro in public? "Naw *suh!*" Would he do it again? "Yes *suh* Would he uphold the federal law regarding desegregatio
230

now that he was governor? "If a man wonts to let them Nigras in his place of bizness that's up to him. I cain't stop him. If he don't then I cain't stop that neither. The system of free enterprise is one of the principles the American people cherish most. They are declaring war on the chillrun of the South. Integration represents an erosion of the rights of the people. We are placin' the Constitution ahead of the welfare of our citizens and the people of Georgia are not gonna continue to tolerate this."

It was all beginning to sound like dialogue from a bad Susan Hayward movie. What were his views on some of the more sane topics, I wondered? How would he handle, for instance, capital punishment? (Four hundred and fifteen people have died in Georgia's electric chair.) "I've never signed an order sendin' nobody to the 'lectric chair. Rather than do that I'd rather walk that last step myself. Some of the people go to the 'lectric chair 'cause juries are afraid the criminals will be back on the streets in seven years if they don't kill 'em. I plan to solve that problem by makin' their sentences longer and keep 'em in jail. Then they cain't git out." Right.

The phone rang. It was a long-distance call from the new head of the Pardon and Parole Board, Judge J. O. Partain, whose first act after Lester's appointment was to sign a medical reprieve for a dangerous Negro prisoner to travel to Louisiana for an operation. The prisoner had escaped and all week the Atlanta papers had been giving Lester hell about it, charging incompetence, demanding an explanation, and even publishing a history of Judge Partain's activities as a member of the Ku Klux Klan. "Yes *suh*. What do you mean we don't have the prisoner's records anywhere in the files? How could you lose a man's prison record?" A frantic glance in my direction. "Well, don't tell that fellow you just named anythin' you don't want to be told all over the place, you heah? Yes *suh*."

He returned from his conversation, ready to quote more political press agentry to his Yankee visitor. "I believe people in high places as well as low places oughta practice what they preach. They talk big but then they git into office and turn to graft and immorality. This state gonna git the best gov'ment under me it's ever had. I just wanted to see what a honest man could accomplish. I have no close ties with any Establishment controlled by any group anyplace anywhere. I'm jes' one of the people. I git out in the streets in them country towns and people yell 'Lester,' not 'Guv'nor!' I'm a big follower of Dale Carnegie, who taught me to follow the

Golden Rule of Jesus instead of jes' admirin' it. My image was like a animal or a red-neck or a beast. That's 'cause of the Communist press. We still have some articles in Atlanta that are brutal. Look here." He thrust some clippings from the *Atlanta Constitution* at me. One was an editorial-page cartoon showing Stokely Carmichael holding a sign, "Don't Obey Laws You Don't Like," and being chased with a club held by Maddox, then Maddox picking up the same sign and marching off with it. Another was an editorial by Ralph McGill, the distinguished journalist-columnist-publisher of the *Constitution*, titled "Defending the Second Rate." A third, titled "A Little Maddoxemantics," was an analysis of the grammatical errors in Lester's public speeches. "They try to make me look like a durn fool ever chance they git," he said. "It's yeller journalism. They won't ferget my past. When I gave up my restaurant, I opened up a souvenir stand in front, sellin' ax handles. You could buy a whole family backlash kit with mama-size drumsticks and junior-size drumsticks—those clubs railroad switchmen used to carry. I was outta bizness and had to do *somethin'*. They blew that up in the papers like it was awful, even tho' the demand fer my ax handles only lasted two days. I bought more'n I could sell and there weren't no Nigras aroun' to use 'em on anyway 'cause the restaurant was already closed down." He raised his arms behind his bald head and stretched his stumpy little legs out in front of him, closing his eyes, remembering. "I'd much rather be ol'Lester at the Pickrick, sellin' short ribs and beans than guv'nor. Everbody lost when I lost that place.

"I still believe intergration is un-Christian. The Bible says so." Where in the Bible? "Wait a minute, and I'll show you." He searched in his desk and handed me a sheet of paper someone had mimeographed for him. "This is proof of the breakdown of the races as ungodly—'In choosin' a wife for Isaac, he was instructed that thou should not take a wife unto my son, who is a daughter of the Canaanites'—that's from Genesis twenty-four, verses three and four. Also from Leviticus—'Thou shalt not let thy cattle mix with the diverse kind.' And in Deuteronomy it says 'Thou shalt not plow with an ox and an ass together.' It's against the will of our God to integrate. The Bible says it right here."

He told me it was high time he got some work done but I could "hang around" if I wanted to and promised me another meeting. "Sorry I don't have more time, but son, I hadn' had a day off since I been here."

Outside, Mrs. Beasley had been replaced by a Mrs. Alexander, a substitute secretary in a bright-yellow sunflower shift who turned out to be the mysterious "Carolyn." She was talking to a Negro woman who looked like Aunt Jemima, leaning over the desk bawling big glycerine movie tears with a bright-red bandanna wrapped around her head. "I gots to have some hep fo' my haid. I'm sick and I'm jes' as free as you is."

"I know you are, hon," said Mrs. Alexander, directing the woman to the free clinic across the street from the capitol.

"Is them the psy-criatists?"

"Yes, and *they* can help you—the governor *can't*."

"I gots ta get my haid out from under my hem," said the woman, shuffling out into the bright sunlight.

"Lord, they come here with every problem known to man," sighed Mrs. Alexander. "I didn't work here during Carl Sanders' administration but the girls tell me he didn't see any of them. Lester comes around twice a day and says hello to everybody and yet they still write the most terrible things about him. Did you read the article in the *Saturday Evening Post?* It made me sick to my stomach. Why, you should see the little Nigra Girl Scouts. He kept the mayor of Atlanta waiting in his office one day for an hour while he signed autographs. . . ."

The man in the white ice-cream suit with the plantation bow tie was still standing nearby, smoking his Havana cigar. "My name's Shine. Please to meetcha. You from a magazine? *Esquire!* You mean ol'Lester gonna be in *Esquire?* Well, kiss my foot. Now if he c'n jes' get in *Playboy* he got it made. You tell them folks up yonder in New Yok he ain't crazy. He got Klan members on his staff, but I never seen ol'Lester at any Klan meetin' I wuz ever at. He's been good to the coloreds. Why, there's been more goddamn niggers in his room since he's been here than any guv'nor in the history of Georgia."

A little girl wandered into the governor's office drinking a bottle of Orange Crush. Nobody stopped her. Then the forty-two Negro school kids from the Jackson Heights Elementary in Albany wandered through on a tour. The president of the fifth grade, a small, grinning child named Douglas Green, sat in the governor's black-leather chair as a pretty, white tour guide whacked out in her best fading-camellia smile: "Maybe that'll inspire *you* to run for governor yourself some day." Lester shot her a withering glance from behind the staff photographer. "C'mon, y'awl smile—say cheese!" A chorus of giggles. They smiled their watermelon smiles as an armed state trooper watched from his post near a window overlooking a menacing Civil War statue standing like a silent sentinel in a clump of peaceful flowering zinnias.

HOW, IN AN ENLIGHTENED POLITICAL AGE full of Kennedys and Stevensons and Romneys, you ask, could it happen? This is the South, baby, where Huey P. Longs can still get elected by appealing to the illiterate lower classes. Maddox is the microcosm of old-fashioned grass-roots politics, representing the legion of poor white Southerners who think of themselves as "just folks" and feel alienated from the growing middle-class society around them. (On the night of his election, a throng of Maddox supporters, including several Klan members and a few Baptist missionaries wearing cotton house dresses and gardenia corsages, gathered in the rotunda of the state capitol. "Well, one of us finally made it," said one, swigging down a Coke.) The real irony lies not in the fact that Lester Maddox made it (in Louisiana, worse things have happened—Huey P. Long's brother Earl used to pee in a Coke bottle at state banquets before they carried him off to the insane asylum in Galveston, and in his second term Jimmie Davis rode to work up the steps of the state capitol building in Baton Rouge on a white horse called Sunshine), but that he came to power in a city like Atlanta.

People there still can't believe the election. It was a queer one, even for a state that once had two governors at the same time. This was a city that had watched Lester's rise to power with the horrified fascination of a crowd at Cape Kennedy that has just witnessed a rocket launching explode in midair. Before he became governor, he couldn't even get elected dogcatcher. He ran for mayor in 1957 and 1961 and people laughed. He ran for lieutenant governor in 1962 and the Negro vote killed him. The liberals denounced him because his background is a study in illiteracy (he is not a high-school dropout, as some political columnists have pointed out—he never even got to high school) but the common workers love him. He appeared to shake hands at every shift break in every cottonfield in Georgia, walked up and down the main streets of the country towns telling druggists "Doctor, I wanna show you my prescription for Georgia," and while his opponents rode in planes Lester refused, saying, "You cain't shake hands from a helicopter." He put every penny he owned into his campaign, even mortgaged his house. People who ridiculed him were often subjected to threatening phone calls from his admirers and one political opponent was even forced to engage full-time police protection at his home.

In the Democratic primary the Republicans cut their

own throats by voting for the Democratic candidate they thought had the least chance of beating their own Bo Callaway, a distinguished Ivy League Atlanta lawyer and the first Republican representative from Georgia to sit in Congress in years. (Callaway even gave up his seat in Washington to run.) With the Republican vote added to the red-neck vote, Lester got enough votes to land in the run-off with Callaway. But the liberal Democrats and the Negroes, who didn't approve either candidate, headed a write-in for Ellis Arnall, a former Georgia governor, who stole so many votes that neither Maddox nor Callaway received a majority. Callaway got approximately 49.4 percent of the votes, Lester came in second with approximately 49.3 percent, and Arnall got the rest. Lawsuits were filed. A recount was demanded. According to the state constitution, if no candidate receives a majority vote, the election must be decided by the General Assembly, which is composed of 231 Democrats to 31 Republicans. One hundred and thirty votes were needed to elect. Since 55 percent of Georgia's Democratic Party is conservative, it was easy to predict. The whole fiasco was complicated by Stokely Carmichael's sudden appearance on the scene, a race riot, and the attack on a local youth by an Atlanta policeman. Lester's racist attitude suddenly became popular. Instead of another election (this one had already cost Georgia more than the state budget) the General Assembly met the first week of January, 1967. That night, while people were still laughing at him, ol'Lester drove his family out to the new one-million-dollar-plus executive mansion, parked his stationwagon, and pointed a stubby finger: "I jes' wanted y'awl t'see where you gonna be livin'."

Few Atlantans slept that night. TV sets blared, waiting for the votes. The people had already handed Callaway a plurality. Now it was up to the politicians. So few Republicans showed up for the count that Callaway got on TV, tears in his eyes, and said he understood. It was the poor plowboy (Lester) vs. the rich liberal millionaire (Callaway) who never worked for his bread and butter, went to West Point, skied on the slopes of Aspen, owned five textile mills, and had a brother who was a Hollywood playboy.

The morning Lester was announced as the new governor, liberal, sophisticated Atlanta awoke to storm clouds. People wore black arm bands. Men stayed home from work. Children stayed home from school. Businesses nervously watched the stock market. Gas stations erected signs near their gas pumps announcing "The chicken man will get you if you don't watch out!"

235

Atlanta bears little relation to the rest of the South and none whatsoever to the rest of Georgia. Of its 1,250,000 population, one-half is composed of Negroes and only slightly less than the remainder is made up of sophisticated, upper-class white liberals brought in by big businesses from other states. With its sloping hills, its richness of foliage (they say three blossoming dogwoods abound to every man here), and its swanky sections of luxury homes, Atlanta looks more like Beverly Hills than the South. Very few reminders of the old South, in fact, still exist. The Ku Klux Klan used to burn crosses on top of Stone Mountain, a pebble's throw from where Butterfly McQueen sold peanut-butter sandwiches to the tourists in her Prissy costume from *Gone With the Wind,* and out at Aunt Fanny's Cabin, a slave quarter turned into a billion-dollar restaurant serving such pre-Civil War staples as Smithfield ham, grits, black-eyed peas, and sweet potato pie, pickaninnies stuck their heads through holes in the wall and sang the menus, then went into a buck-and-wing for the delighted summer visitors.

But all that has changed now. Calvin Craig, grand dragon of the Georgia KKK, has been forced to move out of Buckhead, Atlanta's classiest residential section (where, ironically, the new governor's mansion now stands), by his neighbors, and burning crosses are as hard to find as Confederate nickels. Butterfly McQueen has two lawsuits against the city for using her picture on a postcard without her permission and the pickaninnies at Aunt Fanny's Cabin have banded together to sue for ten years of back federal excise taxes on entertainment. People drive as fast on the Atlanta expressways as they do on the Hollywood Freeway. The old Tara-like plantations have been razed to make room for new $110-million luxury apartment complexes and the city boasts the best Urban Renewal program in the United States. The Klan is still active in the rural sections of Georgia, but in Atlanta it is an innocuous group headed by a local barber, whose activities seldom get rowdier than ringing doorbells and passing out circulars. The only racial demonstrations have been minor. As one Atlanta newspaperman says, "There hasn't been a march through here since General Sherman."

Not that Negroes are treated like kings. Restaurants still refuse to allow them to be photographed inside, Negro babies are kept behind the whites in hospital maternity wards, so they are not visible from the plate-glass viewing windows, and Negro homes in Buttermilk Bottom are being bought by the city for measly sums and resold to developers for millions. I spoke to Atlanta matrons who never knew until a

236

year ago that Negroes had last names. But the situation is much better than it is in most sections of the South and it was improving vastly when Lester came into office. Suddenly Atlanta found itself trusted to the care of a man who had no experience in governing even a crossroad junction, let alone a cosmopolitan city, who had never held public office, who knew none of the right people, who drank only buttermilk and didn't even own a dinner jacket (the only time he has been seen in black tie since his inauguration was the night of the opening of the Metropolitan Opera in Atlanta, when, minutes before the curtain, he was spotted at the Varsity Drive In trying to get ketchup out of a rented tux).

Lester-watching had been a sport second only in popularity to the Atlanta Braves for years. Chicken wasn't all he sold at the old Pickrick. Visitors could also read letters, pamphlets, and a publicly posted letter calling for the sterilization of all Negroes. Tourists could purchase a copy of the U.S. Constitution or a KKK announcement, side by side. Lester also displayed prominently Goldwater bumper stickers, American flags, a wooden barrel of ax handles to use on any Negro who entered the door, and a large booklet called *Kiss of Death,* published by the Christian Constitutional Education League in Ft. Lauderdale, Florida, billed as "a graphic illustration of beautiful white maidenhood clasped in the arms of an African savage" and showing a white girl being raped by a half-Negro, half-gorilla.

The Pickrick had been started with $25,000 saved from Lester's original four-dollar hot-dog-stand investment. It was a brick and board building approximately a hundred feet long and thirty feet wide located at 891 Hemphill Avenue, in a seedy section of Atlanta across from the Georgia Tech campus at the end of a street on which also stood a Baptist church where, every Sunday morning at the height of Lester's pistol-waving headlines, the minister would end his prayer at noon, close his Bible, and say "Amen and everybody eat at the Pickrick."

Gene Landers, now an Atlanta poultry-store owner, was Lester's night cook. "I'll say one thing for the man," he says, "he was always shrewd. He needed a parking lot, so he bought remnant cement discarded from other concrete jobs around town, gave the drivers a couple of dollars a load to dump it on their way home from work, and put it into blocks with his own hands. He was very religious. I remember one night he dreamed he was going against God because he was selling fried chicken on Sunday, so he closed down on Sunday for nearly a year until he nearly went broke. There were six

Negroes in the kitchen and one called Hot Poppa was his best curb-service man. He used to tell all his employees, 'I'll pay you what you're worth.' My first paycheck had ten dollars more in it than I had been promised. When he bought his first Fleetwood Cadillac he pinned a sign on it saying 'Pickrick paid for this.' "

The Pickrick became an institution, not only for its snappy fried chicken sold cafeteria-style at a reasonable price, but because of its ads, placed every week in the Atlanta papers. Everybody else ran their ads in the big Sunday editions, but Lester foxily unveiled his on Saturday, causing more attention and getting cheaper rates and wider space. They began as harmless ads for fried chicken, but as his following grew, ol'Lester saw an opportunity to use them as sounding boards for racial prejudice. Under big headlines worded "PICKRICK SAYS," he editorialized at length to the delight of everyone in town, capitalizing key words to get his message across: "If you want to integrate, then integrate. Just leave me alone. I don't bother you and all I ask is that you be Christian enough not to bother me. Stop making yourself look inferior by taking away something that belongs to others. AND THAT ALL may know, we do not serve INTEGRATIONISTS regardless of race, creed, or color. This means red, yellow, black and white. We discriminate against INTEGRATIONISTS and respect their right to discriminate against us." Followed by the prices of his Sunday-night drumstick special.

When Dobbins Air Force Base in Marietta expanded its staff to include Negro employees, he wrote: "Is it true that the lady employees have been placed under guard to protect them from the savages who have been turned loose upon the law-abiding citizens of America? That some of them have already been attacked and that guards now watch over them while at work and even guard them to and from the parking lots?"

But trouble really started for Lester on July 3, 1964—the day after the federal civil-rights bill was passed. Three Negro students tried to enter the Pickrick and were chased away by customers brandishing ax handles and by Lester waving a pistol and yelling, "Get away, you no-good dirty Communists!" On August 11, three more youths appeared and were immediately surrounded by a crowd of Lester's friends in torn sweat shirts and Bermuda shorts, gas-station attendants in sockless tennis shoes, frowsy Southern white girls licking Eskimo Pies, and Lester's own Negro kitchen help. Lester's people. Among them, his own two fat sisters, shouting obscenities. That night Lester staged a march, followed by 500 local toughs, in front of the Pickrick. He shoved policemen, shouted at the TV cameras with spit running down his chin, and threatened to shoot any Negro who came near him. Police wreckers were called to haul away the Maddox family cars blocking the entrance to Hemphill Avenue and Lester ended up on all the front pages, even rating a profile on the Huntley-Brinkley report. He became more than just an object of curiosity. He became a celebrity. He even posed under the Pickrick sign, kissing his wife with tears running down a face streaked with red-clay Georgia dirt, and announced "Hello, Boss man" over a loud-speaker system each time a local reporter entered the restaurant to snap his picture.

The next day federal marshals invaded the Pickrick and handed Lester a government order to desegregate or else. He went to the Democratic convention in Atlantic City and picketed in front of Convention Hall, to no avail. In the last week of September, a Negro theological student named Rev. Charles Wells tried to enter the Pickrick and Maddox pushed him bodily out of the front door. Wells was the same minister who already had one lawsuit going against ol'Lester for waving a pistol at him in the July incident. With two lawsuits, a federal order to desegregate and the federal tax men suing him for deducting his Pickrick editorials as business expenses, ol'Lester was really in trouble. He wrote in his customary ad in the Atlanta *Journal:* "Because of this ungodly, un-American, unconstitutional and unhuman legislation, we lost more money in the last two months than I earned the first ten years after leaving school. We will never get over this horrible thing that has come into our lives and never recover the financial losses." Followed by:

OUR PRESENT MENU

Long-Playing Record,
  "IF I GO TO JAIL" *by Lester Maddox*......$2.95
  (A live reproduction of our news conference a short time after being attacked by the Communist-inspired racial agitators and just before being sued by little Bobby.)
  CARTOONS: *(10¢ and down)*
  "Bobby and the Gestapo at the Pickrick Door"
  "Get Behind Johnson" (North end of south-bound donkey)
  "Johnson With a Beagle By the Ears"

On top of his financial problems, the Justice Department stepped into the picture and began an investigation of the Pickrick because ol'Lester was violating the Interstate Commerce Act by selling foodstuffs imported from out of state to out-of-state residents in a segregated establishment. Lester's greatest ad appeared in October, 1964, the week Lady Bird Johnson visited Atlanta:

PARENTS

in distant states who have been questioned because your son at Georgia Tech came to our cafeteria for meals, students at Tech who have been visited by FBI agents, men and women who work in Atlanta (with out-of-state license plates) and others who have been subjected to this police state harassment . . . please do not blame us.

BLAME THE PRESIDENT,

the United States Congress and the Communists for this dreadful and unbelievable thing that has happened to Freedom and Liberty in America.

SPECIAL TONIGHT
(No Integrationists)

Order of Lester's skillet-fried chicken—25¢ for drumstick and thigh, 55¢ for breast.

AND I APPRECIATE

the Negro man who called to tell me it makes him sick to look at that picture that shows Atlanta's top Negro political leader being hugged by the President of the U.S.

BY THE WAY

we could use a few more customers but we don't want any integrationists, regardless of race, creed or color. . . . and we DO NOT OFFER *to serve* INTERSTATE *travelers because the government denies your right to eat here by refusing to let us operate our business segregated if we offer to serve you. It is a police state we have; just like Lyndon Johnson said we would have if the Civil Rights Act of 1964 should ever be passed.* OUR SUNDAY MENU—*skillet-fried chicken, 50¢.*

On Feb. 1, 1965, Maddox appeared in Federal Court charged with contempt of a court order compelling him to serve Negroes. On March 20 he was tried for choking and beating a Negro minister. An all-white jury deliberated forty-seven minutes and returned a verdict of not guilty. Lester led the Ku Klux Klan through the streets of Atlanta to dramatize the situation (on the condition that they leave their robes at home) but by September he had thrown in the towel. Several hundred people gathered at the old Pickrick to watch him erect and dedicate a monument to the "death of private

perty rights in America," a small white building with a
enty-foot tower which still stands today. In the base are
pies of the Declaration of Independence and the Constitu-
n side by side in a coffin symbolizing, to ol'Lester, "the end
freedom."

One thing which has never been publicized, but which is
nerally regarded as fact in Atlanta, is the sale of the
ckrick. The rumor is that Lester had already sold it to
orgia Tech for a quarter of a million dollars *before* the
mmotion began over desegregation. If that is true, the
ickrick Says" ads were shrewdly calculated political
aneuvers designed not out of belief and personal conviction,
t out of a hard-nosed determination to make a "name" for
nself before election time. The announcement of his cam-
ign came simultaneously with the closing of the restau-
at.

Since his election, he has seldom exploded in public. He has
pped criticizing the Johnson administration. And he has
t turned Negroes away from the state capitol. The local
ess, which has given him a bloody fight, is most amazed of
. "Perhaps," suggests one newsman, "he's another Harry
uman. Maybe the office is taking hold of the man instead
the other way around." Another newsman has openly sug-
sted that the state require a licensed psychiatrist to examine
ester to see if there is a trace of paranoia in his personality.
ll agree he has yet to be confronted with the kind of
rcumstances that would provoke an outburst. "If it ever
mes to a showdown, I'm afraid it'll be like *Gunfight at the
K. Corral*," says one.

Once the Mr. Hyde character did come out in the school-
nsolidation crisis. The state board of education wants to
nsolidate all the little backwoods schools in Georgia so
urses like calculus and French can be offered and conse-
ently more kids in rural areas can qualify for Georgia
ech. Lester doesn't want it. This interferes with his "little
an" conception of the human race. He wants each little
hool to be its own boss, the way he handled his chicken
staurant. If there is a consolidation, he says, it must be a
ajority vote. Discussing this in his office, one school-board
ember made the mistake of saying, "You're a fine one to
lk about *majority*—you weren't even elected by a majority
f the *votes!*" Lester turned apoplectic with rage and threw
e entire school board out of his office.

Mostly, though, it's been Dr. Jekyll all the way. "Patton
ever became the general Ike did, because he slapped a
rivate in public," he is fond of saying. Although he hasn't

done much of anything in the way of legislation ("I reck
I'll get around to that soon," he keeps repeating) he
shown some action. The first thing he did in public office v
change all the locks on the state capitol doors. Then he issu
an order banning mini-skirts in the capitol and ordering
male staff members to have their hair cut above the ears.
announced a war on gambling in the roadhouses in Southe
Georgia and when he learned bribes were being taken duri
the Masters Golf Tournament he knocked on the doors
the bookie joints and went in himself, announcing "I alwa
knock the first time. After that, anything goes."

He has now promised to close down all the roadhouses
the Dixie Highway by January, 1968. "The honeymoon
over," cried one local casino owner. He speaks to Sunda
school classes warning against the pitfalls of alcohol and ev
backed up his own sermons in a *scandale* which has becor
known in Atlanta as the "Bucky Redwine Case."

Bucky was a young all-American Gary Cooper-type lawy
(Mr. Deeds *before* he went to town) who was like a son
ol'Lester. As a reward for his aid in Lester's campaign,
was appointed executive secretary, arriving almost simultar
ously with a warning to the new staff that nobody was ev
to be caught with liquor either on his breath or in his desk
long as Lester was in office. Two months later two youn
University of Georgia students were picked up in Bucky's c
for driving without a license and concealing six cans of be
in the trunk. One of the boys' dates was under twenty-or
and also worked as a secretary in Lester's office. Althou
Bucky's only guilt had been to buy the beer, ol'Lester c
dered him out of his room at the Henry Grady Hotel an
fired him in front of a TV press conference while the publ
howled. The Atlanta press had a field day angling in c
close-ups of the Holy Bible while Lester fumed and Bucl
sat by with a wad of Juicy Fruit gum in his jaw telling t
reporters: "He reminds me of the father who told his li'l be
'Climb up on this ladder and jump in Daddy's arms.' Fo
times the kid jumped and four times his Daddy caught hin
'Now go all the way to the top and jump all the way down
Daddy.' The child hit the ground with a splat, and the Dad
said, 'Now. Don't trust nobody. Not even yore Daddy. Tha
the first lesson in the big world.'"

It was also a lesson to the Lester watchers. He is a man
his word. Two Wednesdays a month he opens the doors
the capitol on "Little People Day," sings "God Ble
America," his favorite song, and even makes the press jo
in. Shortly after his appearance on *Meet the Press*, he eve

cked down and appointed two Negroes to state jobs, a
volutionary act which caused one state senator to remark:
ester don't care how high a nigger gets as long as he don't
t close." Lester's next area of attack: raids on church bingo,
threat which has the Catholics in Atlanta saying flying
venas.

TLANTA's WEST END is "Niggertown." Here, a few
ocks from the "Uncle Remus Branch" of the Atlanta Public
ibrary, stands the office of Leroy Johnson, the most impor-
nt, influential and powerful Negro in Georgia. Leroy is the
st Negro elected to the Georgia Senate in ninety-two
ears, which makes him the first Negro to sit in the General
ssembly since Reconstruction. He was elected in 1962, after
e won the endorsement of Ralph McGill and the *Atlanta
onstitution* over three white Democrats. He owns more law
egrees and citizenship awards than ol'Lester has diction-
ies, and is very close to the Johnson administration (LBJ
ppointed him as special ambassador to represent America at
e Independence Ceremonies in Zanzibar, Africa, in 1963).
That Lee-roy is one smart nigguh," one Maddox aide had
arned me earlier. I figured he was definitely the man to
ee.

Among the degrees, citations, and plaques which line the
alls of his air-conditioned office, two framed blow-ups beam
own directly above his cluttered desk. One shows him
haking President Johnson's hand (the same photo ol'Lester
ook out a Pickrick ad to publicly denounce two years ago)
nd the other shows him with his arm around a smiling
Martin Luther King. While Muzak plays the Norman Luboff
Choir singing "Be My Love" from a hidden speaker in the
valls, he sits calmly behind horn-rimmed glasses, blue shirt
risply starched and two bright-blue glass cufflinks the size of
Easter eggs staring out from under his Ivy League sports
acket like bloodshot eyes. This is the man who, as president
f both the Fulton County Citizens Democrat Club and the
Georgia Association of Citizens Democratic Clubs, dictates to
he 250,000 registered Negro voters in the state.

"It was our organizations that prevented Lester from get-
ing a majority of votes and forced him into being elected by
he General Assembly," beams Johnson proudly. "No one
ought harder to keep him out of office than I did. It was the
nost crooked election I've ever witnessed. Neither Maddox
or Callaway would make any commitment to the Negro, so
ve said the hell with them and headed the write-in for
Arnall, a liberal by any yardstick. They threw out most of

243

the Negro votes because they didn't spell the name righ
they spelled it 'Arnold' instead of 'Arnall.' There were 10
000 votes never even counted. Maddox was elected by
machine, *not* by people."

I asked him if he thought ol'Lester had turned out bet
than expected since he took the oath of office. "Well, so
I'm surprised more by what he has *not* done rather th
what he has done. He has appointed one Negro to t
executive committee and one to the tax commission, he has
referred to the Negro problem in any of his speeches and
says he intends to be our governor as well as the whites'. T
question is: is the change a permanent one? I don't think
but it's too early to make an analysis. He's a man of ma
moods, impossible to predict. Martin Luther King came
my office one day and we went over to the capitol to discu
job opportunities. Dr. King was mad as hell when he walk
in and the first two things he told Lester were 'I'm not gon
be a slave' and 'I will not beg.' By the time we left, they h
their arms around each other and Dr. King said he wanted
come around to the mansion but he didn't want to get r
away by the state police. Lester said 'Nobody will be turne
away.' I can't figure him out."

Lester has promised Johnson he will appoint Negroes to t
state posts, but he will not be pressured. "That's what
says," nods Johnson, "but I say we give him sixty days an
then we're gonna turn this state upside down. Now here's wh
we want. We are not asking. We are *demanding*. First, w
expect to get two to six Negroes appointed to the Georg
Bureau of Investigation, where no Negro has ever been befor
I have just come from the governor's office this morning
this hot summer heat to present him with three qualifie
Negroes ready to take a cut in salary from fifty to a hundre
dollars a month just to open the door to a new opportuni
in this state. We'll see what he does about *that*.

"Second, we expect to get two Negroes employed *immed
ately* with the Internal Revenue Department. Third, there
an opening on the Board of Cosmetology to inspect beauty
parlor operation. That board has been lily-white ever since
was founded. There's a vacancy now and no reason why
Negro shouldn't get it. Now let me tell you somethin
Atlanta is the most sophisticated city in the South becaus
we have an enlightened power structure, a swinging, liber
press headed by Ralph McGill, and an enlightened politic
machine stemming from Negroes teaming up with the bette
elements of whites over in Buckhead. If it hadn't been for thi

dox would have been mayor years ago. It was the
-oes that defeated him.

There's a big BUT though. We've got the Civil Rights Bill
.tlanta, but it doesn't mean a damn thing in Tallapoosa,
rgia. If a showdown is coming, it's going to be in the
 country towns, where there is still *total* segregation. Get
with the red-necks in this state and you won't find a single
ro on any faculty. They had to integrate to a small extent
hey wouldn't get federal aid, but it's only token inte-
on—one child here, two there, four somewhere else. The
 proof of whether Lester Maddox cares about Negroes
come in the country areas. He has the red-necks on his
. What's he gonna do when we demand *total* integration
 in the sticks? If he does not help us, if he vetoes these
pintments I told you about, then he'd better start right
 to assume the responsibility for not only a very hot
mer but a very hot winter, because it will be very hot
ed."

O'S AFRAID OF Virginia Maddox? Well, just about
ybody. One Atlanta hostess told me, "She never gets
ted anywhere. Well, she won't go to cocktail parties and
 don't think I'd give a sit-down dinner and serve Dr.
per, do you?" Everyone in Atlanta still talks about her
 major appearance in the local news, which took place
ol'Lester's first official Little People Day. The press has
g since tired of covering the event, but that first time got
 much curiosity coverage as Stokely Carmichael's race
. While everyone in town sat in their living rooms
ching, Mrs. Maddox suddenly appeared before the cameras
he foyer of the capitol. Cotton wash dress. Hair a mess.
re you here to participate in the governor's Little People
y?" asked the newsmen, shoving mikes into her horrified
e. "Naw, cain't rightly say I am," came the reply, "I jes'
ne down here to get Lester to sign this check so I c'n go
 some groceries."

Even with the right men hired to moderate his speeches,
ster has a hard enough time with his *own* public image. He
too smart to let Virginia out without a chaperon. When I
ed him for an interview with the First Lady, he peered
er the top of his glasses, turned red as a sugar beet, and
d, "She don't talk much." Somebody at the state capitol
ist have given him a high sign, because after several
ayed messages to state troopers at the mansion, an ap-
intment was made. It was Mrs. Maddox's first interview for
major magazine. She was packing to move into the new

245

executive mansion, but could I drop around to the old ___ about noon?

First, I decided to drive by the new one. Well, you sh___ see it. The closest thing Atlanta has to Ashley Wilkes' ___ Twelve Oaks and impressive enough, probably, to brin___ tear even from Margaret Mitchell, if she were still arou___ Elevated on a sixteen-acre clearing on West Pace's F___ Road in the Buckhead section of Atlanta, it gleams like ___ alabaster castle in the white heat of a Southern summ___ surrounded by groves of magnolia and cottonwood trees ___ the set of an old Jeanette MacDonald movie. Nobody trie___ keep me out, so I walked right in through the swimming ___ and up the stairs past shiny metallic kitchens, lavender-a___ pink bathrooms with white Georgia-marble sunken batht___ lemon-yellow suites overlooking Grecian gardens, par___ and marble floors, sauna baths, ten-thousand-dollar cha___ liers hanging fifteen feet from cream-colored ceilings ___ together by more than thirty fluted white columns on all ___ sides of the house. Two Atlanta housewives were bu___ inspecting the bookcases in the library with a measuring t___ I followed them into the grand ballroom, seventy-three ___ long and thirty-nine feet wide, where 500 can be acc___ modated at state dinners. "Couldn't you just die, Loralee" ___ one of them to the other, "all those beautiful dinner par___ and the crystal full of buttermilk?"

The sun shifted high in a hammock of cotton candy clo___ as I pulled up the driveway of the old mansion. A couple ___ state troopers were leaning on their straw-back chairs in ___ back of the house like characters from *The Andy Grif___ Show*. Guns glinted bright metallic glows from their holst___ "You from some magazine?" one drawled cautiously, squi___ ing his eyes from the sun. "You hafta wait in yore car ___ Miz Maddox comes home. Wait a minute. That's her driv___ up now."

A black sedan burning high-octane fumes roared i___ view, angling in under the shade of magnolia trees tall as ___ Statue of Liberty. A state trooper got out of one door an___ soft, primly dressed woman in a raspberry-colored dress w___ neat matching budget-shop shoes and purse stepped out ___ the other. She walked into the old house from the drivew___ without looking back and the state trooper, measuring ___ distance between us with the end of his thumb, motioned ___ to follow.

Old floors creaked and moaned under the weight of ___ feet. Voices echoed through the near-empty halls. Dark, c___ stillness settled around the rooms. Brief glimpses of plu___

ored light seeped in from the shutters, which ran from the
h ceilings to the floor. Mrs. Maddox kept walking, not
ning around. The walls were pink. The rugs were pink.
e ceilings were pink. Everything was dark, as though the
had never been there. She led the way, like a sergeant on
d maneuvers, to the vastness of the living room, paused
ar an old brocade sofa that had been upholstered to take to
e new mansion, touched it gently, and turned to the state
oper: "I declare I don't think they did a durn thang to this
thang."

"No, ma'm, it don't look like it to me either."

She noticed me for the first time and smiled weakly. A soft
n ray peeked through the shutters and played with her
ir. I took an informal hand, soft and doughy as freshly
oked French bread. Standing close to her, I smelled John-
n's baby powder. "You wont Co-Cola?" she asked, and the
ate trooper went off to the kitchen to get it.

Sitting near, with so many armed policemen within
outing distance, she seemed shy. Skin white as blackboard
alk, nails long and lacquered, hair neatly coiffed in a
nsible manner, with just a slight hint of worked-at casual-
ss. Her face was free of lines, slightly puffy, totally inno-
nt, with no features of any real interest except for a tiny
w ribbon of a mouth which sinks slightly around the edges
ke a woman who wears dentures. Perhaps I was staring
dely, because she blushed so deeply that her skin turned
lotchy with little pink pinpoints of color. "This place is
old and in bad condition and fulla leaks. We don't like it
bit, lemme tell you. You caught me right in the middle of
ovin' and all my stuff is in boxes and the good furniture is
aitin' for the movin' van and everthang is in one good mess.
eems like Lester'n me's been on the go ever since he got this
overnor job. I jes' cain't fer the life of me get use to it."

I asked her if she was excited about living in the elegant
ew house. "Yeah, but you know that's a awful big place for
ester'n me. We got two kids still livin' at home, but it's not
e same. We just sold our own house last week. It was much
icer'n all this. We moved in here January 15th and you
now sumpin'? I jes' wouldn' unpack fer two days. This durn
lace was so big I couldn' even find a percolator. By the time
ou walk from the kitchen to the breakfast room all your
ood's cold. And they got me some prisoners from the state
ork farms and you know them prisoners couldn' cook worth
durn. We had four prisoners, but I got rid o' two of 'em.
till got two left. They colored. But you know they don't give
e a bit o' sass. Them police tol' 'em, 'You gotta do ever-

thang she wonts, 'cause if you don't there's about 300 m⟨
that wonts the job.' I didn' like the idea of them prisoners ⟨
my house at first, but I talked to some of the other guv'no⟨
wives and they tol' me not to worry none. They all ⟨
prisoners in their mansions too. Jes' hafta get use to it. Y⟨
know I never could learn 'em how to fry chicken the w⟨
Lester likes it. Then I got my maid, Martha Jenkins, be⟨
with me for a long time, to come and I felt a li'l bett⟨
Lester still wonts me to cook, but I jes' cain't cook fer ⟨
those politicians he brings aroun' here. He don't like anythi⟨
but fried chicken."

"Doesn't he eat anything but chicken and collard greens⟨
I asked, chumming up.

"Well, you know sumpin'? He used to be right finicky, b⟨
we went up yonder to Washington and that Lady Bird had ⟨
dinner party for all the guv'nors and Lester eat everthar⟨
they shoved in front of 'im. He's gettin' a whole lots be⟨
ter."

The state trooper brought our Cokes, wrapped in napkir⟨
engraved with the state seal, and let himself out the si⟨
screen door. "They're real good to me, them boys. All the⟨
doors stay locked and they don't dare come in withor⟨
callin' up from out back first."

She was warming up. "Where you from?" I told her I wa⟨
born in the South. She got friendlier. "What magazine yo⟨
say you were writin' fer?"

"*Esquire.* Do you ever read it?"

"I b'lieve it's one of them men's magazines," she sai⟨
negatively, adding quickly, "but I believe it's a good 'un. ⟨
mean, they don't print any pitchers of nekkid wimmin, d⟨
they?"

I was beginning to understand why she is never allowed ⟨
see the press. Five minutes with her and you get the whol⟨
picture. The Snopes family did not die with Willia⟨
Faulkner, they just went into politics and moved up to th⟨
Big House. "Doncha jus' love it down here? Lester was bor⟨
and raised right here in Atlanta. His daddy was Dan ⟨
Maddox, and he worked as a roll-turner at a galvanizin' mi⟨
right up to the time he died two or three years ago, bless hi⟨
heart. I was born in Birmin'ham. My daddy was Mr. S. ⟨
Cox. We left Alabama when I was six months old, so I don'⟨
know a thang about it. My daddy worked for the railroac⟨
but he quit durin' a strike one time and opened a grocer ⟨
store and never went back. I don't have much of a head fo⟨
dates, but I'll try to help you some for your story. I marrie⟨
Lester when I was seventeen and he was nineteen. We beer⟨
248

arried thirty-one years. My girl friend and me used to ride
ur bikes in front of his house. He had a li'l pigeon coop
gged up in front where he sold candy and Nu-Grape soda
nd ever time he saw me he'd say 'Virginia Cox from Birmin'-
am, I'm gonna marry you.' He only made eighteen dollars a
eek for a steel mill and I tol' him, 'Lester Maddox, you ol'
ool, you gonna hafta make at least twenty-sumpin' 'fore I'd
ven *consider* it.' I finally gave in. He moved his pigeon
ouse up the street on the corner of State and Fourteenth
nd we expanded it to sell hot dawgs. I didn't know a thang
bout makin' hot dawgs, but I was right there beside him.
We had four stools and mostly a carry-out trade—we added
amburgers and ice cream. Then in 1947 I think it was, we
aw this property grown over with weeds on Hemphill Ave-
ue. They couldn't sell it so we got it cheap. We started a
rive-in. That's where the whole family got started. Soon as
e kids could reach the counter they'd wait on curb service.
We bought the best grade meat and people took a likin' to it.
Most places buy pore meat and stuff it with bread. I was the
ashier. We first started out with hot dawgs. Then we started
ervin' breakfast. Then we opened at eleven and cut out the
reakfast. It got to be too much trouble. We never had a
acation, but we didn't care. Some days I made three hun-
red pies at a time if I was pressed for hep. We made a big
izness outta the Pickrick. Everbody in town came. We had
ur own special recipe—had special pans made up to fry it in.
We never dropped it in deep fat. You know sumpin', I cain't
each the cook how to make it right in the mansion. I'm not
ellin' you a story. He'll put it in beaten egg and milk before
e dips it in flour. My chillrun sit down and say, 'Mama, this
s not *your* fried chicken.' I guess times won't never be as
ood as they were at the Pickrick. You know sumpin'? You
an make a lot more money in fried chicken than you can in
his governor bizness."

I asked her if her life had changed noticeably since she had
become the First Lady of Georgia. "Yessuh. It flat has. I
gotta go to the beauty parlor all the time. I always did m'own
hair but when I got into this politics bizness some folks sat
down'n tol' me, 'Now you gotta dress just right or people'll
criticize you. Yessuh, they *do*. They *crit*-icize. I get letters
from 'em. I said, 'Lester, I don' think I c'n look good all
the time like they wont' and he says to me, 'You jus' gotta
make a effort.' So I try. I had me a seceketerry for a while but
she had a baby and quit on me. Now I have to read all the
letters myself. Now you know what he's gonna do? He's
gonna open the new mansion up five days a week to the

public. He says, 'We only gonna be in there four years, b[ ]
the public's gonna be a-comin' the rest of their lives,' a[ ]
I says, 'Lester, I jus' don't believe I can handle all that. [ ]
them school kids traipsin' in an' out all day long. I would[ ]
mind three days so bad but five is more'n I c'n handle.' [ ]
we got us a man we pay out of our own salary to supervi[ ]
things. He's even gonna make out the menus, 'cause I do[ ]
know nothin' 'bout that stuff. We cain't feed people fri[ ]
chicken all the time. You know that kitchen's got only o[ ]
stove in it. I'd go crazy cookin' for all them folks in there [ ]
one stove. 'Sides that, I still got the payroll to make o[ ]
down at the furniture store."

The Maddoxes have four children: a married daughte[ ]
Linda Densmore (twenty-nine), who helped her father as h[ ]
private secretary during his campaign; a single daughte[ ]
Virginia (twenty-six), who works as a "seketerry fer Dupon[ ]
but you don' wanna advertise *them*, they git enough publici[ ]
without us hornin' in"; and two sons—Larry (twenty), a[ ]
employee at Lockheed Aircraft in Marietta, and Leste[ ]
Jr. (twenty-three), who was arrested in the fall of 196[ ]
during his father's campaign, when police found him robbin[ ]
a TV and appliance store of $3,000 worth of merchandi[ ]
("I offer no apologies and seek no sympathy," said ol'Leste[ ]
on TV, his face turning pomegranate red, "however if th[ ]
Communists and the government of Lyndon Johnson had n[ ]
destroyed my bizness, my family would have stayed togethe[ ]
and escaped this tragedy"). Lester Jr. now works in hi[ ]
father's Pickrick Furniture Store.

"We don't none of us see Lester much. Only time I se[ ]
him regular is at breakfast, but he's gone pretty near eve[ ]
night. I didn't ever like politics, 'cause I always got left [ ]
home, but now I get to go some of the places. I been t[ ]
Washin'ton *Dee* Cee three times. I also went to Delaware fo[ ]
their centennial and Lester got out of the car in the parad[ ]
and started shakin' everbody's hand and left me alone an[ ]
the people in the street jes' laughed at me when they looke[ ]
in and saw a woman inside where it said 'Governor o[ ]
Georgia,' so I tol' the lady drivin' the car, 'I believe I'll ge[ ]
out and walk too, 'cause they lookin' for *him*, not me.' Th[ ]
stories they print in the press 'bout us is jes' plumb awfu[ ]
Where do they get such lies? My oldest daughter jus' cain[ ]
stand it. Lester says to pay 'em no mind, 'cause if you star[ ]
denyin' everthang it only makes it worse. The kids say, 'But i[ ]
they talked about *us* you'd feel diff'rent.' How would you lik[ ]
it if somebody was talkin' mean about your Daddy all th[ ]
time and you jus' knew not everthang he does is wrong. You'[ ]

be plumb mortified too. Everbody wants a favor now. What makes people like that? Jus' for the cake and punch I served at the Old People's Day party it's outrageous what they charged me. I coulda made it my*self* cheaper'n that. If you got a mansion people think you got plenty of money. One man walked up to Lester one day and said, 'I don' wont nothin', I jes' dropped by to say hello,' and Lester said 'Get the photographer quick, I don' believe it.' "

She was laughing and talking now, sipping her Coke over the soft hum of a lawnmower out on the lawn, where one of the prisoners was mowing the grass. I asked her if she had ever tried to interfere during ol'Lester's ax-waving incident at the Pickrick. "Nossuh, I never interfere with anythin' he does. A person oughta run his bizness the way he sees fit. I didn' mess in his bizness then and I don't now. I don' think I been down yonder to the capitol over three times since he's been there. He's the guv'nor and they sure don' wont the wife down there. I figure he can take care of that part and I'd take care of this part at home. Guess you heard 'bout the time I was on TV. We got this Mansion Fund we're supposed to live on but heck that don' hardly keep a cat alive, and I cain't get a check cashed unless I got his John Henry on it, so I figured if I was ever gonna see him I'd get in line like the rest of 'em."

I asked her about his ban on mini-skirts. "He calls 'em long blouses. Well, I didn't know nothing 'bout that till the TV station called me up for a comment and tol' me. That night he came home and I let out the hem on a long dress of mine and he didn't even notice. 'How do you like Mama's new dress?' one of my daughters asked him. 'Well, I think it looks jes' fine.' I said, 'Lester, I don' know if you noticed or not but my ankles are showin'.' I don' think he even knows I got ankles. But you know sumpin'? I don' think the capitol is the place for them thangs. They don' even let 'em wear those in my beauty parlor. I do all my tradin' at Rich's and I never saw any of the clerks dressed anythin' but conservative. Most of the people like what Lester's doin' in office, includin' the Nigras. I went down to Crawford Lawn Hospital to get a checkup the other day and saw this old colored man name of Ozell who used to work at the Pickrick and he says, 'Miz Maddox, we're real proud of the guv'nor but he made one mistake, he hired somebody else instead of me as cook in that new mansion.' I thought that was nice. Lester's a good man, but we been married so long it's gettin' harder and harder to please him. I always give him a real nice store-bought suit for Christmas. He used to smoke cigars right after we got married, but he hasn't smoked one of them thangs in ten years."

We had talked the day into afternoon shadows. I got up to leave and she walked me to the screen door. "I really enjoyed it," she said. "I don't see many folks 'cause I never know what they wont me to say. Not too many of 'em come here to the house. We had the Hubert Humphreys by for tea. She's a real nice lady. 'Course one woman always understands another. I didn' have much to say to *him* though. Then my nephew from up North come down here on his way to the Army with his roommate. I believe he was one of them I-talians. Seemed right nice, though. I'll be glad when this four years is up and we can get back down to normal. I tol' Lester, 'This is the hardest four years I'll ever spend. This is harder work than the Pickrick.' " Hand on the screen door, gesturing out over the gardens. "You know sumpin'? We lived in one little house with one bathroom and six people for twenty years but we never did have a bit o' trouble with that bathroom. Never did one of us wanna get in there when the other'n was usin' it. Now we got seventeen bathrooms and nobody to use 'em."

BACK ON THE MADDOX TRAIL, ol'Lester was stealing the show from the Holstein cows at the Putnam Country Dairy Festival. Riding down the main street of a little hick town called Eatonton, the home of Uncle Remus' creator Joel Chandler Harris, he jumped over the side of his car in the parade and went into action. Shaking hands, kissing babies, and exchanging folksy talk. He darted into stores asking the proprietors "How's bizness?" "Fine, and yours?" "Never had it so good." He leaped over white-trellised front porches to shake hands with old ladies rocking in the sunshine and grabbed an uncountable number of babies from their mothers' arms, thrusting them into the air with glee. "This is where it all began years ago," he told the crowd of red-necks, "this is Maddox country." The crowd cheered while children played tag and pricked each other's confetti-colored balloons and complacent cows mooed in the country grass.

His bald head glistening with sweat, he handed the white carnation in his lapel to a four-year-old who took it, looked at the beaming governor, threw it on the ground, and yelled for his mother. Then ol'Lester told a group of young Negro schoolchildren standing in a frightened cluster on the curb, "You got to make A's in school. That's what we want." He was home.

But the air in Atlanta was filled with anything but gaiety.

Ol'Lester was being roasted in the press for his war on church bingo, which had been unwisely announced at the same time as a raffle at his own furniture store for a "free $299 Serta perfect sleeper set with king-size mattress." ("Meanwhile back at the store," cried the *Atlanta Journal* editorial page, we notice that a furniture store closely identified with Mr. Maddox (so closely that it runs his picture in each ad) is, itself, having a kind of raffle like.")

On another page, a Catholic bishop and Lester's own Baptist preacher were having it out over the mini-skirts: "I do think the rags worn in our slums are far worse than the mini-skirts allegedly worn in the statehouse," said the Catholic. "We do not take our faith from a foreign power," snapped the Baptist. "I don't think he'd know a mini-skirt if he saw one," sniffed one of the governor's own secretaries, summing it all up.

And ol'Lester himself, promising me one last meeting, arrived at Atlanta's WAII-TV to face a stern-looking group of political interviewers. "What are you doing about the filthy conditions in our prisons?" They demanded on the air.

"I invited all the wardens to lunch and conditions are being improved," said ol'Lester, wiping his brow nervously, the sweet memory of the morning's peaceful cheers in Maddox country fading away in the harsh reality of the afternoon's inquisition. Only minutes after his statement, the TV newsroom received an Associated Press flash announcing a surprise raid on the state prison work camp at Rome, Georgia, revealing that Negro prisoners were still being charged 6c for 5c stamps, locked in the cafeterias and not allowed to lie on their bunks on rainy days, fed baloney, beans, and water (no milk) at every meal, and allowed only one two-hour visiting privilege every two weeks. Lester looked like he might faint.

"What is your stand on gambling?" asked the commentators.

"Gambling is bad. I don't like gambling anywhere it is. It can get a hold of ya. I don't even want people playin' cards in their homes. It can lead young people to drinkin' and assault and dope addiction."

"What are your plans regarding George Wallace and his third political party?" They leaned forward. (This is the question plaguing everyone, not only in Atlanta but in Washington. Ol'Lester denies being close to the Wallace administration in Alabama, but it is a known fact that when the Pickrick had problems with the federal government, Wallace aided him financially, calling it "the only American thing to

253

do." Now, when Wallace visits Atlanta, state troopers line th
capitol and liberal state politicos walk out of the General
Assembly, but Lester meets George and Lurleen at the air
port, even gets down on his hands and knees and straighten
out the wrinkles in the red carpet.)

"I hadn't made up my mind yet on this subject. I'r
flexible. Lotta folks up yonder in Washin'ton who wanna se
Georgia on their side. We are the heart beat and the hub c
the South. . . ."

"Sure," said one of the newsmen, yawning on camera.

The Maddox brand of press agentry continued for half a
hour, until they asked the final question: "Governor, you ar
always doing a lot of talking about free enterprise. Just wha
is your definition of free enterprise?"

Ol'Lester fumbled nervously, wiping the sweat off his bal
head. "Well ... when the Pilgrims landed at Plymouth Roc
they tried socialism a coupla years, then they put all thei
corn in one pot and nearly starved to death. They learne
socialism wasn't the best thing after all, and neither wa
Communism. We gotta learn the same thing. It's every ma
fer himself."

He left the broadcast blushing, not sure whether he ha
made a fool of himself or not. "Ever'thang pick rick?" h
said to two blonde secretaries in the reception hall. "Ever'
thang's pick rick," they giggled.

He motioned for me to follow him into the men's room
where he talked to me over the top of the urinal. "How
y'awl like Atlanta, son? Y'awl been gettin' ever'thang ya
need?" He relieved himself, washed his hands with disinfec
tant soap, and asked if there was anything else I wanted t
know.

"One thing I don't understand," I said. "What does th
word *PICKRICK* mean?"

"To pick means to help yerself, son, to choose. And ric
means to eat fastidiously. You pick it and we rick it." I tol
him I had heard some good things about the restaurant while
it was open. "Yes*suh*. You could get all the fried chicken you
could eat fo' a dolla. I jes' loved that place, son. It grieves
my heart not to be there."

In Georgia, a governor cannot succeed himself. It's four
years and out. Did he have an eye on Washington when his
term expired? "Naw *suh*. I jus' wanted to see how fer a li'l
feller could go. I wanted to see if this wuz still America."

He left the john and stepped cockily toward the glass doors
of the TV station. "How you, Charlie? Haven' seen you in a
coon's age, Luke. How's the wife, son?" His bodyguard, a
254

an referred to simply as Lt. Pope, swung between him and
the rest of the room, his hand on his holster.

"Boy, I'd like to hear how he's cussin' us now," said one of
the commentators as ol'Lester headed down the walk.

"Son, you jus' come on back down here fo' years from
now and you gon' fin' me givin' up this here guv'nor stuff,
right back in my furniture store, jus' a pickin' and a rickin',"
said Lester, waving at me.

He climbed into his blue Oldsmobile parked at the curb
and his driver stepped on the gas. "Ride 'em cowboy,"
howled the newsmen from behind the glass doors. But all
they got in return was a "Y'awl be good now, ya heah?" and
a crooked-tooth grin as the car drove away in the dusty
afternoon.